# Some Reflections of My Mind

BIVA BASU

authorHOUSE®

*AuthorHouse™ UK Ltd.*
*500 Avebury Boulevard*
*Central Milton Keynes, MK9 2BE*
*www.authorhouse.co.uk*
*Phone: 08001974150*

*First published by AuthorHouse 10/13/2010*

*ISBN: 978-1-4490-7377-0 (sc)*

*This book is printed on acid-free paper.*

To The Loving Memory Of My Father.

He Was A Professor And An Author.

I Know He Would Have Been Very Happy About My Book.

# Some Reflections of My Mind

# Chapter One

I am so very tired.  I am tired of defending myself all the time.  I wish I could relax a little and enjoy life a bit more!

When I look at a beautiful sky I sometimes wonder what does it all mean!  I like to know if it has any meaning related to me personally.  I am sure it has no meaning of that kind.  It is just there and will always be there as long as the forces of nature will allow it to be there.  It must have been made out of some natural consequences.  But has it got nothing whatsoever to do with me!  Still I like to look into the vast clear sky that seems to be staring at me with no apparent interest!

I have never been given much room in my life!  Every time I tried to be myself things go wrong.  I get hurt some way or other as if I have to bear punishment for my misdeed.

I watch a lot of television. I watch it all the time.  I see so many important and influential people trying to create as much impression as possible in the media.  Most of these people seems insincere most of the time.  They are basically nothing but hypocrites.  But they do their job very well.  They hide their real intention cleverly.  Their true convictions are below the surface.  They are not supposed to be seen openly.

To me, sometimes their pretence seems to show through them as transparent and they appear to be outrageously unkind! They say things they do not mean. These big people irritate me. I do not believe in them! Perhaps everybody feels the same to some extent.

It is nice to have some faith in some people or in something! In time of sheer desolation all of us turn to God. In fact we all want something, some power; some miracle should come over us and rescue us from our trouble. I only wish it would work just like that!

All of us are not that lucky all the time. In real world so many people are so unfortunate! It makes me sad even to think about. Strictly speaking, maybe the thought should comfort me a little because I am not alone; I am one of the unfortunate many.

My life is not full of rare happiness. I live a dull life without much fulfilment. However, people sometimes make me feel even more bored and weary. I rather watch television all day long than meet just anybody.

I do not mind watching television if I have to. Anyway, I can select what I want to watch or not. If there is nothing to choose, I sometimes do not mind watching real rubbish including even the commercial advertisements. Maybe I do not watch them with full attention or interest. However, in absence of something better I need at least the sound and the flicker of light in the background to keep me company. I find it quite soothing on my nerves.

Anyhow the message of the adverts is simple. They all want to sell some product or other. It is really direct, straight forward and fairly honest.

But people are in general very difficult. Their messages are by comparison quite complex. Basically they too want to sell something. But they are rarely direct. They carefully hide their intention from most of us. Once again most people seem nothing but hypocrites. Often they are up to some form of deception or want to take advantage of you but never in a straight forward way. It seems they always want to catch you when you are not on your guard. As if they want to do you but do not want you to know that they have you done! This is doubly humiliating.

I find them always coming to me for pure selfish reason. Yet they want me to believe that they are there only to see me entirely for my own good and simply for the love of me which is far from truth. People confuse me and I find them very often boring and nothing but waste of time. I did not always feel this way. Probably we are all products of our experiences and hence I cannot help but feeling the way I feel!

I am sure I exaggerate badly when I say people are crooks and a bore. I do not mean everybody; but some are though.

Also, maybe over the year I have become bitter. Maybe I never met any particularly nice people in my life. Maybe I draw only the wrong people around me. Or, perhaps it is because I live in an affluent country as a lonely foreigner!

I cannot differentiate the right reason from the wrong. Anyway, this is what had happened and I am very sorry for my fate. There must have been a wishful thinking in the back of my mind for a happier life. I would have liked to meet enduringly nice and genuinely kind person in my life. But I never did. That must have made an enormously empty vacuum in my heart where everybody turns out to be hollow and hopelessly boring!

I thought mind is the most precious thing in a human being. I wanted to improve myself by improving my mind and by making my intellect grow. I did not succeed much. I did not realise that nothing grows without happiness. I was foolish. I thought if I improve everything else I want, will follow. My improved soul will do everything for me. It will draw improved people, without such people one cannot be happy after all.

But it did not turn up like that. People do not seem to care much for improvement. Maybe they do not like improved woman. They especially seem to prefer women without much intellect and spirit, willing to serve without too much question. People preach differently. They say that they admire and worship spirited women and that they like building up relation with such women on equal terms. But it is probably just pretence. Perhaps people do not truly trust spirited independent women, at least not in general. There is of course, plenty of exception in the world. Also if the woman is exceptionally brilliant and spectacularly successful, everybody admires her. She is then given an easy ride. But it is not so for the ordinary woman with an independent mind of her own. People tend to stay clear of her unless of course, they have an ulterior motive.

I am only an ordinary woman. But I earn my living and live an independent life. Probably people do not like me. I likewise am beginning to dislike them. Maybe we only imagine everything! And it is all nothing but a passing mood of mine! I wanted to do some good. Instead I grew to be cold and bitter. Is it not a shame and a big waste!

I wanted to make the world loving and great. But I found myself in a world which has no room for me. I ask myself why God, why is it so! The world is so big and so vast. Why could it not have any generosity for me!

I never knew happiness. It seems happiness is not for me. Maybe one day I will have peace. I say this only because, how can one be deprived of everything in life! Everybody deserves something!

Maybe not necessarily so—how am I to know! For some curious reason I missed out all the fun in my life. It did not matter at first. But now it seems quite a sad thing to have happened in anybody's life. Sadly it seems I have got too old for life too quickly. Life never seemed to have given me much chance. Probably it is not true at all. But this is how it feels to me. Maybe I misunderstood life from the start to the end! And story-telling is a very compelling urge in any human being.

It has not been very easy to live my life. To start with it seemed full of promises. Gradually it has got tougher and tougher. Suddenly it was all over and feels impossibly hard to go on any longer.

Certainly it is not so easy. Maybe it is not easy if it is not meant to be easy! It looks easy for some though. Maybe it is just an illusion and nothing more.

Anyhow life is not easy for many. Just why it happens to be like that I do not know. All I know that it is meant to be difficult for me—very difficult indeed!

I would have loved to combine work and a loving family of my own. I would have liked to give my love to a man who deserves the best in life. I always felt I have a lot to give, to love and to produce! We all create things in life with the love we possess in our soul. Creation does not come out of nothing. Joys of creativity is the manifestation of love in life. To deny this is a great pain to bear.

We alone are responsible for our action. The inability to be happy is my short coming. I know this. But the acceptance of unhappy life is still not very easy.

Perfect life should have perfect happiness. Maybe nobody achieves that. But that does not stop us looking for it. We long for it all our life. Maybe this is what makes us religious. In search of our unobtainable happy state of mind we turn to religion.

I was thinking about religion the other day. What is religion? I feel it must be an inner struggle for self realisation and a total commitment for the service to mankind as a whole. It is not a power struggle and definitely not a competition to get to the top in this life or after.

Also religion cannot be a means to provide some escapism with lots of nice or lovely illusions. It must be a way of life—a help to get into the depth of pain, futility and nothingness of our life and the world around us.

It is not the doctrines or the rituals which is the focus of a great many religions of our world. It must be the holiness in man which should be the object of religion. Nothing else makes a scrap of a difference to man and his world.

Centuries after century man had tried to proclaim him as good. This is the only way he can justify his existence and satisfies his superior intelligence. Only by being good he can set an example amongst his fellowmen and attain peace and tranquillity.

He knows the world is not for him to keep for ever. He has to go. He feels only if he can set an example in giving service which is within him the world will remember him by. So he sets his goal and keeps himself occupied with good deeds and thoughts. So he lives a worthwhile life. This must be the essence of religion and human standard of all ages.

Just talk big or small is nothing. What we do with our lives and how we live has something to do with our religion!

Watching television all the time makes me to understand that Britain is basically imperialist. She glorifies her army and everything to do with her army.

She needs her army and that must be the reason why she has to show, her wars are all righteous and her army is full of wonderful men and women. The army is shown as full of glory and the best and exciting place to be in. It is the right place to show up all the divine qualities of human development, character and personalities.

Britain wants her people to admire war and army. It is quite a lot of self-fulfilling for her interest and purpose! A kind of religious sophistication one might say!

This ideology and its manifestation must have been many times more before than what is apparent at present. Mass education and the projection of values are tied up with the power and the policies of the land. Maybe this is how the society functions. However, everything does not always go the way one would like it to go.

The British and all the other imperialists plundered the world freely for centuries. There was no body to stop them and they did not stop for a long, long time.

When at last things have changed and straight forward looting was over, they became specialised and very sophisticated in preserving their self-interest. First they wanted to keep the booties for themselves and themselves only. When they have to share they were prepared only to share with friends and used collaborators if needed. So they formed a club for the rich and the privileged nations. Within the club they looked after each other's interest. United they tried to get as much as possible from the whole world for themselves. Together they were even more a mighty potent force to reckon with for anyone outside their camp.

It is very interesting though to notice, how the law of greater nature plays a very important part which is different from what they would have liked it to be but could not stop.

History takes its shape from all the elements and not just from those which are strong and domineering. It seems incredible how it happens but it does and that is all that matters. The world is no body's personal property and the power never stays in one's hand for ever. Maybe nature does not like to be anybody's fool. It may do us all good if we all learn this basic truth but we never do. We all like to play God and feel mighty powerful. We wish to control our own destiny and make a mess of this world over and over again and never learn our lesson. This is history and it repeats itself. History reveals itself sometimes very slowly almost imperceptibly and another times very fast and very sudden, taking everybody by surprise.

For many years, in fact for about two centuries British occupied India. They kept Indians under their thumb. They used India, exploited Indians as many ways as suited them. However, this is nothing unusual. Exploitation is truly the name of the game in this world. Everybody does it everywhere as long as he is not somehow forced to stop it.

For a long time in India, British encouraged the rich Indians to suppress and exploit the poor ordinary people of the land. The rich in their turn helped to protect British interest there.

Over the centuries the rich got better and better in using the poor and the helpless to their own advantage. They are still doing so. I am sure they will keep going the same way until the poor gather sufficient strength and able to put an end to it. Until such time the power struggle will go on in one direction or other.

It is incredible how people become so hard and ruthless in their job of using defenceless people. The pattern is more or less the same all over the world. Amongst these shrewd people the best of those who had most opportunities and longer practices. Without a doubt the British nation may be regarded as the most outstanding in this respect.

Maybe one day long time ago they too were quite simple and innocent. But they are now the product of their own history. Maybe they were once subject of some cruel history of their nation. They might have been treated very harshly at some stage. They were thus forced to grow matured and cunning in many respects indeed. Gradually they acquired the skill to match up and master their world.

They became strong and shrewd and ruthless in dealing with the rest of the world. Suddenly they were in a position to use the whole world to their own advantage.

Maybe this is just nature at work and this is how things occur in real world. We are all nothing but just victim of history of one kind or other! The world makes history and history makes the world!

We are just what we are! No need to be proud or ashamed! No matter what part your history makes you play in your life, you are not much more than just a pawn in a game of Nature's chess.

Once one learns to exploit others, one finds reason for doing so. Exploitation becomes no dirty word in one's way of life and thought.

The British people became very powerful and privileged. They learnt to use the underprivileged people. They begun to consider them as lesser people and found justification in enslaving them. They brought the slaves to work for them. They only wanted the slaves to look after their interest, their booties and newly acquired wealth. They thought they remain the master race for ever.

They never imagined that the history could turn on them one day. But it has. As it happens that they are now forced to share their privileges with unprivileged people to some extent.

By one way or other they gathered riches from all over the world. With the help of their inventions, discoveries and sheer determination they acquired power. They made their home, country and nation the envy of the world. They built it for themselves alone. They did not want to share it with anybody, let alone the member of the poorer nations who, in their opinion, are nothing but inferior people.

The British brought these lesser people from their colonies and former colonies. To maintain quality living for their own people they needed these people to do the menial job and all necessary dirty work which no one else would like to do. Because of economic reason they opened the door for these poor people. The poor people of the world came, worked for them and eventually made their home amongst the affluent host society.

The host community now more or less despise them amongst their midst, but are unable to get rid of them.

The Americans suffered from the same fate. They wanted to use the Negroes. They bought the Negroes as slaves. They wanted the slaves to look after their interest, comfort and riches. But the white Americans did not want to have any regard for their Blacks. The Blacks to them were no more than a kind of mindless tool which is to make fortune for them, but is not to demand anything for their own welfare.

The Whites had no love for the Blacks. They did not feel that the Blacks deserved any love, affection or much attention. They wanted to keep them as shadowy background figures, which have work to do but nothing to enjoy. They thought the Blacks are nothing but contemptible and no more than a kind of sub-human species.

Now it has turned. The Whites could not escape entirely the fate of sharing life with the people they regarded so low. To some extent, they have to share their fortune with the unfortunates. Most of them perhaps, regarded this as a misfortune and would wish not to have happened. But it has. Gradually everybody is bound to except the reality and be glad to compromise as there is little choice. The law of nature presides over all in the long run.

The powerful people made the less powerful subjected to an untold amount of miseries and suffering. They were bent on keeping everything good for themselves. The lure of cheap labour forced them to bring the poor in their own homeland, and so some of the power of the powerful country has slept into the hand of these unlikely people.

Coming back to the history of my own life I must say I wanted very much to make my father happy but I did not succeed. Often it feels that I am born hopeless and unlucky. When I am feeling low it seems I am forsaken by God for some reason. It feels just like bearing a punishment, for some misdeed I may have committed, by the hand of Providence!

Maybe no one can escape destiny. It is perhaps my destiny to be unhappy in life in many ways. Maybe I am the greatest looser of all times. It feels like that anyway. In some respect, I just cannot succeed. No matter how I try I am to fail! I always fail. My misfortune seems even more of a misfortune as I always fail just an instance before it feels the success is at hand. This makes it so hard to bear. My anticipation and my expectation all turn out to be wrong. Maybe I have a very poor finish in store for me! I wish it wasn't so poor indeed!

I am sure nobody can understand me or my unhappiness. Could lack of love be the root cause of all my trouble! Love is everybody's birthright. When you have it in your life, it seems just one of those things—very ordinary and nothing special. But as I never seemed to have it, it seems very special indeed. Life without love seems like a life without any meaning and very tragic indeed. Maybe what I mean by life without love is something quite a strange reality. I cannot help feeling a bit resentful and upset. Without love the unfairness, the unjust insanity and the injustices in life is too much to bear. I resent it all. I wanted to aspire and reach high. But I have been forced to stay small. Life has belittled me. Fault must be in me but I do not quite know what or why!

May be all unhappy souls think in this way and so I am no exception! But I have no knowledge of that either!

Human capacity to endure pain surprises me. It is enormous and incredible. Even then, the fact that one has never been loved hurts me very badly. This is a very painful thing to come to term with in one's life. I am born to this world but the world does not care for me, is not at all easy to cope with. This pain burns into my heart. I am repeatedly forced to ask myself why things are the way they are. Why couldn't it be different, however slightly!

Just a little bit of honest love and affection in my life wouldn't have been wonderful! I do not doubt it. But it was never to be. I suppose one has to be really lucky to have that fate! I am born unlucky. So it is no wonder that I am singled out to be unhappy in life. Pain and frustration is the story of my life. Little tenderness and some affection always has allured me from a distance like mirage but never been real to me.

To put up with my loneliness I was watching a television programme. It was on that instant, about Indian history when a small section of Indian military took up side against the British. Subhash Bose known to the Indians as Netaji, was their leader. Ideas and opinions put forward in the programme were a bit irritating for me, some one of Indian origin. It seems very much one sided. Maybe it could not have been helped; because, it was produced by the British for the British television.

However, I am of Indian origin and I cannot help feeling vexed by it. Probably I am simply biased. Most probably they are very much biased too. Maybe I should be just grateful that they put a programme on India anyway! But I do not feel that way. All I can feel is that their way of thinking does not do a great deal of justice to my people or our point of views.

Centuries after centuries the British plundered India freely. At any rate they had free hand in misusing India for their own interest. They exploited India and the Indians as much as they possibly could. In the name of their own country they destroyed India slowly and systematically. If they thought that they were doing good for India too, that was beside the point. First and foremost they were in India for their own sake and not for India's.

They enslaved Indians thoroughly, ruthlessly ruined their moral fibre and ability to stand on their own feet. The British occupation in India for so many years was no less than a rotten air for the Indians. They took away all the responsibility to govern their own affair from their hand and made them just puppets on a string. The string was pulled only by the British hand to satisfy only the British interest.

As the British Power was able to do all these why should not they please themselves! Of course they should. After all everybody looks after their own interest and there is no reason why British should have behaved differently.

What surprises me though, why the British cannot imagine that any Indian could possibly hate them and somehow could try to liberate India from their hand. They make one to understand that it is an evil-deed, outrageously immoral action and only possible by an ungrateful inferior race like the Indians. I know they pretend but do they honestly believe that they were in India for the good of the Indians! Do they truly think that they were the salvation of all the inferior races of the world!

It is incredibly difficult for me to understand how a clever race like the British could possibly be brainwashed like that. Maybe they did think like that. Maybe they still do. Perhaps they feel they are superior and it is their rightful duty to dominate the world in any way they ought to dominate.

I am not trying to criticise them. I am trying to understand why they acted the way they did. Maybe anybody in their position would have done the same. But we do exist as well. Our emotion, aspiration, interest and progress are not theirs. Us and them, are both a reality. The world may be in the hand of the powerful. The poor lives on this earth too and they have their story as well. One sided story is just not satisfactory.

I know there isn't much point in feeling heated up about history. None of us know exactly what the alternative history would have been if some thing did not happen the way it did.

Anyway nothing is good about you if you do not succeed! The Indian leader Netaji failed in his mission and therefore in world's opinion everything was wrong with him. Indian nationalist opinion, however, worshiped him as a very precious hero!

Everybody needs to boost their nationalistic moral ego. The privileged nations do it by projecting constantly in the media the images of the heroic characters they admire. This need is no less for poorer nations. In fact, they need it even more than the others.

The rich nations are educated to believe that they are superior and the poorer nations are inferior. It helps the rich. But there is no education for the less fortunate. The education they receive from the hand of the rich teaches them that they are born inferior and should stay inferior for good.

Over the centuries Indians were stripped of their responsibilities and made virtual slaves to foreign imperialist domination and interest. In the end they were obliged to observe the differences between themselves and their confident, self assured, resilient foreign masters. The deep shame and moral degradation for their own nation, was overwhelming. The awe inspiring respect and fear for their rules on the other hand was formidable, this must have been the secret of success of the British Colonial rule in India for such a long time.

Superficially it may not seem too bad to-day. But the British rule in India for the Indians was very serious indeed in many ways. The deep impact and influence on the Indian character and culture must have been devastating in more ways than one.

British opinion always exaggerates the benefits of British Empire for the natives of India. As if, a handful of Indians being able to speak English and a few hundred miles railroad, out way all other ill effects of slavery in large scale for centuries. Maybe it was good for the Indians being ruled by the British! Doesn't it then presupposes that the Indians are born to be slaves. Anyhow not many people talk about the Psychological ill aspect of foreign domination in India. Perhaps there is no point talking about it. Still it helps me to understand the transformation of the Indian personalities during British rule. If today the Indians are to be stamped out for certain characteristic nature I want to know where did it come from!

As the Indian suffered from the complexities of an inferior nation and was trifled by it some rebellions rose from the ashes. Some persisted. Some disappeared in the thin air. The fact that the India was trying to assert herself, mattered to the Indians.

The fact that Netaji could stand up to the invincible British and exert a blow was enough to steal him a place very dear to the people's heart. All the argument that he tried the wrong way, he joined the wrong side or he asked for help from the wrong people, was immaterial to the people of India. After so many years of suppression at least one of their sons dared to overthrow the rule of slavery. Disregarding everything else this was the only fact they cherished dearly and still do. Netaji himself did not survive to tell or justify his story. His attempt to liberate India did not succeed. India did not escape her subsequent misfortune. Indians went through catastrophic bloodshed and was engulfed in the blaze of communal hatred and massacre. India did not remain whole. She was mutilated.

People of India just remember Netaji as someone who wanted to spare them from all these. They think of him as a martyr who tried to save India from all theses disasters, calamity and unbearable suffering.

Of course, British saw him as a subversive enemy. They naturally had no love for him or his cause. If they now can discredit him in any way, is a gain for them on moral ground. As an academic argument if one wants, it is now quite easy to show lots of faults in him and his desperate attempt. In spite of all these Indian on the other hand, do not seek a perfect man in him but seek consolation in his motive and courage. To them he came as a saviour but was destroyed and his memory is now indestructible.

The British people were perhaps accustomed to take it for granted that everybody should be happy to accept their authority. They used to consider it was good for everybody. It might have been unforgivable to them if anybody did not want to do so. This psychological make up is the product of the colonial era. It is very different from the nation of the people who is not a protégé of colonialism.

Still with India and her straggle for political freedom Gandhi took a very different path. First of all he was not a militant. He was non-violent. He perused an extraordinary moral means to stop domination and injustices. He became a unique and universal figure in all struggles for human right.

In more than one sense, Gandhi did not fail. The world will remember him for a long time to come. So he must have been right and his actions must have been right in one way or other. But in terms of the struggle for India's freedom even he was not able to save India from her misfortune. Is it possible then that even he was not right every time? Maybe he was too saintly to counter act the cunning authority of British colonialism in India. Some of his failure to judge the situation correctly may be the reason why India ended up in bloody civil war.

In spite of all the goodness and greatness of Gandhi it may be his lack of deceitful tactics which caused the miseries of India at the end of the British rule in India.

Of course no one can blame him for anything. One cannot blame a God for not being ungodly sometime when too much evil in action. In the face of too many conspiracies, too much power struggle and too many hands to pull the string, it is of course humanly impossible to guide the boat safely ashore. Naturally blood is bound to flow, helpless perishes in vast number and disaster follows disaster. Power to destroy is within individual. But the power to stop it is not necessarily within us. Once the chain reaction starts it must work itself up. This is the way of evil. Gandhi was heart broken. He tried to prevent it. But he did not succeed. India was not lucky. She was cut to pieces. Her people faced crushing agony. Many did not survive. Even

Gandhi was assassinated.

To sum up the history of the end of British rule in India, it can be said that Gandhi was pushed aside. Deals were made between interested parties. Finally British left India but set the stage ready for her to hack herself to pieces. Perhaps it was a kind of vengeance to mark the end of the empire!

Still we can now look back on its bright side. Thanks to the British-empire Indians are now able to share a bit of wealth in different parts of the world. Without the empire Indians would not be in England, South Africa, America and quite a few other places. Out of great suffering was born something which must be great too. Whether it is a joy or a happiness, that I do not know. But it is bound to be something of great value that I am certain.

The British played with the fate of the Indians for about two hundred years. They, however, had not much feeling for these people. They did not really care for the Indians. When they left India, they did not leave with any thought of Indian welfare in their heart. Centuries old "divide and rule" British policy in India worked as a time bomb. Just before British departure from India, India started to explode in a massive scale. British did not try to stop it. They did not provide any protective measure for the Indian people.

If they did so much killing at such a large scale could not have gone on so freely for so long. Nobody cared. The whole world watched and the Indian population was left to kill each other in a blind rage.

If the British cared they would obviously have given a little thought. They should have found a way to leave the Indians in more peaceful situation and not in a state of dreadful chaos, confusion and self-destruction.

To them India was nothing more than an object to exploit. When at last they came to the conclusion that India was no use to them anymore, they lost interest in India as a whole. They simply washed their hands of India. They pretended that the law and order in India was no more to do with them. It was someone else's problem!

In spite of what was said and what was not said Jinnah, the Muslim leader, must have been a British invention! They used him to destroy India in the most dangerous way possible for them to damage India.

It was truly India's hard luck that the Indians were no match for the British political expediency. Indians were unable to escape cruel fate! They were played by the British and driven to the terrible destiny. Britain was perhaps India's master without a heart and any real affection.

Coming to the point that Britain has probably kept all her love for herself and given very little, in fact, hardly any to her Indian empire; cruelty and selfishness perhaps is the name of the game as far as India was concerned for the great British political conscience. British did learn all the tricks of politics from the Romans.

In many ways British must have believed in themselves as the moral gods on earth. They might have reason to be conditioned to such an idea. Their education system and cultural values were planned to reinforce it. It seemed quite right to them that the whole world should want to serve them and pour out all the riches at their feet. It was as if the world owed it to them. The people of the world should only be grateful at the privilege of being able to do so.

This was in their opinion the best of the civilization the world could possibly aspire to attain. Anybody else wanting to take such a place, however, was unspeakably wicked, intolerably wrong and must be stopped at any cost.

Only the British were allowed to be the world's overlord but not the Russians or the Japanese. Any over step by the Japanese must be stopped even with the use of Atom bombs. It was and still is morally justified in the eyes of the world which is really the Western eyes.

As long as the people of the west and their allies are the world's number one exploiter that is alright and they must be allowed to remain so.

People belonging to the poor races must fall backward to please the people of the superior races in every possible capacity. This ideology seems quite reasonable and not at all peculiar or strange to the most people of the European origin.

They want to believe in it and they did their utmost to practise it at every parts of the world. I wonder why it does not strike wrong or disturbing to them at all. Then again I am born to a poorer race and stamped as only an inferior people. Maybe my mind is not sharp enough to comprehend it. One may really need to be superior to grasp all these quality thinking. Who can tell!

I may not be quite right if I say that American success and prosperity was built on the sacrifice of the American Indians and the Negro slaves. Maybe I am not too far from the truth in saying this. Maybe not! Anyhow history does not depend on my opinion. But people make history. And history stares at our face! We cannot help but taking note of history. In making of the modern America land and labour both were taken by force.

People blame the Germans for the Nazi uprising and the Jewish holocaust. But that is definitely not enough. It is the whole of the Western culture which is really responsible for it. Nazi culture belongs to the West as a whole and the West produced the Nazis.

Western nations are not different from the Germans in their outlook in general. It was their conflict of interest which brought out the war between them and the Nazis. They ostracised the Nazis because they happened to won over them in the war.

The idea of using the poor nations for the gratification of one's own greed and satisfaction is universal amongst the rich. Thinking of the less powerful people as less important than themselves and regarding them as lesser race too is quite customary for the people of European origin. Having the upper hand in conducting the fate of the unfortunate people of the world is regarded as a divine right vested upon the West by the God almighty himself.

All these notions are very dear to the heart and very deep in the conscience of the whole of the Western mind in general.

The reason Germany got the blame, is only because he was not able to make a good job of it all! He just lost his head completely and became too beastly amongst the beasts.

I am sure it maybe said that the savage inhumanity of the West manifested and exposed itself in the shocking deeds of the German Nazis.

Making a great scapegoat of Germany is not now going to get us anywhere. We maybe made to feel better by thinking that all the blames go to the Germans alone. The rest of the West may rest absolutely clear of all conscience and all the horrors of the war may seem to have nothing to do with them.

It is a bit too simple to think that Germany is the bad guy and the rest of the Western nations are the good guys of the world.

The second world-war is over; all the hell, the misfortune, the suffering, the loss, the death are done and gone with the dead. We can forget it all if we want to. We can choose to learn nothing from all these if we like.

The Germans are still here. Germany is still in the West. Germans and the rest of the Western world are in good terms and great friends. What is one to make of it all these? Who is clever enough to try to fathom out of all these mysterious history?

I just do not know what words to put in to express what is in my mind. I do not even know what questions to ask, let alone try to answer anything. Coming from a poor nation as I do, all I can feel is that we should not trust anybody—definitely none of these Western nations. We must be on our guard all the time!

Otherwise one just does not know when one will be sent to the gas chamber by the clever nations of this world. Whenever they feel like doing so the poor must have a little time to run for life!

This is not a talk for imagining safeguard. This is for real! The West massacred the American natives, enslaved the Negroes, gassed the Jews, almost annihilated the Japanese and God only knows what else they have done to whomsoever people through out the history.

It simply proves that they never think twice to misuse their power whenever a need arises in their mind. Also they know quite well how to justify their action. They are very good and clever in mobilising world's opinion on their side and do so whenever they need to. They dominate the world by conceit, coercion and concession. They do anything as long as it suits them. They never care even if it may be harmful for the people who are not part of their camp.

They think they are infallible and never make any mistake. But they do make mistake like anybody else, for they are no more than human. So when they think they are doing something for their own interest they may easily be misjudging. Unknowingly they may even kill themselves by mistake.

They are so powerful, heavy handed and used to ignore all opposition their very own survival is now in grave danger. The trouble, however, is that if they kill themselves they will kill the world too. It is very unlikely that they will leave anything behind to survive when they themselves have perished. This is the tragedy of the power in the hand of the powerful and proud Western superpower.

They have everything they need. They have things they do not need! They can lay their hand on anything including other people's things and lives.

It is now these other people who need to stop being stupid. They need to be saved. They do not need to suffer humility.

Ability to exploit the weak is admired in the West. Shrewdness, insincerity, ruthlessness and sophistication are the great Western virtues. No wonder it turns them to monster in the end!

But these Western people are quite unaware of the fact that other people can see them now as they are. They do not think that anybody is able to see them through the shield of their pretend goodness. They have been successful for a long time in using their pretence as a good musk for them. They pretend that they are as good as God and are very superior! And this gives them the right to rule the World!

The world lived with this Western domination for a long time. It was perhaps not due to just one thing or other. There must have been a great many historical reasons behind it all. Also it would be quite silly to think of one person or one group of people responsible for all of it.

The whole of the dominant culture must have produced it and the whole of that culture must bear the responsibility. But the reality of it all might be that the existence of the entire weak world must have made room for the dominant to predominate. This must be the lesson to be learnt from all the consequences of historical imbalance between strong and weak, if there is any lesson at all to learn.

From all the misfortunes of the past centuries human race must realise that the weak needs to overcome their weakness. Also they must have sufficient muscle to safeguard their well-being. They have to have the means to stop the strong from over ruling their lives.

If these are not learnt and put to practise in real sense then, all were lost for nothing. All the sufferings were in vain. Future humanity will have nothing to thank for.

Brutality was brought to the surface and all hell was let loose in this century. The world must ask seriously why! The whole humanity should be shocked, stunned and ashamed. If this is the only reality of this world and if the future has nothing to look forward to, then what hope is there for the hopeless humanity. Why don't we all give up living? If we do not have a purpose, is it not better to stop breathing rather than share the same world with the monstrous humanity.

Is human race is destined to choke humanity to death? Is this why human kind is attributed with so many ugly racial and social cruelties? Greater races teach the lesser races how to be destructive and self-destroying.

Too much power, feeling too important and too superior, inevitably drives one to a ruthless brute. The standard of morality gives way to self interest and selfish action.

Humility and morality are most needed in the depth of human soul. Everything else is nothing more than superfluous.

People are so keen to do even the impossible for God. Why don't they leave God alone and do things for their own sake! Surely God can look after Himself! Heaven can wait eternity if needs be! Only the poor mortals need help from each other. It is our time on earth which is running out! We are short of time. Why not make humanity the sole cause of our good deed.

Also who cares for super powers as long as they leave the rest of us in peace! It fails me how they justify that their freedom is precious and noble but the other people's freedom is not. They preach the Gospel of double standard! They happily dominate, captivate and enslave others but think nothing of it. When someone else threatens them in any way, they expect the whole world should be horrified at the prospect.

It may be very comfortable for them to be conditioned this way. But I must admit it is thoroughly confusing for me.

Nations with power dominated the world for centuries and was brainwashed to think it was their God-given right. However, when the Japanese tried to play the same game, the challenge was too much for them to bear. The Japs had to be stopped with nuclear bomb without a shred of doubt or hesitation.

Why is the right of powerful divine? Is it because the weaker world did not possess any atom bomb and was not able to stop the powerful from showing so much contempt for the rights and the lives of the less powerful nations?

The Western nations had enjoyed one-sided history and also God on their side for so long. It would perhaps, be too hard for them to give it up ever. The world belongs to them and them alone in all sense and purpose. To think of anything else is a great shock to their system.

I wonder if the world will remain the same for them for ever! Will they rather finish it all if they are challenged to face a change?

These nations know all about machine, especially about machine to kill. They are expert in war technology. This power made them the master of the world. Their possession grew bigger and manifold over the years. They are very good in their skill.

They are proud and self-possessed. However, their greed and skill to cheat others successfully knows no bound. They know very little about spirit of love and compassion for people who are not in their power-camp.

These powerful people make me feel guilty for the poverty in my country. As if the poverty amongst my people is my doing. I am responsible for this misery. All my countrymen alone are to be ashamed for the disgraceful sufferings there. We produced it and so it must be our fault. We are to blame for it. We are born poor. There must be something genetically wrong with us. We are to be left to perish in utter squalor and hopeless misery. Only duty the rich nations seem to have is to enjoy in pointing out all these to us.

At the same time they feel or acknowledge nothing about all the wrongs and injustices inflicted on my people by their people. They make one to understand that they personally have nothing to do with any of these activities and hence no guilty conscience of any kind for them to bear. They do not bear any responsibility either.

They are trained to wash their hands off when things are not very nice.

But they are very effective in taking all the pride and glory when things are right for them. They have made a very convenient world for themselves. Probably one has to be very superior to live a life with selfish heart and soul.

At every age amongst every nation some think and behave differently. That is really besides the point; also that is not enough either. As long as the majority or the people in power think and act very selfishly, the world as a whole is to remain a very wretched place. The human race or the human history has very little chance to improve.

If, on the other hand, enough people were kind, thoughtful and genuinely not so selfish, the world would have been a better place for everybody to live in. There would have effective machinery to stop so much misery and oppression in such a large scale all over the world for so long. So many atrocities of one kind or other need to be avoided if the grotesque history of man's compassion for his fellow men is to take a more safe-shape in future.

At the moment, all, people do is enjoy the spectacle of black tragedy committed everywhere away from their home and people. At least that is how it looks to the others.

No body holds power for ever. Everything evolves and it evolves from within.

The history of white supremacy is a history of unparallel violence and brutality. Power and possession may make a man formidable but not necessarily a man of quality or greatness in human term.

# Chapter Two

Imagine if the British really were philanthropist and truly wanted to help India unselfishly. Britain would have been the greatest nation on earth. They could claim to be almost godlike people.

With their skill and superior administrative capacity they could easily make wonder in India. A great friendship would have born between two nations. Enormous sufferings and pain and anguish could have been avoided for a section of population on earth. However, this is nothing but an idle dream. This sort of greatness is not to be found anywhere anyway. The world is not yet ready for this type of fair-minded people.

The history of the world is still the history of greed, deceit and just the grasping power for one's own kind, and nothing more.

But the meanness breeds meanness; violence creates violence. In the end nobody gains all that much. So Great Britain did not become all that great. She more or less burnt herself up in developing the great skill of diplomacy in keeping the weak for ever weak and the hungry struggling for ever to stop the pain of hunger. She was all the time thinking of her own advantage and interest. I am sure she thought she was doing all for the good of her own side. She was doing the best she could.

Perhaps this is what everybody does and Britain was no exception. Maybe we will never know! To send missionaries to save the souls from damnation is one thing; to make serious effort to improve the material condition of the down trodden people of an occupied country as one does in one's own country, is altogether a different matter. Is it not so!

The poor people are never lovable. The people who are degraded by the system, who are reduced to an emaciated state of one kind or other, always look ugly sub-human and very repulsive. Everybody feels quite justified in feeling contempt for such lives. No one asks question who or what is responsible for such an inhuman consequence. No one feels shame, sad or pain in such a sight of eye-sore. It rarely occurs to anybody that the world which produces such a tragedy is on the whole degrading for everybody who lives in it.

The people, who go through severe sufferings, are victims. We may shudder at their sights. The shame is not theirs. The shame is for all who see it happening but do nothing to prevent it. They are the criminals. They are committing crime against humanity.

Whenever I see the picture of the concentration camps of the second world-war in television, the inmates make me feel full of horror and utter disbelief. Then I remember the picture of the famine victims in India.

During British rule India suffered from quite a number of dreadful famines. Most of them were man-made. They were to serve British interest in one way or other. Countless Indians died unaccountably as a result of the deliberate action taken by the British authority at the time in India. It was part of their war-efforts to win the war. They did not think necessary to give a second thought for the poor dying Indians.

It was their right to win the wars even at expense of pitiful death of other people. No one ever talk about it. At least there has not been much mentioning of these catastrophic events in India. It has on the other hand, given to half-understand that famine in India is nothing more than a natural consequence for the famine-stricken Indians.

I am sure it is beyond the imagination of most average British that the famine in India has anything to do with the British.

However, the thought about the untold miseries and misfortunes of the millions of Indians haunts me and makes me feel very sad for my people.

The bodies of the people who died of hunger look like the bodies in the concentration camps. In any case what is the difference? Both groups of victims must have gone through extreme pain and degradation of slow and painful death. No body cared. No one paid much attention to their death.

At least the world mourns the loss of the camp-victims. Everybody knows who were responsible for the wicked deed. People now try to do all that can be done in honour of the memory of that awesome misfortune.

The famine victims in India do not have such luck. They have been destroyed by a mindless system which may have been very different from the system that produced those camp-victims. I wonder if the Indian victims knew the difference and felt happy about it in any way.

How many Indians died in the famine? Did anybody keep any record? India never recovered from these devastating famines. No real help was ever given to rescue her from these devastations. So many Indians are still hungry and are today living in the hell of constant pain of hunger. The rest of the world outside and inside India thinks nothing of it. They have grown to believe that it is natural for the Indians to be hungry.

These poor Indians look wretched and unlovable. No one feels sorry for them. No one likes doing anything for them. They are left to rot in their miseries. The common feeling amongst the non-poor is that it must be the poor's own making and so they deserve to suffer. Perhaps some people even feel that it is only normal for the Indians to go hungry. While they themselves must spend a long time working out how to enrich their own diet so that they can live a longer life in comfort and luxury. No one even acknowledge any responsibility for the dying poor of India. World public never shown any true concern or compassion for the helpless millions of India, who were and are sacrificed for their war-effort to win right over wrong. But their death and sufferings have hardly ever been honoured. No body shows much respect for their memory. I am sure this cannot be right and the world will one day regret it. To the contrary of the popular belief the pain for an Indian is no lesser pain than that for anyone else on this earth.

Pain never feels less painful just because one is a poor Indian or someone similar. I should know. I am an Indian. I don't want to deprive anybody of any smug feeling. It is really surprising though how people become smug if it suits them in any way

The poor people of the world are usually ugly. They are small. They do not have nice skin or appearances. They lack hygiene and often smell bad too. The poor in India and in many other places are driven by their hunger to eat scraps of food even from dustbins. It is no doubt an awfully repulsive sight for any people who are themselves quite well-fed.

Maybe these poor unsightly creatures do not look like men on the whole to most people. It does not seem wrong to oneself if one feels that these obnoxious filthy beings are only suitable to be thrown into dustbin and forgotten for ever.

It is fairly easy to play one's part for the people who are reasonably comfortable. It is, however, not so easy to have love and compassion for the people who are not lovable. That is a bitter fact of life!

Nevertheless the world is what we make of it. The inner quality, honesty and sincerity of man can produce wonder on earth. The pretence, on the other hand, is like a grotesque mask which only makes us look ridiculous. It does not do very much for our happiness.

There is no ultimate truth in this world. But we can all still strive to achieve it and progress towards it closer and closer but never actually attaining it. This is a good enough reason for desiring to go nearer to it.

I am not talking about each and everyman individually becoming saint. That would be very unrealistic. Man is made of good and bad qualities. That is not possible to change.

However, if the politics and the vested policies of the authorities in power are in favour of greater good for the human race in general, things will change for the better beyond recognition. But that is too much to hope. The world is full of people who are ruthless and reckless and determined to benefit themselves at the expense of others.

I was wondering why art of India did not flourish much under British rule. Maybe it was because the British were not a very good patron for Indian art. Art is a self-expression, creating new frontier of one's own innermost feelings and identities. One cannot be a patron if one has no feeling for such thing.

Art and culture of India is much more known now amongst the British people than it was ever been during the British period in India. The British did not pay much attention to it. They naturally did not like anything Indian too much.

They were brought up and trained to admire their own civilisation. Anything else was simply unworthy and uncouth to them. The British in India were mostly rigid and inward looking as far as their own culture was concerned. They lived in India but always looked towards their far away home in Britain. They felt homesick and looked down on everything which is not really British.

Nothing ever flowers without encouragement, honour and respect. Poor patronage and poor understanding can produce only poor results. India had a very impoverished period in many respect in many spares of creative activities. It was as if India lost her own way of saying things and became almost invisible for a while. India, as it was before the British, came to an abrupt end. She lost her power. She lost herself and was quite confused for sometime.

It was long time before she could recharge herself and emerge as a new India. But the old India is gone for ever. Also this new India is not quite the Indian India either. This is really a kind of conglomeration of Indian experiences past and present together with the outside influence which is in fact the domination of the Western culture. India no longer has her own unique Indian voice. She is now only a part of the whole world. She speaks, works and makes mistake in a way everybody else does too. The art of new India is now no more than an expression of the world culture. And it is in many respects still quite a weak one too. In some field, however, it is gaining ground and found something worthwhile to say to the world. But it is not Indian anymore, it is international!

The conflict between Marxism and Capitalism is really a conflict only for the bourgeoisies of the West. In Marxism, it is their freedom and privileges to do what they wish, is at stake.

They enjoyed their freedom almost as the overlord of the entire world for a long time. They do not want to give it up or loose it, which is quite understandable. This is naturally appropriate to their true nature. But what has it to do with the poor and under privileged people of the world or the world's poor nations! They have no freedom to speak of. They rarely have the chance to enjoy even what is rightfully theirs.

The poor are usually forced to serve the causes which benefit the rich. They do not have much choice. They hardly even have the democracy which is genuinely for their good at heart. The democracy they sometimes share, is nothing but a sham, a pretend democracy which is built on a conspiracy. Its entire purpose is to have a symbol and a stick to beat them with and not being discovered by anyone that they have been beaten.

Why should the loss of this democracy be a war-cry for the lot of the poor kind. The poor do not have democracy. Neither do they have freedom. How could they therefore loose any of it?

It is in fact a great, great world war for the protection of the riches for the rich. The rich use the poor in their war with all their sugar-coated ideology which maybe true for themselves but not for others.

The poor are materially underdeveloped. They are usually intellectually immature too. So they are not to discover the true nature and the purpose of all these logic and necessities of the battle of ideology.

The poor should give their lives for freedom. They must also not die of hunger and deprivation. The poor do not deserve death and they should not die. Who decides that they must not ask anything more in this world? Above all why should not they rebel?

They will have a good place in Heaven? What more could they possibly want! Material achievement is not good for their souls! It is only good for those who have it always! Others should see to that the rich do not ever loose their possession but must never desire any possession for themselves though.

In one way or other all of us want to take more than we like to give. This is very silly of course. As no one can ever take any more than one gives in life. When will people ever learn this basic rule of life!

Everybody wants and no body likes to give. This is perhaps why the world is what it is. Many men want to make love but do not like the responsibility of children.

Whether we like it or not, we all have to pay for the precious gift of life so long we have a life. The more the life is worth the harder we have to pay. Higher quality of life costs even more.

I do not know who made the law. But it is impossible to break it. Higher form of life costs such a lot of pain and suffering! In fact, without hardship, pain, loss and severe sufferings higher conscience does not even come to the surface or take some shape in anybody's life.

Mostly most people live a lower grade of life. They usually want to cheat. They want more than they are prepared to give. They think they are clever enough to get away with it. However, everybody pays in the end in one way or other for everything in life.

Everybody wants to be happy. For the lure of happiness in life we compromise and do all manners of mean deeds. But where is happiness? When at last we come to our senses that there is no happiness, we begin to know the loneliness of life. We begin to understand there is nothing to gain by being greedy or mean. Maybe that is the moment when we begin to touch greatness within us and become ourselves quite great sometimes.

There is no short cut. It is through tragedy and pain we learn to do good. We learn that there is nothing we can do for ourselves and it is good to do good for others.

Love for others is only born out of loneliness of heart and through realisation of the tragedy of life. This is perhaps the creativity of our inner most soul. It only works when one comes to know the futility of one's own life.

We are born on one day and die on another. Also we can not do very much for ourselves in between. We do not bring anything with us to this world and neither can we take anything with us from this world. By nature the only thing for us to do in life is to work for this world and make it better as much as we are able to. That is all there is. It is quite a lot though if you think about it seriously. This gives us a reason to be born and a purpose in life. Even for this we must go through a lot of pain and suffering in life.

It seems as if we come to this world to prove our worth not in terms of our possessions but in term of our qualities. The possessions we accumulate are not ours anyway. It belongs to the world. In some way our quality is something which belongs to us; because we ourselves create it in our consciousness. Only quality appears to count as we leave the mark of our quality behind us for our species to uphold.

However, more people are interested in possession of wealth than anything else. If it was fashionable to do good for others—real good—serious good work—if the best brains would devote their efforts for the good of the world—the world would have been a good place. Unfortunately the world has not yet evolved to that stage. It still enjoys being selfish. To inflict cruelty to others is regarded as a smart act—a sign of great civilisation. So the civilisation creates nothing but a rotten world for us. It is a great pity no doubt but that is it.

People by nature love to be rich and better off. The more poorer they see the others by comparison, the happier and prouder they feel for their own achievement.

In the Western world people in power sometimes talk about Third world. They seem so very bored. They talk about something which is without any serious interest to them. They pretend of course that they are concerned but that is no more than just pretence.

However, they forget that they were not always without interest in the third world. When the third world was for them to be taking they came there with great enthusiasm and in great number. They did not hesitate to plunder it to their heart's delight. They found plenty of justification and energy to do with it whatever they felt like. No place in the third world was too difficult for them to reach.

As long as it was profitable for them to venture in the third world nothing and no effort was spared. Now that they managed to suck it up dry the third world is no longer profitable for anyone and only just liability . They have therefore lost their interest in such a world.

They are not interested in the welfare of the third world. But that does not stop them talking big. They like to keep up their pretend concern as a political gesture. They are very good at that. But in reality they could not care less for any part of the third world or any of its unfortunately poor population.

They may feel that they must continue to talk and show concern about the poor nations; otherwise it may make them look uncivilised. They may also use it as a clever political trick in order to strike a bargain with any third world commodity or favour. Maybe they talk their empty talk due to their hypocritical prick of conscience! I do not know.

I can not however help hoping that one day, maybe in not so remote future, if it would be possible for the poor inhabitants of this third world to improve themselves and their countries, and if it would rekindle the interest of the rich nations once again. Would the rich nations change their tune and find enough interest to get involved in it again!

I am sure they can not ever resist the temptation of finding a way to share the fruits of any nation anywhere. No doubt they will have any difficulty in justifying their action and making themselves simply indispensable for the cause. Most probably they will have the whole world praising them for their honourable motives and deeds!

The rich and the powerful all the time want to own everything. They want to enjoy the whole world as a rich man's club at the expense of the poorer nations and poorer people. They do not mind using the poor for their own whims; but they never wish to do much for the poor.

Of course they would not admit it openly. In fact they would go a very long way to convey the message to the world at large that they have taken the problem of the poor in their own hand and they will in near future deliver the poor from the peril of poverty and all other sufferings.

Obviously, it is nothing but a simple trick so that the poor do not get worked up and do remain for ever undeveloped. They do not wish the poor to acquire the intellect which will help them to see clearly that they are just a pawn and an object of exploitation in the hands of the rich nations.

Now-a-days the poor nations may understand their position in the world to some extent. But they are still politically much immature, intellectually under developed and more than anything else, sociologically very divided. They have not got the muscles or the means to stop the hands of the rich from hitting them. The rich on the other hand have all the power to keep the poor under their own control. So far they only wish to keep the poor happy with just empty words and nothing more.

Evidently this is simply a human nature. The one, who has something, wants more and wishes to be a giant. A giant wants to grow even more of a giant. For a giant it is simply a pleasure to be able to and also to wish to crush the little ones around. The small ones on the contrary can not protect their things and so loose more and more, and thereby become smaller and smaller. They so remain a pigmy under the thumbs of the giant!

Is it not very strange that the rich wish to ruin the poor and even kill them if needed for their own profit and selfish reason but at the same time wish to be seen as the selfless benefactor and even the sole savour of the world! They desire to enjoy life both materially as well as spiritually.

This is so contradictory! Why do they aspire this way? Is it because they are not so highly developed at some psychological level of conscience and emotion? Their outward sophistication maybe no measure of their inner imbalance! Maybe they are not as strong and as invincible as they think!

This psychological make up is not the prerogative of the rich of the rich nations. It is more or less the same for the few rich belonging to the poor nations as well. The rich and the powerful anywhere take the riches of the world for granted for themselves only if they can get away with it.

They are everywhere very good to help themselves if no one to stop them. Perhaps the greed and the possession of power make them less susceptible to the prick of conscience or the consciousness of fairness for all.

However, everything is part of the mother-nature. The weak and the poor cannot be ignored for ever. They may have to wait for their turn to come. But it will come one day. Maybe they will need to wait until a crack or breakdown appear in the rich man's world through which the poor maybe able to turn their fate. At least the world may change for the poor and the rich may not be able to keep all the privileges to themselves anymore.

Centuries after centuries the poor cried in pain all over the world. God never seemed to pay any attention to their prayer. One might think that God is partially deaf to the poor.

It may not be so. It may be that He does listen but He needs a long time to make up His mind! When the situation is over charged with injustices and the air is badly polluted with pain, He does at last decide to shake the world for a change. Things are no longer the same after that.

Until then the power seems to be in the hand of the powerful. The contempt for the life of the poor seems to be almost universal. Many Indians are desperately poor. Western people generally appear to hold the Indians in contempt.

They do not think the Indians are worthy people. They do not regard that anything the Indians possess is of much value. Indian art, Indian culture, Indian religion, music, dance, values, life-style, ways of living—everything is of no consequence in their eyes. They hardly think it deserves any serious consideration. They are brought up to ignore it altogether.

They also teach and convince the Indians to neglect it. Indians loose faith in themselves; and so become worthless in their own eyes. They perform and act as less of worthy human and become inferior in all acts and deeds. The tragedy of a nation takes birth.

The greatest tragedy in life is the loss of faith in oneself. Every other loss is less serious by comparison.

The western mind has always been engaged in making the world comfortable for them to live in. Their science and technology are devoted for the purpose. Their religion is to give them spiritual comfort and uplift so that they can enjoy their comfortable lives to the fullest extent. They do not want to miss anything and neither do they want to leave anything. But anything uncomfortable they do not wish to know.

They love their pets only as long as it is not any bother. When it becomes inconvenient they quite comfortably put an end to it. Their culture and way of living give them all the moral justification for their action. They believe life is to enjoy and not to suffer. However, the suffering of others outside their doorstep does not often move them too deeply.

They simply consider this as a part of unavoidable natural order. To them it is only natural that some are to suffer to make others happy as long as these others are themselves. They believe in the survival of the fittest.

They are the most powerful race and that must give them the right to be comfortable even at the expense of the less powerful ones.

If this order is ever changed I do not know how they will feel. If one day the less fortunate people become fortunate at their expense I hope they will accept it as only natural. I hope they will give others the same right to be happy without any protest or resentment.

In any case, who knows how the laws of nature really work. It may turn around! Everything seems to go in a circle!

One may notice that the children of doctors, engineers and professors, often do not want to be professionals. They do not wish to work hard and be somebody. They simply aspire to be ordinary and nobody.

The children of nobody on the other hand desire eagerly to be somebody. Someday some of them even succeed.

Perhaps this is the law of nature. This is how nature keeps control over the smooth running of the social order. Nothing goes to the extreme. Somehow everything is brought to the level of average. Balance in nature must be restored. Even though some fluctuations between certain limiting values are bound to occur all the time

Our sense of values must have deep functional role. It keeps us content sociologically and thereby physically.

At some stage we work very hard. We want to improve ourselves and our world. Humanity leaps up. We feel proud and we relax. Decadence sets in. We fall back. Others then catch up with those who have gone ahead. This is perhaps how the world tries to function and progress steadily throughout the ages. With it we go up and down the ladder of human achievements.

Until about a little more than a few decades ago, most of the English people in England, would have been found to be terribly prejudiced about Indian food

Maybe because the people of India are poor, the English people associated Indian food with the food for the poor people. They looked down on such food and were very proud of their own. They felt exalted in eating plenty of meat, butter and cream in rich English style.

However, things have changed quite a lot since. They have found out that they can be proud of their food habit if they want to, but they may not have very long to live and enjoy their proud life. They may have to leave their wonderful world for others to enjoy.

Of course, they did not like the idea one little bit. Vigorous research and medical investigations soon revealed the harmful nature of their dietary system. They searched hard for alternative ways and found certain beneficial goodness in some eastern food habits.

They now associate a lot of eastern food with long and healthy living. Most of their people caught up with the idea very quickly and will not be left behind with unhealthy eating. They have everything to live for and wish to live longer than ever. For that there is nothing they would not do.

Eastern food, vegetarian food, wholesome health-food shops have sprung up everywhere like mushrooms. Suddenly people appear to be quite madly keen about wholesome food. They are no longer short of good wards in favour of these food-stuffs which they once thought only fit for the poor.

They are now educating their public about the goodness of the high-fibred food which they never thought of having the misfortune of ever to eat it.

People change. Sometimes they change very quickly. It is truly incredible how quickly these changes can take place in the established dietary pattern of a society. Suddenly some food become popular; some go out of favour. In the end it is a question of motivation. Given the right motivation man will eat anything!

Our quest for the right nutrition for our body and mind goes on. Theories and ideas come and go. With these come the changes in our concept of good food. There starts the notion of preferable food for our health and beauty.

I have always been very suspicious about processed food. I never liked any tinned food, especially tinned meat product.

Maybe it is because, I come from India. I do not mind eating poor Indian food, but I feel tinned product is unwholesome.

I always had a strong suspicion about convenient food. I have a peculiar fear that there maybe a close connection between tinned meat products and cancer in the body. I do not know how it started. No one ever admitted it. No one has proved it or pointed this way. Everybody uses convenient food of some sort sometime. They do not all die of cancer. I know that. Nevertheless, I cannot get rid of this notion from my mind. It maybe simply an obsession of my mind!

Several years ago I lived in some place. My landlady had four very nice and healthy cats. I am not fond of cats and was not overjoyed to have them around me. But some years later I was very sorry to hear that each of those four cats died of cancer. They did not all die at the same time. At different time they developed cancer of one kind or other and so they were put to sleep before the disease got too far. Several other people told me that their pet cat and dog died of cancer too.

It confirmed my fear that there might be a link between preserved process food and cancerous diseases. After all, the pets in England are fed mainly on tinned food. Maybe any living body fed on this type of food stuff for a prolonged period of time naturally would develop a cancer of some sort sooner or later. Many dogs do die of cancer if they do not die of something else earlier. I feel dog-food is responsible for this in some ways.

Perhaps my fear is entirely irrational. Perhaps it is not so. People in the west are too free and easy with convenient food. However, many fold doubt is beginning to set in people's mind. Fresh and natural food are becoming more and more health-food in people's estimation. Obviously an occasional meal of convenient food is not going to kill anyone. But too much of it taken too frequently must be quite harmful for all of us. So much additives, colouring, processing, preservatives and high technology go in food industry, food manufacturing and food science, it cannot be entirely free of harmful effect of some kind. Many people are becoming more and more suspicious and trying hard to find an alternative way.

# Chapter Three

The Western world has everything. They have health and wealth to enjoy themselves; ability to protect their interest and technology to improve their world. All the power of a fuller life is in their hand. Understandably they wish happiness too. But a lot of violence and bitterness is exposing itself amongst them. This cuts short of their enjoyment in many ways.

British society too is becoming more and more violent for no apparent reason. This outbreak of violence may not stop simply by more severe punishment for the culprit or by improving social securities.

Imposing more security may not be the answer to social disorder. These disturbances may be the manifestation of some of the qualities encouraged by their system of education and values.

Throughout their long history of progress and prosperity they have always encouraged their thugs and hooligans against other nations, especially against the weak ones. Their teddy boys and most of the unruly characters were sent to conquer the world for their country. Their ruthless personalities were on great demand and needed for managing their empire. England needed an endless supply of such characters to ensure the smooth running of her vast colonies.

European culture thinks highly of selfish motives and shrewdness amongst human attributes as long as they help them as a nation and an individual. So long they had their empire they could not have enough of these people who could skilfully repress and exploit the natives of the colonies. Their education had to be geared to produce vast number of such people. As these people were always short supply for the number needed, such people were admired and highly prized in the society. The misfits, the aggressive characters and the trouble-makers, all had a very useful role to play in looking after their country's interest in far away places. They became the brave and bold patriots. They found great purpose in their lives in making, maintaining and guarding the empire. The vanguards of the empire were never the sweet gentle moralists by any standard. But they were the heroes, the source of strength of their country.

They made the history of their country. Their people look up to them with great admiration. The more rough and ready elements were about the better it was for the war-efforts and the innumerable battle-fields all over the world.

The drop-outs and the unskilled had plenty of opportunities, provided they were adventurous and willing. They were not left to rot in an unseen corner of the society.

England had a vast empire to manage. She needed all her people. Even her anti-social characters had great use in great many ways. Some of them managed to enjoy a great deal of freedom of choice and self-expression. The whole world was for them to explore. They built fame and fortune for their nation in the remote parts of the world. Their country acknowledged them as rare heroes. These rough and ruthless elements stole nation's heart and were worshiped in a most romantic fashion.

Their eventful history was made by their restless aggressive nature. They had to be aggressive. They wanted to be aggressive. They admired aggression as it helped them to become the overlord of almost the whole wide world. The aggressors had a lot of places to go to. There were great many pipe lines all over the world to channel all the aggression the society could generate.

For a long time the west was very privileged. The western societies themselves did not suffer much from its own aggressions. They were not at the receiving end. They were able to channel most of their aggression and aggressive qualities for the expansion and maintenance of their empire.

In their colonies they had lots of room to let loose and exercise a lot of their dark ruthless-aggression. Later the western nations entered into a period of history when they engaged all their might, power and people in pinching and overthrowing each others empires. There started a dangerous time of mindless violence and self-destroying competition against each other. One empirical power wanted to test the strength of another. Death, destruction and downfall followed in an unprecedented scale. All devouring hatred broke loose against each other. The whole world was dragged into world-wars, one after another.

Western nations seem to nurture hideous hatred against one another and are capable of incredible violence and destruction. Now they are sitting on a time-bomb bent on destroying the whole world in a flash.

Their culture took great pride in killing. Their science cultivated the power to destroy. Their civilisation is based on gun-powder. They persuaded the power to master the war-machine. Now they are powerful. They have opened up the secret to destroy the universe. Everybody is waiting for the end of the world. It is now no more than a question of time.

One more world war means the end of us all. There are not many colonies for the west any more. The overflow of cruel characters has nowhere to go to. The vast industries of war and the multi-dimensional games of cruelty against humanity are at last under stress and an ultimate threat. There is not much room for expansion any more.

Lots of people in the west have nothing to do and no where to go to. They have no excitement in their lives. They are bored to death. No wander their society is beginning to suffer. The game of violence, cruelty and deception is now out in the open in their own society.

Without change of heart, education and philosophy it may be impossible to eradicate these tendencies of serious social disturbances in the west, and also it's follow-up in the east.

Maybe it is the price of civilisation every nation has to pay. Maybe it is simply in the nature of things that in making the advanced stage in social development, dark destructive forces set in the nation from within. Maybe refinement makes a nation spent and exhausted.

A great deal of violence is exposing itself in British society. It must be the manifestation of something!

There seems to be a lot of discriminations amongst the British people. Quite a lot of mindless, selfish and shrewd hooligans are engaged in attacking the minorities and the weak. More and more it is taking its role in their society as an ugly force.

They think they can stop it by making some slight changes here and there. It may not be so easy to do without altering the society quite seriously and sincerely.

Without a fundamental change in their behaviour and without an improvement in their basic attitude towards people in general it may turn up to be a national sickness. It seems a deep seated disease. To cure it they need to change their values.

They need a lot more compassion, kindness, gentleness and morality in the society. The respect for their fellow human and a genuine recognition of humanity are needed to be placed firmly in their conscience.

Otherwise they are bent on destroying their society and themselves. The effect of double standard is serious. One set of behaviour pattern for themselves and another one for the others, bound to produce complexity and mistrust. This practice has its ill consequences.

Lack of respect for others is a serious problem in a society. For many years the British believed and made others to believe that they were the best. Faith in themselves, helped them to become the best.

Faith in oneself or the lack of faith in oneself plays a big role in making a man no doubt.

Now that the British no longer believes that they are the best, they may behave in an inferior manner. Also once the complex sets in history may take a downward course. Self-respect and the respect for the others is the only salvation for any nation on earth.

Mankind as a whole has come a long way. Man is now standing at a crucial cross-road and is in danger of actually leading himself to become extinct.

The underlying cause of it all is greed. The greed is natural in man. It is the rise and fall of mankind. The greed of man has gone too far. It is now high time he learns how to put the harness on the reins of his all pervading greed.

Once up on a time man found out how easy it is to profit at the expense of his down-trodden fellow beings. His greed caught hold of his imagination. Soon it became a great virtue—a quality of high value for him. Before long it knew no bounds and instead of man controlling his greed, greed is now controlling man.

However, it has gone too far. There is just no room to go any further. He is actually standing on the verge of a precipice. One false move may be the end of him altogether.

Now that it is no longer possible for mankind to profiteer by oppression or other evil means without a great deal of harmful repercussion, it is high time man must relearn how to harness the evil within him. Otherwise he will probably destroy all including him.

In spite of all the doom and despair there seems to be a glimpse of hope. If one can motivate people correctly and catch their imagination, they will perform miracle. They may even turn this world into a paradise. Who knows and who can tell!

People of the Western world, talk about compassion. They often play act compassionate from political motivation. Usually they do not know very much about genuine compassion on the world-wide basis. The only thing they really know is to live in comfort and luxury. They like talking about compassion as it makes them feel good.

However, it is very important to feel good. People do not always realise that sooner or later the power of moral conscience catches up with everybody. Life without morality is not much of a life! It is a kind of certain death in the society. If one looses moral values life gets out of control and it starts to go astray. The purpose and object of living dies in you. The meaning of life gets confused. The entire structure and strategy of living becomes crumbled and destroyed. It is a very serious business indeed. Our life and our social health cannot survive without moral fibre. It nourishes our ego, helps us to justify our existence and makes us to live as best as we can to the very end of our natural life.

Without it we are doomed and our existence is threatened. We loose our reason to survive and are bound to go crazy in one way or another.

But what is morality? Nothing is fixed in this world and nothing is perfect either. It is different in different people and in different places. As long as we are honest and sincere nothing else matters. The morality therefore depends on one's own education and culture. Behind it as always goes on a lot of pretence, manipulation and dishonesty. Uncovering of these evils to the caring people could prove a great service to the human kind.

It is not an easy task for anyone in any country. Yet people all over the world, naturally assumes that our spiritual leaders, the men of so called religion should be able to give us a helping hand. But they do not always do so. Very often they are nothing more than an instrument of the state. They are simply officers to control the mind and behaviour pattern of the simple people. In spite of all the careful dressing up of the truth and morality, certain amount of the real thing does filter through to the ordinary people of all nations. It is perhaps because our need is the same all over the world. No matter, who we are and where ever we may be, the basic need of our life is universal.

Yet the men of religion are not always the same in their conviction. In my own tradition of Indian culture the men of God were not regarded as men of God unless they renounced the wealth and worldly possession for the good of the world. Ritualistic gesture is understood differently from religious action.

In the West the men of God are employed to do paid job. They hold highly paid office and high status indeed. To carry out God's work is a profession like many other profession and some people follow it as a kind of living. Renunciation of worldly possession is regarded with scepticism. It is a bad thing in their eyes. It is more or less regarded as an act of people who are clearly out of their rational mind. They do not believe that it serves any useful purpose and so no one in their right mind would dream of doing it.

Generally, people in the West like gathering wealth for themselves and for their family. Giving away all for others is looked upon as unhealthy.

However, small charitable acts are very fashionable amongst them. They are used to small charity. So long it does not hurt at all and so long it makes them look good in other people's eyes, it is praiseworthy—it is alright.

Unfortunately, little charity, little good or pretend goodness does not produce much mark, neither does it change anything. The rotten world stays rotten all the same! Still, little is better than nothing at all!

Amongst all nations there is a long tradition of doing some good deeds for the benefit of their own poor and oppressed. But there is not much of a history of doing real good for the people of other nations. There has never been many Mother Teresa of Calcutta. There are usually quite a few Billy Grahams. They are very keen to convert people to a set religious order which they consider the right one. They pour out their energy for this purpose. Their actions appear to be overdramatic, hypnotic and well acted. They produce some interesting short lived results which have all the characteristics of a Hollywood film. They do not hold much reality for people outside of their group of friends or influence. It is only now there is one Bob Geldof trying in a big way to save Africa from the hunger of famine and desolation. Even this may not in the end amounts to very much in spite of all his efforts and strong will.

Each of us upholds our own values, tradition, rituals and memories in our own ways. In doing so we feel good and we identify ourselves to a particular group, nation or community. This works as a kind of group therapeutics. We all need it. Feeling good is all that matters while one lives.

People of one race do not usually feel the same way about another. In fact, the beauty of human race is that everybody laughs at everybody else. Everybody finds everybody else is in someway funny, amusing and ridiculous!

The dominant culture makes you believe that nothing else is of any consequence. It uses up things it has some use for, but ignores the rest as if it does not exist.

The world is full of misery. So much misery is every where. Yet no one wants to leave this world at one's own free will. But you have to pay the world for your life even though it may be a rotten life. That is the message of life to the living. We cannot escape it.

To pay for our life we do all we can! It is our nature that we like to get on the band wagon. The children and the adults are both alike in this respect. So far the Western side seems to be the winner and so everyone wants to be seen to be with the West. The battle between east and west was never been a fair one. But things may have come to a full circle and the luck at long last might like to change side.

The world is changing now. The children of the world are refusing to accept things at their face value. They have begun to question and compare different values with questioning mind. They are being surprised at the revelation of truth in front of their eyes. These children are not the same as those in the olden days. Their education is different. It is soon going to be impossible to pull any wool over the eyes of these children. No one will be able to exploit or manipulate them to the advantage of one over others. These children are ready to fight for the truth—the truth they themselves have discovered and not the truth they have been told of.

The world seems once again ready to leap forward quite a distance along the path of fairness! Real battle is about to start. This is going to be the battle on equal terms. The survival of the fittest is to be settled. No one will be able to fix the win on unequal terms.

The west takes advantage of both worlds. They use either of the worlds if it serves them right to the best of their advantage. They know how to exploit the best of both worlds—the world of naked cruelty, ruthless brutality and the world of morality, high spirit of holiness. They can act as compassionate spiritual super human if it would serve their purpose.

Their act of pretence is so perfect, it is almost impossible to detect by any untrained mind. The only give-way is that it is always timed rightly and it is always to serve their own interest, and never any one else's!

The ordinary people anywhere are just ordinary and varied. It is difficult to put a label on them. But the power which pushes the ordinary has a special nature. The power-block of the west always follows the ideology of serving self-interest and nothing else. Though, they have indeed mastered the art of pretence. They have learnt to play-act and help themselves whenever and however they have a need to. If they need to boost their morality they know how to behave. If they need to improve on their physical strength and if they need to perform some treachery, they know exactly how to do it. They can lay their hands on a right source of abundant supply of their necessity in the right way at the right time and feel very superior!

I suppose superiority must be the ability to give best possible justification of one's own selfish motive and the capacity to dress it up as the most glorified deed of action!

Maybe it is our destiny that we are either, simple, honest and primitive or cunning, shrewd, dishonest and superior. We just cannot be both!

I know I am too simple and straight. It is obviously no good. One has to be a bit bent if one wants to be smart.

The most powerful people are the capitalist of the Western world. The capitalist world always seems to safeguard its interest by favouring the elite. I am not sure how it works. But it does. Maybe the elite of the society are interested in the values of the capitalists. Somehow the elite need to exploit the poor and that in tern serves the capitalist hands. This is perhaps why the imperialist always appear to hand the power over to the elite and never to the common mass of the land. Before handing over the power the imperialist always seems to make sure that the common people never get the chance to share real power and prosperity so that the country can never improve generally and peacefully. At the departure of the imperialist rule common men are usually plunged to their death in an instant.

Actually the weakness of the west shows in their strong attachment in the richness of the rich people. They take great pride in their wealth and material possession. They claim close friendship with the people who have a lot. They, however, disown any relation with the people who have none. The west have two sets of rule—one for the rich and another for the poor.

It may mean that they are only human, but it also means that they are simply not superior. They are capable of going up and down like any other people.

They may think that they are infallible and good luck is with them for ever. It is simply not true. Their fame, pride and glory are just as brittle and fragile as anybody else's in this world. They might have their good days. They might have a good run of it. The others can have their fortune too. Maybe the others have their good days ahead! When the table is turned the world may not even remember them as it has forgotten many before them! The western people might be proud of their power today, but they do not have the magical power or the imagination to grasp what lies ahead! Because no one has!

Thinking of people of different origin, Negroes must have been a very resourceful race. It is not a small wonder that they did not simply give in and die of broken heart. They had to bear incredible misery, disorder and injustice. But they are still alive and kicking. Perhaps one day they will claim their fair share of this world and take up their proper place. They may even prove to be the fittest race amongst all races. Who Knows! The potential of their race is still intact!

Talking about the black people of Africa, the cruelty of slavery immediately comes in my mind. The history of slavery is long and cruel. Africa is not the only country to suffer from this savagery. It has been world wide. But the slave-trade of the Africans must have been particularly brutal no doubt.

People know of it as evil now. But the curse of slavery is not so easy to cast off. The slavery of one's own people is perhaps relatively less evil, as it dissolves away with the progress of the country. Once the economy improves, poor get better and the problem of slavery goes away without much trace. However, the slavery of another race amongst the people of a different race is entirely a different matter. The consequence of this evil deed is far reaching and probably for ever.

Subjugation of one race by another might have been very exciting amongst the powerful people. It might have been like a cat and mouse game to them. Probably the powerful nations enjoyed playing this game because they were the cats and they were always to win. They thought it was their right to win and could not think any other way. They knew they had very little risk of loosing anyway.

The subduing the weak by the strong was not regarded as wicked. It was thought to be perfectly normal and the right thing to do. They were not at all squeamish to get away with anything they liked just because they had the upper hand. The strong is always very good in dressing up lies and deceits. Just because others are unable to stop them from their wilful work, they think it is alright.

Very few people realise that deception or thoughtless provocation is a boomerang. It is only a question of time before it comes back and hurts the promoter most.

Lack of justice creates volcano deep down in the depth of human heart. It may lay hidden for a long time. But there comes a time when irruption takes place. It comes out one day for everybody to see and suffer from. It changes a lot of things around too.

The submission of the poor by the rich and powerful is only a historical phase. As long as circumstance is in favour of the rich, they are the winner. No matter how unfair it may be for the poor. This can change though.

The winner may think that the winning spell is to last for ever. He may think that the credit is his and his alone. He may be convinced that his strength is because of his genes which must be vastly superior to the rest of the mankind. But there are two things to think about, the genes which have gone to the top and the genes which are going to the top. Nothing in this world is likely to be permanent. The power of the powerful is most certain to change hand. The poor is not going to remain poor for all times. The world changes around; too many factors and too many dimensions make our destiny for us, rich and poor. Nothing stands still! That is against nature!

It is quite understandable that the western people should be so proud of their culture and incredible achievement. Self-respect is fine. But there is no need to become conceited.

They love portraying all other nations as imbecile, hooligans and devoid of any moral virtue. They like robbing other nations the pride of their nationhood whatever that may be.

In contrast the west is very keen to make their own people think of themselves as virtuous, fair-minded and full of many goodness. They are very thorough to educate their public in this respect. They become almost conditioned to think of themselves as very righteous people even though the facts may not always support this.

As far as the quality of their people is concerned they are very complacent, very smug indeed. They like to believe that the whole world looks up to them and there is no better example than themselves for the entire population of this earth. Maybe they are right in some ways; but what about their faults, misdeeds and wrong doings? Is it a good thing to overlook them completely? They seem not to remember anything which is not to their credit. But what about the people at the receiving end of their wrong doing? Is it easy or necessary to forget the sufferings and the pains?

Anybody tries to point out their short comings is not popular. Any attempt in this respect rouses bitter suspicion and point-blank disbelief.

One such attempt was the television programme, "the Denara Boy", on channel four in British television. It was not acceptable to the British public. It was supposed to be based on a true story of British treatment of the Jewish refugees in Great Britain during the Second World-War.

The revelation of the true nature of the British feeling towards the poor alien in their country is a very bitter truth and is obviously not palatable to them.

It would have been very entertaining if it was a programme, about some other people, and not, about their own. They are used to playing magnanimous. They could not swallow that their own people could easily sink so low. Of course it did not do much good to the national image of superiority they like to believe.

For a long time the view of superiority is firmly established in the mind of the western people. To them it is just right. It suited them in many ways. However, every view is double-edged. Superiority is no exception.

To be superior in technology was fine. They had superior power, arms and wealth. They could do whatever they liked with the lives of the people everywhere. It was very intoxicating and inspiring for the west for sometime.

But they wanted more. They wanted to be superior on moral ground too. Otherwise, the image of a superman was not quite complete. Without moral superiority the ego was overshadowed by something not so happy in their mind. There the conflict started to go wrong for them. It soon got out of their control in many ways. At last it started to serve interest, other than their own.

To be almighty is something, but to be all humane and more in real sense is something quite different. They began to realise that they were not the master in the true sense of the world. They had never been truly the master race. So the superiority started to elude them. Instead of being an advantage it became a serious handicap for them.

They have accepted that life without moral superiority is no superiority at all! But to become superior in that sense they have to give up so much that they are not prepared to do so either. Hence they have to do with less superior image for themselves which is not too good for their own moral! As superiority begins to loose its shine, it undermines their faith in themselves.

Morality, superiority, God and religion! These abstract words are not easy to live with. We aspire to these ideas. But does anyone really know what they are supposed to mean? Yet in many ways they cause a lot of havoc in our conscience.

The idea of religion is particularly difficult for many. Yet everybody seems to have a religion of one kind or other. People seem to take refuge in their religion. But what is it? What exactly is it supposed to mean?

It may be that only the superficial, selfish and happy people cling to ritualistic religion. These people are contented, easy in their mind. They found what they wanted in life. So they think that they are special. They are rewarded by God because they have been good. They think God follows the carrot and stick rule. They feel they must not make God angry by forgetting or ignoring any of the rituals of their religion.

It feels all wrong to me! It irritates me to no end seeing people so vain and empty. I really dislike this business of religion. I actually hate it. In my opinion nothing is more harmful than this deceitful attribute of human mind. Nothing is more divisive of man than this silly notion of religion. It makes man a perfect hypocrite. The organised religion has helped to promote more violence, cruelty, self fulfilling interest in man than anything else. It may have absolutely nothing to do with God or Goodness. Yet men all over the world have fought over it to the death.

Anyway how is anybody to know anything about God? What is this human notion of God? I have no feeling for any of these rubbish aspiration of religion except perhaps a faint weakness for a kind of mysticism. In my quiet moments the universe seems such a great mystery!

I cannot help feeling mystic and awe towards all creation. One has to have simple wonder, great admiration and deep respect for the whole of this world and everything in it including the bad and the good and all in between.

It urges me to do all I can for this world before I have to go away to who knows where! All I wish is to be of little bit of use to my fellow men while I live!

Do I care if I was made in God's image or something else? I do not think so. In any case, what difference does it make? Not much I am sure!

Some way or somehow I was made and I had no saying in the matter. Why waste time now in the speculation of images? Is it not the very fact of existence itself important enough for me?

Also what about the animals, the tiniest insects or all the other things on this earth? Are they any less important? And which image, do they proclaim? What a deceit! What an arrogant idea! Maybe it just projects the self-importance of the dominant culture of the western mind. Will man be able to live in the world which is unfit for animals? Don't we need the animals and plants more than they need us?

I have very little in common with this culture. I do not share much of this view. I regard it as negative and very harmful for the mankind in the long run.

We may have our eyes glazed over with all the talk about our spiritual state or the bellyful of the psychological interpretation of God. We are not ever going to know anything about the Absolute, spiritual or otherwise. Did not someone say it already that, it certainly is a dream and an illusion! We are all destined to travel towards great unknown!

Maybe God is the poetry in our heart. Some of us know about this only by the grace and goodness in ourselves. That is all there is to it!

Some of us live inside of ourselves and rot there. I, for example, have been dead in my heart for a long time. Long before I reached the dead end in my heart I began to feel great pain and sadness.

Some people have all the luck. But I was not one of them. Some people are lucky. They get what they want. Some are not so lucky. They cannot get what they want. I am one of these people. Never have I got what I really wanted. Simply unlucky me I suppose!

It is very easy to be trapped in one's misfortune. It is so very easy! It is a surprise that everybody is not. Yet people pass judgement on the unlucky one so easily. We all do! The thing is if only we have a way to know what lies ahead of us, we would be wiser and we would know what we are talking about!

My better days were such a long time ago it almost seems that it was another life. It feels that I never had any happiness in my life. I wonder if I always have been miserable as I am now.

It is not really true. Certainly my life started quite well. Early life was very happy. Maybe I was a bit of a glazed-eyed girl, lived through innocent haze. In my youth I was a dreamer, dreamt of ideas, high morals and happiness. I thought the world was a wonderful place and I was born to have a wonderful life! It seemed impossible then to miss the best life possible! I thought I was the luckiest person known to me! But it did not last. Happy days disappeared into oblivion.

Sad and lonely days came to rein in my life. Suddenly everything looks different. I now realise that the fault is mine and mine alone. I had too much of an unreal air about me. I made too many mistakes. I never learnt how to make good compromises. I just ruined my life for nothing and no apparent reason.

In my utter ignorance I always went after the rubbish and never a real thing. The lack of ability to differentiate real life from unreal must be the cause of all my misery! I do not know why rubbish should make me go overboard. Why I have not been as sensible as others and made a good job of my life that I shall never know. Everybody should enjoy life to the full. But I managed to miss life altogether.

I made costly mistakes and paid dearly with the happiness of my life. Perhaps it was my destiny to be left on the shelf and be content with unhappy living. Maybe there was nothing I could have done to alter this fate of mine. In any case it is absolutely no use now crying of spilt milk! It is all over and done with!

I have bypassed all the emotion, excitement and happiness of a normal woman. Every woman needs to live to the full. So did I. But it did not work out for me. My expectation did not materialise. My wishes did not come true. It feels as if I wasted my life. It should not to have happened. But it has. With hind sight I often think I could have so easily avoided this. But at the time something must have pushed me to it. Anybody can be wiser after the event; but that is no help.

I never have thought I was going to end up like I have. It still seems unbelievable. It still seems unbelievable. I always had a strong conviction that I will live a worthwhile life. But that was simply a pipe dream. I have not been happy.

I was born but never been able to feel good to be born. I would have liked to feel loved a little by the world. But the love of this earth can only come from a man for a woman. That has never happened to me. This loss of love is so sad for anyone to bear in life! It maybe just a human imagination and nothing more! But I do not know!

This sadness brings loneliness and loneliness makes one depressed. Because of this I slowed down so much. I could have done so much more, but I did not. I ended up living the life of a freak recluse—not much use to anyone.

Now I have the luxury of feeling sad and miserable for two days a week at the weekend. Also I live a miserable life for the rest of the week, that is, five days a week from Monday to Friday when I have really no time to feel anything, because of the pressure of work.

Enough of this wallowing in self-pity, it never does anybody any good. It cannot make my grief go away. However, speaking about it might do some good to my mental health. People do say that it is better for you to get it out of your chest! To keep it bolted up is bad for you! I do need a strong mind to bear my sorrow.

I must say I am getting better in coping with my depression. It was much more acutely painful earlier. Maybe everything including pain gets duller with age.

I remember quite a few years ago I could hardly contain my grief I felt then. In desperation I started to scribble a little now and then about my sad feelings. Sometimes it helped to calm me down inside.

On 22 June 1972 I wrote about my life and doubt as follows:

There must have gone something wrong somewhere in my life. I wish someone could tell me what it is and why! I know it started just over two years ago. Since then I realise that I suddenly become unpopular at work.

Perhaps nobody ever has anyone really to turn to when one faces one's hard time in life. Life is so hard! I wish it was not so hard! Would it not be nice if it were a bit sweet!

I wonder why it feels as if everything is changing so radically. Even the place of work seems to have changed.

I am wondering quite frequently if the college I work in, is functioning as it always does. Maybe what I face is just a part of the policy here as I do not fit in for some reason. Maybe they just want to get rid of me.

I ask myself if it is because I am an odd one out here—a foreigner and a spinster! Maybe it is because of my sex—a woman and not married! Perhaps I am simply academically inadequate! But why is it now and not earlier?

But I was not inadequate when I came here and when the college needed more advanced work. Until over a couple of years ago, there were quite a lot of advanced work here, and I happily carried out all my duties since I joined.

My record of work for the previous four years, that means, since I joined, does not show any inadequacy. In fact I think I have done a very good job. Very few of my students have ever been unsuccessful. Only people I could not help are those who did not want to be helped and were totally unwilling to work. Doubts arise in my mind why then I never get any credit.

Is it possible that some men of the powerful British nation do not or cannot show regards and respect to people who do not belong to their own race or something like that! I cannot help wondering if they have mastered the techniques of undermining and belittling the confidence of the insecure person. Surely they have practised it on the underprivileged races of the world for centuries. Maybe it is now simply a part of their national instinct. Maybe they are just conditioned to believe that any such outsider is nowhere near their equal in capacity. With this inborn subconscious prejudice the rest follows just naturally. They may act differently when they need you desperately!

I am certainly loosing my confidence everyday. My functional capacity as a competent teacher is getting ruined. I feel suffocated in an untold but non encouraged undertone of some kind of atmosphere. However, the colleagues and the students are no problem at all. I wonder where the troubles are from and why!

Is it all my imagination? Why do I imagine such dumb thing for myself? I admit I am getting too touchy and dangerously sensitive. But I was not an unfriendly person and I was not like this before! Constantly I feel I am not invited here and I am not trusted either!

# Chapter Four

I keep talking about the same thing over and over again. It is only because I want to let my emotion out.

On 26th June 1972 I was feeling very upset. I even wrote about it.

Today I received an internal memo from the Head. It is about the administrative duties at work. There was a list of names for different responsibilities. My name was not anywhere in the list. I will have no administrative duty in the college next year. Until this year I have had at least the responsibility as a course tutor for one or two courses. It was not much. Still I was counted as one officially. After this year even that will be gone. I feel there must be some strange secret policy against me here. The colleagues are fine. The policy seems harsh!

I wish I knew what it is and why. I am working here non encouraged, unappreciated, unwanted and unloved by the authority. I feel rotten and isolated. Often I am in despair. I get so much depressed. Yet I do not see how I can escape from this tight corner. I have somehow got trapped in the situation.

It feels as if there is no one in the whole world who would or could help me to get out of this rat-trap. It seems to me that there is a deliberate policy to take away all the power from my hand.

No one asks my opinion anymore about anything now-a-days. I feel I am so much unwanted here. Gradually I am being deprived of every bit of my responsibility at the college. Everybody seems to ignore me. Everyone overlooks my presence more often than none. I am becoming almost invisible. I am so belittled! I cannot help feeling hurt.

Maybe I am letting myself to be intimidated. I am vulnerable. Why should I be treated badly though! Should I not know why?

Maybe it is all my imagination. Maybe I am becoming too touchy! That is what I keep telling myself. Otherwise I will go mad!

After all is said and done, one question remains unanswered. Why the people at work do not want me! I must have done something. But what is it? I do wish I have a friend to tell me, what is the matter? I am so alone in England! Perhaps I am alone in anywhere. Perhaps that is what wrong with me! Maybe not, perhaps everybody is the same as me all over the world, suffering quietly and knowing nothing what to be done.

I believe in cause and effect. My pain and my problem must be coming from me. Life seems so worthless and so full of pain. Maybe it is so only for me.

It is me, it is me!
I wonder how long
It is going to be!
It seems so unbearable
And yet it goes on and on.
I wonder if it will stop!
Do I or don't I want it to go on?

I have managed to accept and adopt this painful existence of a lonely life in a foreign country. For another fourteen years I suffered and endured in a vain hope that it will stop and I will find happiness in something or someone. But it did not materialise. The pain, however, feels less painful now. It has lost some of its intensity.

I learnt to survive, gained some respect and understanding amongst the people I work with. Some of the lost responsibilities were restored. But never managed to achieve much power, I lost interest in it altogether. Day to day life without a massive disaster of one kind or another is all that matters to me in my present state of mind. Future is gone, past did not help much! So I only live for the present!

I still resent a bit now and then. But it does not hurt me badly anymore. Maybe at last I learn to compromise with life!

Life is so full of treachery and confusion. It is impossible to know what is right or what is wrong at the moment of importance.

Why should anybody, of any real sense, would like to live any longer in this wretched world—it is the real mystery of life!

None of us know what we do or will do in life. Most of it is like a chain reaction. One spark creates another. There is a lot of room for a lot of random changes. We do not know who or what guide us through our life. But we all take the credit for our successes and blame our fate for all our short-comings.

We live our life as best as we can. But I made my life miserable in many ways. I did not want to. But that is the way it has turned up to be. This failing is bad enough. The worst thing is that I made everybody else in the family, miserable too. I disappointed my mother in many ways. I made my mother very unhappy.

My father had high hopes about me. I managed to shatter them. Last few years of his life were very miserable on my account. He thought I was wasting away my life far away from home and friends. He was right no doubt. But I was unable to change it for the better.

Probably I make my brothers and sisters quite uncomfortable in my presence. At least my interests and purpose in life do not seem real to them. They probably think of me as one fairly odd in nature or perhaps an eccentric in outlook no doubt. I do not share their life style and that sets me apart from them.

My youngest sister is very sweet and nice. She is very domesticated and does not take part in any intellectual pursuit. She does not share any of my interest. Also Didi, my elder sister has nothing much in common with me either. Neither have any of my brothers except perhaps my youngest brother.

They have no time for me which must be very understandable. Why should they and how could they! As a matter of fact, they do not anyway. My second sister is no different from the rest. Yet for sometime she made me believe that she wanted to help. Of course she was not able to help and she did not. I did not discourage her from trying in her own way. In any case, God willing, she might have been able to help in some way. But god was clearly not willing. So I got nowhere and nothing had helped me ever. More misery and more disappointment were added to the already heavy burden of sorrow in my heart. It is all in the past now. All the hurts, all the humiliation, disgrace and shame—nothing lasts for ever!

I have a feeling that I have always looked on the world as if I am no part of it and I am only a spectator. It is almost as uncanny as though I am watching a play of another time in the television.

One takes certain interest in a play and yet one knows fully well that one has no real relation with it. The time, place, the event and the people are not real and not one's own.

Nothing has ever happened to me to change this feeling of unreal reality. I do not know why I have this detached view of the world. Maybe everybody has this detachment towards this world until something forces us to accept it as our own.

I suffer from illusion. It is as if my world is as yet to come and I am as always waiting for it. But it has never come and life has passed me by. I have wasted it all! The reason; maybe the possession of a foolish mind is the cause of it all! I do not have any other reasonable explanation except considering a supernatural intervention!

I must have wanted drama in my life. So this is the way God thought fit to punish me! This must be God's judgement! I have no choice but to bear it.

Is it not strange though that some one's pain means so little or even nothing to some one else? We feel so important to ourselves and yet we are really nothing at all to others. This is life no doubt! Life on earth is so strange in so many ways that it is really incomprehensible!

I am sorry and I feel sad for what I do not have. I am not thankful for what I have got. So I should say that forgive me god, I cannot help the way I feel. You made me, so you should know. It must be the human nature! I am, being only human, very sad for not having a fuller life. In any festival time, even on the New Year's Day, my mind is usually quite heavy with some sad feeling.

I come to realise that the worst thing in life is the suffering from guilty conscience. The best thing is the feeling that one has done one's best for one's own world and that there is not anything more one could do.

I wanted to please all and ended up making everybody unhappy. I think now that it is perhaps best not to expect anything and just keep doing what feels right.

I do not know why I wanted to be perfect. But is there anything which is perfect in this world? I thought that nothing could beat me in life. But I ended up beaten badly.

Maybe I did not hold my ground. So it was taken by the others and I have ended up with no place! I know I may not have any originality; I simply pick things up as it catches my imagination. Also I fear that I am probably a great bore. I talk and think about things everybody might already know.

Well, every one of us perhaps thinks we control events. Yet events overtake us always. We are after all nothing but victims of our circumstances.

I do understand that spirits are lost in women. No one really likes to trust a spirited woman, at least not in one's own free will! Most people secretly long for a woman who would serve them in their terms and not in hers. They would expect her to play the role of a kind of servitude but feel happy, grateful, satisfied and contented for having this opportunity alone.

On the whole men do not like women on equal terms! They may not admit it on the open but this is how they feel in their heart. Woman with a mind of her own is simply a kind of nuisance to men in general.

I think it is very sad and awful that such women are usually kept at a distance by most men. This situation may never change if men were given a choice. So far they do have a choice. But this choice may not last for ever. At least it is a possibility!

It is possible that the men may one day grow to like women with a strong mind. But it would be from lack of choice and only when they are forced to do so. However, once they start they might find it a most fascinating and worthwhile experience in life. They might one day wonder, how could they, have ever done without it!

Seriously though, I fear that nature does not favour woman with an independent mind. For a woman to be capable and courageous may be against nature in some ways. Maybe humanity sees its doom in such women! Maybe it is the destiny of our human race as a whole to grow clever and destroy ourselves in the process. Maybe it is simply nothing more than a prejudice of an ancient kind.

No one can be certain about why, but everybody including the women must march on. No one can stand still. It is in our nature that we must progress. Maybe we have to progress before we perish.

I admired American ideology that all men are created equal. Of course this means all women as well. It is a very fair and noble ideology indeed.

The British and most of the Western Europeans on the other hand, believe deeply that all men are born unequal and should stay that way.

Even the Americans may not have meant all men of all races. By saying all they may have wanted to say all of them only, that is, all men of white origin. Surely on many occasion that is what they have expressed in their action. They may feel that way on occasion but they would not or could not say it openly. Besides something is just not right and something sets the fire of inspiration amongst all men in all races. American ideology is one of such rare visionary speculation which helped the humanity to achieve a higher step towards a higher goal.

British heritage and history is different. They do not share this ideology. They do not believe in equality. They had to be superior to rule the earth. If you are not a British origin and you live in Britain for some reason, you are bound to have a very strange experience indeed!

Sometime something does not smell right to me. But I have difficulty to understand what actually is wrong. It must be some lack of comprehension on my part.

People seem so nice on the whole. Most people here look good, wear good clothes, speak well and behave fairly sophisticated in all sorts of manners. They are polished and seem to have good manners. It is not easy to believe that they can be uncharitable. But in their subtle ways they are so uncharitable! There is nothing they would not do to suit their own interest.

I do not want any favour from them. But I do want to be recognised and treated as their equal. I try to convince myself that I am not really treated differently. But I have a sneaky suspicion that they do not regard me as their equal!

Somehow I am often made to feel small. They do now and then talk down to me. I do not know how and why I do not get the moral support or the encouragement I need. It feels hard and difficult at times. Deep down in my heart I feel hurt. May be some of it is my imagination. That is what I tell myself and try to keep my sanity in its place.

I shall not be surprised if it is not entirely so. One's instinct, feeling and awareness cannot be wrong all the time.

They are so complacent and patronising. It is truly hurtful. I do not know how but all these do something to you and you become in a way invisible! I have suffered a lot from this disease of invisibility.

Is it what people call racial prejudice? Does everybody suffer from racial prejudices? Is racial prejudice inevitable? Is there no way it can be avoided? What is a race?

Most of all I feel so isolated here. I know it must be very bad for me but what is the alternative! One needs friends. Without friends life becomes very miserable.

All of us are some way racially biased. Everybody is perhaps genetically conditioned to adhere to one's own race. It is in our nature to feel proud of our own race no matter whichever race we may belong to. We only see all the loving glory of our race and racial culture where as others can only notice all the negative side of us. We always appear inferior in other's eyes and almost wonderful in ours.

We all gleefully exaggerate each others faults and shortcomings. Why should one's failings, make another feel great, is a sheer mystery of human nature.

Industrial success in the west unleashed a great power in their hand. Lack of muscle in the power struggle in the east made them much inferior in the western eyes. The west feels very superior and boastful by comparison.

The eastern nations are by no means impressed by their superiority. They consider it nothing more than a gleeful exaggeration of the western world.

No one is perfect. It may appear almost perfect only in biased eyes. The west may be powerful but their standard of moral strength is not a lot to be desired. The eastern eyes see in them the exploitation, the treachery and the deceit. The poorer nations of the world cannot help feeling choked with emotion and wonder when will the richer nations answer for all the social injustices they committed against people of other races. Also the assumption that the other people are inferior and willing to please the superior race is too patronising and socially unbearable to accept.

Maybe racism is the legacy of colonialism. Imperialist thoughts are still deep rooted in the subconscious mind of the richer nations. Re-education is needed. The younger ones are already much more open minded.

The rich may be proud to be rich. But do they like to acknowledge that they sucked dry the world and extracted wealth from the colonies! They boast of giving civilisation to the poor but do they ever admit what they have taken away from the poor!

People are generally narrow-minded. No one wishes to cross the frontier of their own race without a strong reason.

We are no exception. We did not want to change our national narrowness. We did not want to be international. But we were dominated by foreign power. International values were imposed upon us by a sheer brute force of colonialism.

Over the years we learnt to live with it. We have now grown a kind of liking for it. We no longer want to remain as little us in our little world. We want to be a part of the bigger world. We participate in the world culture.

However, our big brothers still want to stay as they were. They do not want to loose the role of a conductor, conducting the world orchestra according to their own rules and whims. They want to lead us, handle us but do not want to include us in their own clubs.

They created the notion of internationality but it is hard for them to be internationally minded. They do not wish to be real part of this spirit. The meaning of this idea they used it for, is different from the meaning it has become for us. They want to keep their power block. They want us to be under it but not in it.

The western world has acquired an insatiable greed for power. They consider themselves as pure thorough-bred amongst the human races. In their opinion other races are no more than just strays. Any contact or intimacy between the two, they fear, can only produce human mongrel which they consider very degrading and hateful.

In my opinion it is very strange that they should think this way. Should they look for real logic, they should expect something new but only better to come out of the interaction between races. Breeding within the race follows already known pattern and potential. Inter racial breeding can surprise us all with new result. Why should it be base by any standard; evaluation of nature is a random selection and life force is natural evolution in deed.

Thorough bred humanity may be a comfort and wishful thinking for the well off western ideology. It does not really help anybody. It may even drive the rest of us to actual extinction. It is really inhuman in all respect.

The law of nature does not obey any club-rule. Neither is it afraid of the magic of any white skin-colour! There is an endless possibility in nature. Why should one expect only the worst!

Everybody is afraid of the unknown. Our instinct of self-preservation forces us to stick to what we already know and the fear of the unknown makes us behave in strange irrational ways.

The rich and powerful people make much of an issue of their own heritage. They defend their identity with all of their might. They consider this effort as noble and admirable quality.

However, they have a way to treat others as nothing and of no consequence. Anybody who does not accept their evaluation is no friend of theirs. As an ethnic minority if you make a stand on your identity and if you consider it an important issue, you are automatically branded as one with a chip on the shoulder. Defence of minority culture is a constant source of irritation for the dominant white public.

If, on the other hand, you give way, compromise and try not to stand out as a different individual, you are regarded as a lesser person. Everybody will walk all over you and never take any notice of you. You then become very conveniently transparent in everybody's eye. They will look through you and not at you. You can never please them if you want to live your own life in your own way.

As a matter of fact, the people with power are happy with you if you are meek, timid and submissive. They can then run your life exactly as they wish so that you are useful and profitable for them.

The British now talk about their stay in India with affection and a lot of nostalgia. Indians are generally passive, fearful and good natured people. It suited the British very well indeed. This gentle character is what perhaps stopped Indians having any really bloody revolution. This is probably why British were able to rule India for such a long time.

None of us can help our nature. It is probably the product of history in some ways.

We all have our heritage. Everybody has heritage of some strange tales and stories. We all draw nourishment from such heritage. Without it we are no longer a full human with enough self-respect and pride. History has a great power over men and men make their history. Sometime we are sorry for what we are not and what we have not achieved. But it cannot be helped. Also all of us in this world live and grow against all possible odds. It is certainly a miracle that some of us grow old and achieve some of our aspiration.

For every successful and fulfilled life there must be an innumerable number of unsuccessful life and premature death. So we should not feel sorry for our unfulfilled dreams, under achieving our goal and unhappy living. This is an inevitable part of our natural norms. Anything else is nothing short of a profound miracle and deserves our monumental admiration.

But it is not entirely in our hand to achieve this success for our own life. We may not like to resign to this fatalistic approach but we cannot often escape from it. Only a few very lucky ones can claim to have experienced a different fate in life.

We live our life but we do not go through the same stages of experience. Quality of life varies from person to person. We are at different stages of human experiences. Something may be vital to somebody. It may mean absolutely nothing to some others.

India bypassed several industrial revolutions over the period of a couple of centuries. Destiny enslaved her to the British and the British cheated her as they pleased. The history they mostly taught their people about India is all the erotic customs, the cows and the bulls, the elephants, the barbaric ritual of "Sati" and the useless romantic notions they built up about India. They never taught their public anything serious, respectful or beneficial for the Indians. Maybe they do not know anything else really. So their obligation stopped at their self-interest and never extended to the Indians. They enjoyed ruling the Indians but bothered very little to provide any care for the Indian people. They rarely hesitated to interpret negatively about India which they did not understand at all.

They freely presented India as pagan and heathen to the rest of the world. The moral values and the spiritual aspects of Indian culture seemed very grotesque to them. It might have been demoralising to the Indians. Indian culture might have been seen as of no consequence to the outside world.

Centuries of aspiration to reach God and desperate efforts to understand the meaning of life cannot be all in vain. Human efforts are never in vain. It shapes our life.

The ancient people of India desired eagerly to know the spiritual meaning of life. It could not have been just the pass time of the faint-hearted. It may have seen useless to some. It may not have produced a nation of world-conqueror. Nevertheless its manifestation may yet be coming long time after its seeds were sown amongst the men and women of India.

Whenever the effect may come if it comes at all, that will be more than something. It may one day come in manifold amongst the men and women on earth and it may even save the mankind from moral deprivation and self destruction.

We cannot judge or dismiss the soul-searching efforts of the ancient Indians as failure or frivolous, just because it did not save their descendants from the subjugation of India by the British who came over the sea. It is never worthless just because some ignorant people did not understand their noble effort. The arrogant foreign opinion mocked India of her profound learning and endeavour. India's pursuit of spiritual knowledge was regarded by some as an idle pursuit. It must have been all a misunderstanding. One day everybody will come to their senses. Surely men all over the world will speak differently in time.

It was not very lucky for India to have a foreign overlord for such a long period of time. They kept her natural growth checked and restricted. They wanted her to stay dependent on them and remain underdeveloped as long as possible.

Even in the last minute just before her independence the ruling power was able to stick the knife in. They literally butchered India. They cut her to pieces before they left. Their policy of divide and rule somehow succeeded to poison the whole of Indian political atmosphere. The unity of brotherhood between the fractions of the community was shattered and lost for ever. Massive blood-bath, poisonous bitterness, soul-destroying suspicion and civil war ripped through the country. The unity amongst the people of India was confused, misguided and never to be regained. India was at last divided in pieces.

How and why it actually happened, and why no well meaning people was able to stop it, is not very clear. There remain a lot of unanswered questions. There must have been a British hand in the matter. They must have cleverly planted a time bomb in Indian socio-political structure. This bomb must have come of age in time and exploded. Of course nobody admits it and no one speaks of it.

I wondered if the political figure of Jinnah was actually planted by the British power in order to bring about a political upheaval in the Indian political scene. Maybe Jinnah was a personality who suffered from some severe personal crisis. Maybe he had some inherent personal grudge against his compatriots. He might have born a personal vendetta against his fellow politicians. Perhaps he had inherited or built up deep rooted inferiority complex of some violent kind because of social set up at the time in the country. Maybe because of any or all of these reasons he succumbed to the temptation of destroying India. He may have easily fallen in the eager hand of the British who were happy to use him as a political weapon to suit their purpose. Under British indulgence everything worked out in his favour. He was very successful to take revenge against whole of India which produced Gandhi and which was represented by Gandhi. With relative ease he managed to destroy the united image of India once for all. He enjoyed the sectarian troubles and revolution as far as he could manage. He must have had a lot of malice in him! He could not have been a healthy or a happy man!

It is obviously no good speculating about the past. Nobody is going to admit the real truth. I simply smell a lot of wrong in the air. Lots of secret manoeuvre behind the scene must have produced that part of our tragic history. Lot of it seemed to be shrouded in silent secret. I wish the true history of the division of India was unravelled and revealed to all by a true and unbiased historian. Perhaps it will always remain a wishful thinking. The people with the necessary information, probably, will never disclose them as it might be against their national interest. Also the records of the truth might have been wilfully destroyed. Some probably are now naturally lost. The people, who personally knew or dealt with some of the facts, died or are dying away with time. So there is not much of a chance of the whole truth for everyone.

It is pointless to grieve now over a meaningless historical tragedy. There are so many of them throughout the ages all over the world. Even then, there cannot be any harm in thinking that it should not to have happened.

Gandhi was India's moral conscience. He wanted to correct the tip of the balance on justice. He tried to strengthen man's moral fibre in no uncertain terms. He gave new meaning to the man's idea of a man of god. India had him as her son as if it was a gift from God for all her yearning towards higher goal in life since ancient time. Maybe he was born in India in order to save her as she was then ripen with injustices and sorrows. Indians do believe that God sends his man to save the world when it is too full with miseries and ugly sins.

Yet he was unable to save India even though he gave his life and full attention for the purpose. It was like a fight between the God and the Devil over India. The Devil snatched a part of it and defiled the rest. In the end no one can stop the free flow of the blood-letting of the innumerable innocents in the vastness of the Indian sub-continent. The world at large did not pay much attention to the matter either.

Watching the film Gandhi made me think. The film is made by a well known British man and is obviously over dramatic in many ways. The real thing must have been, much less dramatic, but much more painful, serious, drab and to the point. He was no doubt a genius and a professional in goodness and godliness.

The British are very good in presenting them as big in the best possible light. The world has changed politically a lot since the days of Gandhi and the British imperial era. They now bend over backward to exaggerate their best possible points which were in sympathy with the Indian struggle for independence.

People do not know or do not now remember the bitterness of the struggle. It is now quite easy for the British to get away with their inverted morality. They are always pretty good in serving morality in their own term.

After all is said and done, it is in the end a question of acceptance. India was in servitude. The yoke of the British imperialist rule was pressing her harder and harder. People of India tolerated it for many years. Yet there is always one who would not put up with injustices. This is the miracle in the nature of man!

It is sometimes very indignant to follow British patronising propaganda about Indian past. Obviously not many of their public would want to know more. But I do. I would like to ask just one question. What were they doing in the country for two hundred years if my people were dying of starvation and in abject poverty during this time and always? Why were they so poor and why nothing was done to stop it? No explanation and not much points of view are put forward about the callous treatment of India in the hands of a rich superior nation!

India is unfortunate. Everything strikes India hard. Even terror in the air blew hard for India. 329 Indian lives vanished in the mid-air in the Air India plane disaster quite recently.

Massive explosion must have made the whole Air India jumbo jet blew up high in the air. So many lives ended so suddenly for no apparent reason. The incidence of the disaster struck very distressing and alarming to me.

If it was a bomb it must be the work of some madmen. It is so easy for a madman to kill so many innocent people for no good reason whatsoever. What a terrible waste of lives!

There must be an international terrorist force for many different colour, shape and form which is causing death, suffering and hardship for hundreds of people all over the world all the time. Where are the people who should be looking after the law and order? Are they fully alert? It is true that it needs only one madman with a bomb to slip through the hand of one sleepy security man for a major disaster of such dimensions.

So many terrorist activities were in the news in last few days. Even then, it needed the Indian ill-luck for the Indians to fall victims of such catastrophic degree. By comparison other nations seem to have escaped with much less loss of life so far. I know it sounds wrong! But that is how it feels to me. India always takes the first place in the list of tragedy and disaster.

Why is it so? There must be a reason. It cannot be just a coincidence every time. I do not know. Maybe it could!

Earlier in the year British Prime minister survived a major terrorist plot. She manages to continue her premiership even though shaken a little for a little while. Her cabinet remains unshaken.

Indian prime minister, by comparison, gets assassinated in a real flash. Everything seems to crumble around her death. India plunges, into a spell of civil war, with a great many loss of lives all over Indian soil.

Once again Indians are driven to madness. People are thrown into despair and endless sorrow, so often and so easily India gets engulfed in endless violence.

Also lots of industrial disaster occurs in different parts of the world. By comparison the Indian Bhopal-chemical-plant disaster exceeds them all. It has to be devastating in enormous scale for India. The destruction of human lives and appalling pain and suffering occurred there, is beyond anybody's comprehension. It has to be a disaster of such dimension if only to fit the Indian fate!

Everyday one hears of terrorist activities in different parts of the world. But India gets caught up in the most appalling kind. India's people loose their life without a faintest idea of why or what for. Is there not a cause for all these sinister outcomes! If there is no reason at all and if fate simply selects India at random every time then, that must be a matter of more alarm.

I have a feeling that India is too trusting. She has been putting her trust in the wrong hands for a long time and it has not helped her. Indians do value much in other people's eyes and opinions. But people do not usually care for Indians. In this world it is not fashionable yet to care for the poor. Indians, in reality, belong to the category of poor people.

People, on the whole, are negligent about those who are not in a strong position to use their muscles. So, generally speaking Indians do not yet draw high regards, care, interest or attention from other people. They are usually indifferent and more used to ignoring the Indians. People of India belong amongst the underdogs of the world. Not many people worry about their well being.

I may be wrong because I am just upset. I may be biased too. Whatever the reason I cannot help smelling some negligence on some one's part in the Air India disaster. Canadian airport security would surely have taken more care if it was not an Indian plane. It may not have been so easy for the terrorists to pass the bomb on board the plane if that plane belonged to a rich nation and the passengers were mostly of some other than a poor nation.

No one likes to pay much attention to the fate of the poor. Yet the poor are the most vulnerable. They need all the help they can get. Sadly though, help is in unusually short supply for the poor.

Poor people are unprotected. They are easy target. They get hurt more frequently than the rich as they get the diseases before others too. They are always exposed to disease and danger.

Interestingly people feel good in helping the rich and the privileged. With help and care from many corners the privileged nations get by with minimum loss and tragedy.

With neglect, indifference and lack of care the poorer nations get bogged down in undue amount of disaster and untold amount of suffering of many kind.

People sometimes appear to show some concern after the tragedy has already struck. These concerns, mostly verbal, do not change anything. No one seems to offer a helping hand with a view to prevent any real mishap.

Underprivileged nations should learn to trust no one and be on their guard twice as much or more if possible. They should be constantly aware of the faults and the facts of their ill fate. If only they could be truly vigilant about their position in this world, they may not have their poor fate so badly burnt every time!

The poor always needs extra careful vigilance, all around all the time. Unfortunately they are the very people who lack training in this respect. By nature and by condition they are too trusting, unguarded and dependent.

Truly they need to be at least one step ahead of everybody if they are to prevent exploitation, disaster, suffering and too many misfortunes. To acquire such a degree of competence, maturity and capability, one needs considerable growth and development of all kind in national level. So we are really in a so called chicken and egg situation.

We are in a vicious circle which is not easy to break through. I do not know any answer.  I only hope that one day enough people will become fair minded and will sincerely try their best to look after the ordinary people all over the world.  One day people may help people not because they are somebody, but because they are just anybody and nothing else.

I do not know if this is just a thought of a utopia on my part.  It may go against basic human nature.  If so then it will not happen and the world will remain as hell as ever.  The people are then born only to go through hellish injustices and sufferings as they always did.

This must then is the purpose of life and so there is nothing more to say or hope for in our own life.  Human life is then nothing but a manifestation of sorrow and suffering.  In that case we should not be sorry if life becomes extinct whenever it may.

Maybe it is not so.  Maybe there is a purpose in life.  We suffer to grow strong and strength comes from pain.  If we do not believe it life becomes unbearable!

Coming back to that air disaster once again I remember the news left me numb for sometimes.  That was quite recently in the past.  Little by little I began to feel sad and very distressed.  During this period, for days I felt very bad and suffered a bad headache.  The more I thought about the people died in the disaster, the more upset I became.

At my working place no one said a single word about the incident.  A major international disaster involving 329 innocent lives, of Indian origin, did not seem to draw much attention from anyone around me.  I do not know why I felt badly surprised.  Not even a single person uttered a single word of sympathy to me.  I cannot help taking it personally.  After all I am Indian and the dead people were my country people.

I do not know why I half expected a few wards.  I thought my colleagues would say something about it.  I felt hurt as if they did not care because the people died were Indians.  They probably do not care for anyone unless it actually hurts them personally.

If one English woman lived amongst Indians in a place in India and there were a disaster involving English people, I am sure the Indians would have said a few words of sympathy to her.  They could not have ignored the whole thing as if it is of no importance.  I am sure, I definitely would have.

I just cannot imagine how the people around me could be so indifferent! I felt the same at the time of Bhopal disaster.  A terrible incidence like that goes by without a single world of concern from anyone here.

I work in an educational institute.  People working here are all educated civilised well-off people. Maybe it is in their custom not to waste any word unnecessarily. Their interest is different from mine. I cannot help feeling alone and isolated on many occasion.

My Indian prime minister was assassinated. Thousands of my people were killed and wounded in a gruesome industrial catastrophe. A dismal air calamity wiped off a few hundred innocent unsuspected air travellers. They all happened to be of Indian origin.

These mishaps occurred one after another within a small interval of time. I could not believe that no one will mention a single word about it to me.

I would have liked to talk about it a little with some one. But I have no one to talk to. I live alone. I rarely see or meet any of my people. It is therefore my fault. I should have lived amongst my people. Now I have to pay the price of not living amongst people who share the same interest with me.


At first I did not think it was so important. I was perhaps never very nationalistic minded. I thought people are people. I felt people are basically the same irrespective of nationality, colour and culture to some extent. I am not so sure now.

More and more I am becoming aware of some disturbing facts. I know now that for some reason I am invisible to too many people here. It is a very uncomfortable and depressing experience. For many years I suffered from it. Being timid and undemanding I felt I had to learn to live with it and I did.

Perhaps the western civilisation has no time for anyone else. Maybe the west was not always like this. Maybe it is only lately the western people have become a little inward looking and maybe it is a sign of decline of the west in some ways. No one can blame them for it.

Civilisation comes and civilisation goes. It is a natural occurrence. People take pride of course. Everyone has a civilisation of one kind or other. Everybody is proud of his own civilisation past or present, whatever it may be. They attach themselves to it with great nostalgia.

No matter how nostalgic we may feel at the ancient ruins and historic monuments, they are now no more than just empty shells. Life from them is gone and gone for ever. Civilisation is a form of creative life force. It only appears when the right circumstances are just right for it.

When it comes it flourishes with great vitality for a while. It then burnt itself up and nothing can stop it from its decline. It goes out of favour from nature and so it disappears into thin air.

Some where else appears another out burst of some excellence of another kind when the moment is right for it there and then.

People will never forget any of it. It builds up the steps of the history of our progress as a mankind on earth.

As far as human race is concerned, mind is most incredibly the strongest instrument in the world.   All our inspiration, aspiration, revelation, enlightenment and everything else comes from there.  Our subconscious mind is the watershed of all our activities and evolution, creative or otherwise.

It is the source of our life and living. It generates too many ideas, sometimes dormant, sometimes not so dormant.  It explains away too many things in too many ways, always exactly the way it suits our mind and purpose!  It tries to make sense just the way it wants to and also ready for!  It is always full of too many mystery and strange magical phenomena.  It has its own world in addition to its inheritance of the physical and the metaphysical worlds.  The culture and the tradition around play some part in some way over it too.  Nobody knows exactly why or how it happens though.  Maybe it is because one feels that one needs it!

# Chapter Five

Quite a few years I went through intensive pain in my mind. I became aware of the depth of sadness in my heart as I was approaching the end of my youth for ever.

I remember near about December 1979, I was so sad that I had to write down a few lines about my feeling. Otherwise it was too hard to bear.

I wrote the depth of my sadness is only getting deeper and deeper for me. I could never have been happy. Happiness is just not in my nature. I feel I understand almost everybody, but nobody really understands me. The loneliness of being all alone in life is very hard to bear for anyone! But I never had any choice in this matter. I have simply always been very much alone!

This sadness has always been with me. The only difference, however, is that I was younger earlier and I had hope. I used to think that I will one day be very happy and I will get what I want exactly. With this hope in my mind I had the strength to bear any passing loneliness.

But it never passed! I am now older and getting older everyday still. I have now come to face the fact that I did not get what I wanted. My life seems going to end as empty as ever. I do not feel I achieved any victory of any kind in my life. I am bitterly defeated. It may not sound very important, but it is a great pain to me. I have born this pain in my soul and I suppose now that this is how I am going to end!

I do not know for certainty, but guess quite easily that there must be many people like me in this world. But this knowledge alone does not give me any satisfaction or contentment. I just cannot help wishing still some joy in my life. Is it not a great pity that a whole complete life is being lived without a worthwhile purpose!

I wonder why people like me is born and why should they live such a meaningless life! Is it just simply a simple waste, or is it supposed to be something else! I wish I could use me for something useful. My whole being cries out bitterly against my seemingly useless existence.

The year of 1979 is soon coming to an end. So another whole year of my life is coming to end. I remember the beginning of the year clearly. I remember the crushing pain of disappointment and despair I experienced at the beginning of the year. My life felt shattered to pieces, my loneliness seemed unbearable.

Life is so resilient. I lived each and everyday of the whole year with the same such pain, depression and sadness in the soul of my heart. The year has come to end, but those painful feelings are still with me and still getting heavier. I still wish my life was not like this!

I may be just a sucker for feeling sorry for myself. It may be a big passion in me to feel sorry for myself, sorry for my country, sorry for everything I know on this earth!

Sometimes I feel that the men in my country are living in fools' paradise. They still appear to talk only about middle-class values and do not seem to realise the depth of reality of life to-day. In my opinion many of them still seem to be quite happy being mother's boy and do not mind behaving as if the world exists only to please them.

To these people women are born only to gratify men's need and not at all for their own. They see nothing wrong in women's suffering because of men. They consider it to be a great virtue bestowed upon women by God. They believe it to be only natural that women should be manipulated by men. Men's wish must be women's command!

Of course men like women. They seem to admire women placed in a cage. To shut women up in a cage is perfectly alright with them. Women are no more than a kind of possession. Women's physical beauty is fine as long as it is pleasing in their eyes. Everything must be to satisfy men.

Some men like women more or less in the same way as children like their play-dolls. Some just want women as masters want their slaves. I should not blame the men of my country though. Given half a chance, would not men anywhere behave just the same in this respect!

Whatever way I look at it, the average women in my country still appear to play a very inferior role. But the women themselves do not realise it and the men do not seem to understand it either. Maybe each is trying to pretend differently or something like that!

However, the truth remains that the women in my country in general, live a very ignorant life denied of dignity and freedom to choose for themselves. They are usually dependent. They depend on men who are not always dependable.

Boldness of character, strength of mind, clarity of thought, grasp of reality and ability to act promptly when necessary, do not come out of life lived in darkness or in a cage.

Women with mind, capable to think and understand, are on the whole fairly rare in my country. All the big boys and girls, who are in the lime-light in my country, seem to be still totally occupied with only paper-talk. They love talk and empty gesture.

The country seems flooded with second-hand ideas, concepts and ideologies. Superficial knowledge and trivial pursuit of material gain is taking up everybody's entire time in a country where spiritual aspiration was once considered to be the highest purpose of life.

There seem to be a big waste of materials and enthusiasm over unimportant matter. People are blind with excitement over trivialities. Some are brooding over the stale ideas of yesterdays. On the whole, they seem yet to learn how to think fresh for themselves and stand firm on their own feet.

Most men do not like a thinking woman. They pretend, of course, that they do; but truly, they do not. Perhaps, they are a bit terrified of such women whom they think they cannot rule and control. They appear to keep themselves clear of such women. Many men do everything in their power to despise, discourage and speak ill of such women.

The trouble is though that, men alone cannot create quality. We need both men and women for that! We know that in real life, stupidity breeds stupidity; ignorance can make only ignorance. Misfortune or ill-fate of a nation always runs in full circle! Effort to break this circle needs clear strong mind which is still more or less absent from this national scenario.

Fathers and husbands do not miss lack of qualities in their lives. Fathers do not feel the need to prepare their daughters to be free-thinking dependable human being. Clear mind with sound intellect is considered utterly misplaced in a woman. Husbands do not have any necessity to prepare themselves to match courageous mind with dignity and self-respect. They are mostly quite happy with wives they can manipulate easily. The average breed of such women, breed in thousands. But this breed with the history of such parentage is usually very mediocre; and this mediocrity in their turn repeats more mediocrity. This vicious circle and the lack of quality in people may never be broken unless something drastic happens to the society.

If, for some reason, people's life becomes unbearable, then, of course, many things will change; and that will change the people with it too.

I am not saying that every woman in the land must be full of unique intellect. What I am saying is that if the spark of intelligence in a woman is not sought after in a society, the society may be deprived of such women. That may be a great loss in terms of human evolution!

I also feel that Indian hierarchy did not look after Indian population with due care and serious thought. Over the year aristocracy learnt well how to live on the back of the poor without giving them much in return. This must be one of the reason why so severe misfortune engulfed India for such a long time.

Ordinary hardworking Indians have all the quality a country should be proud of. They are able to make themselves great and strong. But they gave their lives to the service of their high-born superiors, who were uncaring and indifferent to the well-being of this dedicated population. This is unsupportive of laws of nature and so brought about such downfall for the entire social system throughout the country. When a country falls, it is the poor who suffer; the parasitic high-society section somehow manages to survive one way or other!

After all is said and done, the fact remains is that for an awfully long period of time, the topmost people of India did not look after the interest and the well-being of the not so top people there. These heads of the society never thought twice to use or misuse the toil and the produce of hard labour of the lesser people amongst them. These higher mortals, more or less, behaved and believed as though all others simply exist in order to gratify their need and nothing else. The existence of the other people is of no consequence otherwise. These superior people did not learn or think it is necessary to thank, or acknowledge or appreciate anything offered by anyone. They simply took without paying proper remuneration.

This sickness, this irresponsibility and lack of fellow-feeling towards all who were below one's own social strength, was not just at the top of the society only. It permeated throughout all the social strata. So each class considered its lower ones of no consequence and therefore did not hesitate to misuse, mishandle and misappropriate them whenever possible. Everyone was devalued by their superior. In the end no one really learnt to value themselves.

In a land where so much spiritual evolution, devolution and philosophy have been persuaded; simple all cohesive social love for fellow beings did not take any strong root. This must be a great pity indeed!

The truth that one cannot take anything from anyone without paying the appropriate price for it, did not for some reason evolve strongly and realistically in my country. This might have brought on the history of our miseries as we know them. We make history and history makes us!

It is impossible to tell what exactly made us what we are! Yet it is very important to try to understand ourselves as much as possible. After all it is us who have to live with ourselves. The pain and the social injustice do not come out of the thin air; it comes from within ourselves; we made our caste system and we made everything which lives within it. The reasons what brought it on, may have now sunk into oblivion; but we ought to analyse its power, effectiveness, influence and consequence. It may be high-time for all of us to outgrow it in real term. Oppressive societies never flourish. Oppressed people can hardly attain their full potential. Besides, ability to be self-critical with open and alert mind is an important maturity which no nation can do without. After all human mind is nothing but what one understands and believes socially and individually. We should use our history as a modifying force behind us in the rebuilding programme of our new emerging nation. Unfortunately Indians are still far too elitist for their own good. No section of a society can live a super-life with total disregard of the welfare of the rest of the society.

I seem to suffer from self-pity a lot. I fluctuate between feeling sorry for myself or my country. Maybe wallowing in self-pity is simply my providence. I seem to do it too often.

I do not know if one should believe in providence. But it feels as though it was my providence never to meet any good man in my life. Also it appears to me that it was the providence of some of my people to pick up only more or less little bit like junk-woman as their companion in their life. None of us has been too much lucky in life!

I am full of grief. I grief for the man I would have liked to meet but I never did. The deep sorrow I feel in the depth of my soul for all my unborn children, I might have but did not have any at all. Who knows what they might have become if they came! Might they have been some kind of assets to this world! All the work, I wanted to accomplish but never been able to, might have been carried out well by them. They might have been able to serve the posterity more successfully. Who can tell, my children might have been my best contribution to this world.

Maybe that the act of bearing no children makes one indebted to the world for all eternity! Maybe this thought is just a sickness of mind and nothing else. I do not know. Anyway, I cannot do anything about it now. It is too late. I cannot even share these lonely thoughts with anybody anywhere I know. They are my sadness and mine alone.

I know many people must have fallen to the same fate as me. Should this knowledge of shared misfortune make one feel any better! It does not help me in anyway whatsoever. I cannot see how it could. Perhaps I made a virtue of my sorrow!

I felt sorry in 1989. I was sorry in 1980. I remember I wrote in January 1980 admitting the following to myself:

I wanted an interesting life. But I ended up in having a very boring life indeed. There seems no point in living it through. The pain is enormous. The pain of not being able to grow old gracefully is severe. We all have to grow old. This is a process of living naturally. Any attempt to resist this natural process at any stage of living in any one's life is a sheer disaster to say the least.

Going against nature never brings anything good. It invariably brings some kind of sickness in the mind which can be impossible to overcome or cure. One thing it can do quite easily; it can make one die a living death. Often it makes one die much earlier than one would in nature or in natural way.

To tread against nature brings too many complications in life. It feels bad. It feels like bad luck and ill-omen engulfing one from all angles. Perhaps it brings curse which in the end crashes one to death or, a kind of death, much earlier than one is due to reach one's natural end in the natural way. It is so much better to grow old in the ordinary way and then die an ordinary death.

I know I wanted to be independent. In my youth I thought it was great to be independent in life; and I have really become so.

I have become independent; the world now seems independent of me too. The world does not need me; no one seems to have any need of me. I feel I am left out. Suddenly I become one of world's rejects. It is no more any fun. There seems no room for me in the living aspect of real life any more. Maybe I was always a misfit. Perhaps I never fitted to this world.

I never thought it would turn up like this. At first, I thought, I could make my own world which will fit me well. I now understand that was nothing more than a pipe-dream.

I can see now that I am incapable of making anything. I am with nothing at all. I have nothing. I can now only produce some "Brooding-Monologue of a Self-imposed Exile" and nothing else:

An enormous world of nothingness is around me. The dead weight of emptiness is crushing my heart to nothing. I have become one of the negative people of this world. I feel I am driven to emptiness of enormous nothing. The world is not mine. I am no one. Nothing comes out of me.

I suffered from the same feeling for a long time. I wrote about very similar emotion through out 1980.

I am terribly stupid. There is no doubt about it. I keep on thinking of the things which are of no use in reality. I dream of the things which will never come true in my life. Still I do not give up. I keep on at it. I must be a nut!

I have never been in love! I understand you have to be very lucky to be loved by a man you would like to love! I did not realise it in my early youth. I used to think it should be easy and no problem at all! I imagine now, I must have been ridiculously simple! Still, realised or not, I might not have been able to do anything about it though. I must admit if such a person is not there for me - it simply is not there at all! Maybe I do not possess the sense of quality to acknowledge the existence of such a man. If that is the case what could I have done—perhaps nothing much indeed. In any case not everybody is really destined to be truly lucky in life! Maybe I should consider myself as one of those people who are not to be lucky!

I may not be a lucky person. But that does not stop me wishing for the best for the world I live in. I do wish for the day when the people of the world are well-educated, well-informed and well-balanced. I look forward to the time when it would not be possible to incite one nation to go to war against another nation. It would be a time, of great rejoice when no nation big or small is any longer a victim of any ignorance.

If people are able to think and understand for themselves, I am sure they will no longer allow themselves to be manipulated or exploited by anybody. They will know what is best for them and will do it. Big powers will no longer be able to use less powerful people. They will then give up hope of perpetuating war constantly amongst the poor and small nations of the world.

These wars and disagreements between different people are mostly nothing but a simple trick for keeping the poor and the weak for ever at a desperate disadvantaged, and hence at the mercy of the big powers. These constant bickering, amongst each other, serve only the interest of the big. People are always used by the hands behind them. The sooner the people of the world understand this, the better the whole world will be for everybody! I know I may not be entirely right in all respect. But I am sure there must be some truth in what I have just said!

I often wonder, why, do the Americans think of themselves as big people! They behave in a way as if they are some sort of gods on earth. All the people belonging to the poor nations of this world appear to be regarded by them as small people. These small people are here on earth as though only to please Americans. Their entire existence seems to have one and only one purpose in the eyes of these big people: the lesser people are somehow to please and oblige the big ones. These big people are not just the Americans. They include most of the west as well, in fact all those who are a bit powerful.

The muscle of the world at the moment is usually United States of America. If the people without much power do not oblige the big muscle, the big muscle will get angry and the angry muscle will have all the moral justification to annihilate the weak ones from the face of this earth.

It seems to me they are almost blindly, play-acting, many of the mythological god-stories known to mankind. Does that mean secretly the Americans and the Western nations believe that they are really the incarnations of those gods people came across in their mythology!

I wonder why do these people think of themselves so big; why should the rest of the world regard them so great? They are powerful no doubt, but where is their greatness? Where or when did they ever have shown any true greatness? Does talking big and loud make one big too? Or does eating a big steak produce a big man as well?

Americans and the Western people do eat plenty of good wholesome food, but do they really care if the rest of the world have any at all! Sometimes they act as if they do. But surely for those in power it is no more than just a little make-believe. It helps them in their power-politics. If they were truly sincere in their act, it would simply be impossible for the world to have so much poverty as it has.

Maybe in a way they prefer the rest of the world not to have much to eat at all. Because this then helps them to keep up with the façade of well-meaning towards the poor; and maybe this creates a kind of superiority in their mind too. It perhaps brings out a sort of faith that to have plenty of food to eat and play with is a special kind of divine virtue which they and only they are to be endowed with. No one else should have this attribute! Otherwise there will not be any difference and that cannot be right!

Of course they like to live big, eat big and talk big. It is simply magical to enjoy a life of plenty and power. So they say and think that they are big and great as well. However, are they really?

In stricter sense they never have done anything of great value for the poor people. They pretend plenty. But wherever they went they brought about spiritual desolation together with some material comfort for some.

Wherever the west put their finger in, everything, the whole society got rotten to the core. Whichever country the Americans went in the pretext of granting help, the whole set up is usually disintegrated to pieces. Whatever society Americans touched, is rotted away. They may not mean to do so. Some Americans may be truly kind at heart. But that is not enough. The powers of America somehow always manage to ruin the people in their vulnerable position, their environment, their culture and so their entire country.

However, it seems important for the Americans to make a lot of diplomatic noise in an attempt of convincing everybody that they only have the best of intentions in their heart. They have done all there is to be done as a great favour to the people in need. Because they are the friends in deed! They expect these people should absolutely be thankful to them and must work only for their benefit and no one else's.

However, the poor friends of America have nothing to be thankful about. They simply do not feel happy for the privilege of being destroyed by America. There may be a great rivalry between Americans and Russians. Even then it is very difficult to find honour in being killed by Americans and not by Russians. It may be to the Americans but surely not to the people who are killed!

Of course there are many ordinary citizens of America, who are kind, understanding and compassionate. They are not the cause of this trouble. The people in power are the trouble. They are so ruthless, aggressive and good in exploitation, it has its own tremendous momentum which almost automatically crushes everything in its way! To stop this crushing influence, to preserve the identities and interests of smaller nations and to counteract this much too dominant force in the correct way, a completely different type of worldwide sincere conscience is needed. This unfortunately does not exist as yet in sufficient strength. So the perpetual battle of good and evil goes on all over the world without anything to check it up. Maybe it is just inevitable and a simple consequence of the natural process of changing world. Only time will tell!

Everybody has a lot of problems of their own. It is simply not practicable for one set of people to think and work out what is good for another set of people. No one has the time, incentive and motivation for this. It has to grow from within the set of people themselves. With a lot of efforts, mistakes and corrections one has to grow step by step. Anyone else will simply upset the balance and ruin the prospect in the long run. Other people can make many make-belief promises. But it is not genuine. It works like a kind of charade. It fails to produce anything worthwhile. It is truly the process of growing up; and one cannot do it for anyone else.

Do people realise what a big mistake it is for the poor nations to be in a confrontation with the interfering Americans. No body except the Vietnamese people would ever know what exactly the Americans have done wrong in Vietnam.

Behind the shadow-screen of the American puppet, Shah of Iran, the Americans must have had quite a free hand in the horrors and the tragedies of that country for quite a prolonged period of time. Otherwise such strong passion of hatred could not have been stirred up amongst Iranian people against America and everything American.

Americans do not show much tolerance towards others if the others are not beneficial for them. Do they have ever done differently? Maybe they would not like to co-exist with the weak, the poor and the incompatibles. Would they? They systematically massacred the American Indians and made that enormous continent free of its earlier indigenous inhabitants. There after they consecrate this enormously vast space of land for their own race, culture and interest. They seriously dedicated their lives to build that country beautiful in all respect, but only for their own people. There was no room in their heart for the people they replaced.

There was not even a spark of slightest gratitude for all the kindness and help of these original people of the land which really helped them to survive in this new land in the earlier time. They had nothing in return to offer for the earlier friendship of these original races except, they wanted to wipe them out cleanly from the face of their land.

Is it not quite extraordinary that they could not let these Indians to survive by their side, there was plenty of room, and the country was vast; what would there to loose by a little act of tolerance or may be a hint of charity!

The whole history of the American Blacks and their pitiless exploitations do not shade any light of greatness in the depth of American heart and soul. At least one can safely say that the Americans and the race of people they originated from, are no more great and generous than any body else in this cruel world of ours. The history of Australia, New Zealand and many other countries, points in the same direction.

Anyway, another ruthless cruelty from the American side is quite a bit difficult to condone easily. After all America is the most powerful country of our world at the moment. It is not easy to overlook the fact that they did not hesitate to use atom-bombs on Japan. Americans are the only people who used atom-bombs with clear-conscience on another nation. They and the other western nations in their group, advocate loudly that it was correct to take that horrendous action. They do not see anything wrong in it. If it is such an admirable activity why then so much uproar of condemnation when there is a fear of someone else preparing for it.

Americans violently condemn Russians developing atomic weapons in the anticipation that it may be used in the sphere of their interest. The whole western opinion is in paranoiac phobia against any outside nation who has any slightest capability of developing such weapon. They do everything within their power to force that nation to give it up and bring it to its knees.

The logic behind this attitude is selfish enough no doubt! The Americans would not mind at the slightest to have a go with their own atomic-might on the Russians and on the Russian sphere of interest, if they could possibly get away with it. Maybe they would not in truth do any real harm to the Russians. After all Americans and Russians are now belong to the same racial stock in reality. In spite of great rivalry they have a lot of respect and good wishes for each other. They would never like to do any serious damage to any fraction of their own race.

But for any outsider it is quite a different story. The weight of the whole western-might will be brought to bear without a second thought. Whoever it is, will be singled out, ostracized and heavily punished to teach a lesson once for all. So that no one would dare to try it again in future. The western powers consider it as their rightful duty; and they will preserve it at any cost.

It is not a problem that the west wants to do its duty. It could be a very nice and reassuring that the west is so adamant and dutiful. But the trouble is they have double standards; one for them and another for the outsiders.

The west often acts in a way that the races who do not belong to their own race, do not count all that much in their eyes. Maybe they consider people of non-white origin as expandable. To them it is probably not a great loss if these people are unable to survive or preserve their identity. Their non-white culture, interest and values are of no consequence to cry about. If they cannot defend themselves against the dominant power of the world, it is their own fault.

One should understand that it is only natural for anyone not to have a lot of fellow-feeling for people of the origin which is not the same as one's own. Love, trust and desire to share are very rarely forthcoming across the racial barrier. Maybe this is how all the races are biologically programmed. It is hurtful to find that the high human ideal like love thy neighbour, does not work if thy neighbour happens to be of different race. However this is the way of human nature!

People belonging to western culture, managed to make themselves very powerful; they are very pleased with their achievements. They are extremely proud of their race. They feel big, important and supreme!

By comparison all other races appear to them of much less value. It is no wonder therefore if they do not want to share knowledge, benefits and honest creative activities for the common upbringing. The western people probably find it much more exciting and enlivening to make the most of these less important nations for their own use. They have always done so and they cannot help but continuing so, provided they are not stopped to do so.

Americans are big and powerful. It is in their nature to overpower anything and everything in their way. The small people do not stand a chance!

However they regard the Russians big and one of their own kind; so they like to play match with the Russians. They like the game of playing the role of big power. They play on behalf of almost all western nations. They use the rest of the available world as their play ground. Russians are their opponent in the game of power. They are very annoyed if outmatched by their opponent; even though they find it greatly stimulating as well. Another highly charged game is their propaganda-war. They are supposed to be the Good, Russians the Evil and the whole world is divided between the two!

Of course they are able to brandish their side with firm conviction that they are the Right one. Surely Right must override the Wrong! Otherwise darkness would follow and the world would come to an absolutely dead-end! Who knows; maybe it will eventually come to just that and surprise both good and bad at the same instant.

Perhaps the mind behind the western political power in general, is yet to realise that the physical-might or the material-might does not serve everything in life. It may be too simple to think that these are the things which make a man big!

It is one thing to pretend that one is concerned about the world at large, but it is quite a different thing altogether to be truly bothered. Most people, in fact, do not give a damn about what happens to the rest of the world so long their own interest and whims are safely in tact.

The helpless poor-underdogs of this world are mostly underdeveloped, under-nourished and may be only half-grown. The super-powers treat them as half-wit children of no consequence. They do not fear that these children will one day ever grow up. They probably do not imagine that these poor people will ever be able to stand up to them and hold them responsible for not treating them properly.

In the power-struggle between the super powers poor nations are caught up as poor pawns. These pawns are sometimes cheated, ruined and destroyed ruthlessly by the whims of the big-powers. It is so easy for the big-powers to pretend. These simple pretences and fake promises to the people without much power are no more than just some strategic steps in the power-game of the big people. The big people do not even need to pretend that hard. They know quite well that they do not even have to be too convincing. The underdogs of this world have no power, no muscle and so no bargaining strength. There is therefore no body yet to look after the interest of their side.

Rich people of the rich countries have too much. Poor people of the poor countries do not have very much. Riches make the rich selfish, decadent, bored and conceited. Poverty makes the poor vulnerable and desperate to survive. The rich suffer from an awful obsession of making more riches and also get a powerful kick in stealing from the poor. They are never satisfied. There exists so much, misfortunes! Is anyone ever happy!

One thing strikes me strange, men are regarded highly desirable if they are quite matured, in fact, the more matured the better. Young men are sometimes considered immature, childish and not so attractive. Women, on the other hand, are only attractive so long they are very young. The more young, and more frivolous, they happen to be, the better. Matured man with a very young woman is regarded as ideal match! Nothing seems to be considered wrong of such a pair in people's eye. However, an older woman with a bit younger man is not generally acceptable as alright. Is it not quite strange!

Maybe the men are thought of increasing value as they grow older. The older men represent status, security, wealth and all the worldly possession, even though they may not have any such thing; that is why perhaps they are so greatly sought after.

Women do not necessarily present the same picture for themselves. Their only possession, youth and beauty are both lost for ever as soon as they grow older. Sad though it may be, that is how it is thought of in life!

Thinking of the fate of women in general, I think woman should go to work for a living. If she does not do so and stays at home always to look after the family, she is in the end bound to loose touch with the greater world outside. Effectively she will then grow narrower and narrower until her mind stops growing and becomes dead inside.

Looking after one's family is very important and precious but to stay alive in body and spirit is precious too. One without the other is not really a life in full. Men and women both need it if they are to form a society with growing souls.

I wanted to be a career woman; but not at the expense of the joy and happiness of life, having a fulfilling family life. I thought I would like to have a truly satisfying life in the deeper sense. I imagined it would be something lovely and nice. It did not turn up like that. I did not fulfil myself and become complete in the sensible sense. Everything worthwhile remains as illusive as ever in my life.

It seems to me now that all I had was just a faint wish, but never the ability to act rightly for the attainment. I had been far too passive and did not pursue my goal relentlessly. So I have to reap the bitter harvest of life!

I live alone. All my life I lived alone. Perhaps I will continue to do so until I die. Of course I did not desire it but unluckily it has turned up to be my fate and my misfortune. I do not seem ever to have any effective power to make a change in the circumstances.

No doubt this is sad to happen to anyone. I should feel sad too. Perhaps many people pity me and that is surely a great regrettable feeling to bear in addition to the loneliness of heart.

Loneliness is destructive. It destroys generosity of soul. I get worried in case my loneliness will destroy my soul. Maybe it will make my heart and soul, all dried up. So I fear that I have got a big problem, the problem of my heart. Maybe soon I will no longer feel generous any more to anybody. I know it is wrong to feel this way. It has never been my aspiration. I cannot help feeling very unhappy about this; and my conscience is troubled by the fact that may be I will stop being kind and close to any other people.

In time no one probably will touch my mind. My heart will perhaps slowly but surely dry up rock hard. As I become aware of this possibility I get scared and disheartened. But what can one do? Is this what people call the illness of mind or the shrinking of heart? I do not know how one can escape from such sad fate. Maybe it does not truly happen to anyone! Maybe it is one of my imaginations, just playing a trick on my feelings. Maybe I will not face this fate after all!

If everybody had aspired to be good and if everybody was strong enough to pursue good, the world to-day would have been a wonderful place. The whole human race could have been something on earth to be marvel about. However, as things are in reality at the moment, nothing could be further from the truth.

I used to think the world is full of love, laughter, honour and respect. It was then only up to me to achieve my own goal in my life. I thought everything depended on, myself alone! I never thought there was anything on earth to worry about!

In those earlier days of my life I used to believe that all I had to do was getting ready for high aspiration. If I aspire sincerely I will be able to contribute to the high values of life!

I must admit now, I was too simple and quite childish in those days. I did not grow up for a long, long time. When eventually I did, I found out that those virtues were no where to be experienced! They must simply be the product of human imagination; and therefore anybody with proper sense of proportion should soon grow out of it.

In my later life I have now realised that I must make peace with myself. I do not know exactly how though! But I am going to try! All my life I wanted things which do not really exist for, me. In the end I found myself where there is nothing but loneliness, disappointment, and humiliation. Also dark depression and despondency now often loom over my entire being!

I feel that I cannot survive like this. My life seems to be choked with grief. Joy, happiness and contentment appear to have disappeared from my life totally. There does not seem anything substantial in my life. Have I just lived my life for nothing! Is my life entirely empty! I find the thought is very painful to bear. I feel that I must get out of this frame of my mind. I must find something worthwhile soon to make me alive again! Everybody needs a kind of meaning in life worth living for!

After all we are, in a manner of speaking, simply victims of our own experience. Different things mean differently to different people. From our own world of experience we seem to build up different receptors in our brain. These receptors most probably form the magic of our imagination. This is perhaps what makes us look for the meaning, purpose and excitement of our life in different ways. No two people seek this exactly in the same way. We call it the truth of our life!

It is the truth of our life. It is, in fact, the hunger of our brain cells we create out of our physical and emotional experience. We simply cannot escape the trap we are forced to build out of our own life. This is our destiny! We are born to make it and we are also to die in it!

Without identical receptor in our brain cells we do not react the same way to the same thing. Maybe we start our life with not entirely identical experience; so we build up slightly different base receptors. These then receive further experiences in life in different light and texture; and that promotes the formation of new receptors in furthermore deviated manner. This is probably how we start and live forming our life differently in many different ways and fashions suited to our each individual destiny!

After so many years of my life I am so discontented. I have realized that I do seem to have spent a lot of time gathering rubbish. I have done many things in my life. But I never have made anybody really happy. I disappointed both my parents and I disappointed myself.

Now I spend a lot of my time shading tears in private. I do not think many people know about the pain I bear in my heart. Maybe this is best, what good does it do, if everybody comes to know it or not!

I hear people do heal. I wish I do too. But my painful hurt seems to be going on and on for ever. I do not see the end of my hurtful soul so long I should live.

People seem to have ups and downs. Mine's appear to be only down. Even when I thought I was having my ups, it was not really up. I simply did not comprehend that I was at my down still. I was always at my down.

There is, however, a slight difference between my past downs and my present downs. Before I had some hope. I used to think that I will surely come out of the unhappy situation one day. I firmly believed that nothing could last forever, not even any unhappiness. Now I am not at all so sure. I have lost my hope. All I know and feel that I am doomed to my unhappy life for all eternity.

In any case we are all so sorry for not having the same fate as everyone else. But if we do, then again, we are so sorry for having to have the same fate as others. We fail to find excitement in that fate. We do like to be like others; and at the same time we do not wish to be like anyone else either!

Maybe this is just human nature. One cannot live without being sorry for one thing or other! Or, maybe I need one sort of escape after another. However, I feel, I have used up all my escapes; and I have no refuges to fall back safely any more.

Now the question is how to keep myself occupied and busy. Somehow for some curious reason or other I happened to have cultivated a life of some particular style and quality. I did wish to find a man of similar quality who would be truly interested in me. But as it turned up, there was no such person to be found anywhere by me!

Maybe men do not appreciate any quality of my kind in any woman. Perhaps it someway undermines their confidence and quality. They seem to prefer woman without the quality and capacity of my sort. Anyway, as it happened I was never successful in my quest.

# Chapter Six

I imagine different people marry for different reason. They look and hope for different kind of fulfilment in their marriage. At the start of the marriage or in the beginning of the married life these aims and purposes may not be too apparent, and the partners may not be fully aware of each other's way of thinking in the matter.

After a few years, that is, after the initial period of glamour and excitement of a newly wedded life of a couple, the quality and strength of each of the couple become noticeable to others. The aims and purposes of one's life show through the way one lives and reacts in life. It is usually in the later part of one's life in marriage, one can be sure if he or she has got the right kind of partner or not. The quality, needed to enrich each other's life, would certainly bring happiness and security in conjugal life. On the other hand if the differences between the partners and their ways of thinking are incompatible, then that will definitely destroy the peace and prospect of happiness of one or both of the married couple.

These ways of looking for things in life and these hankering for purposes in living are very deeply rooted in one's own conscience. They may stay buried in one's sub-conscious mind. One may not be aware of them as long as one is not upset in any serious manner. As soon as one is bothered and distressed in some kind of deeper way all those deep rooted feelings and sense of values come up on the surface. One suddenly becomes fully conscious of what is essential for one's own happiness of mind. Any hindrance is only going to bring out more and more awareness of what is felt so deeply in the heart.

Without the encouragement for expressing those feelings one is bound to get hurt and disturbed. And this disturbance would inevitably produce serious split and unhappiness as well.

So one has to be very lucky indeed to find a partner in life with whom one can have the fulfilling happiness. Many people are not that lucky. They sometime end up in bewildering tragedies with shattering experiences. All hopes of happiness go, out of the window; and life becomes, more empty than it was before!

Married or otherwise, most people go through their life as best as they can. They just put up with whatever comes in their way and hope against hope for the best happiness they would love to have.

It is interesting though to notice that some people make happiness out of nothing at all. Nothing can hold them down for long. They expect almost nothing for themselves and provide joy and gladness for others. If it was not for these people the world would have been a very sorry place indeed!

Some people, on the other hand, are simply born miserable. They, perhaps, manufacture misery within themselves. They are not to be happy ever! Great sad feeling comes out of the dark recesses of conscience without much of a call!

I wonder if I may be one of these people miserable by nature. I often am sad and unhappy. Quite frequently I am inclined to feel sorry for myself no doubt. Many a time I think of my little brother who died at the age of three. The memory overwhelms me with grief every time.

At the time I was very young. I remember though that his death was a great sorrow to all of us in the family. It was particularly a severe blow to both of my parents. Mother's health deteriorated ever since. She never did overcome her ill-health again. Also father became a changed man! None of them spoke much about it. I do not remember to hear any at all.

Many years later I was a grown woman. I thought everybody had forgotten all about that loss of a little boy in our family so many years ago. One day quietly my mother started to talk about the death of my little brother. He died quite unexpectedly of serious infection with some sort of deadly dysentery. Doctors prescribed barley water and other medicine for him. No solid or other liquid food was allowed. He used to refuse taking his feed and ask for milk. Mother could not give him any milk in fear that it might do him more harm in his illness. He did not get any milk. He died. Mother must have borne this pain over the years in silence.

People, probably didn't give a second thought on the matter of this sad incidence. They might have thought the death of a little boy of about three year old, could not be that serious; it should all be forgotten or at least eased off in time. Perhaps it had; but not before it had left a permanent hurt in the heart of my mother and damaged her health very seriously and for ever!

I do not think people realised how sensitive and deep was my mother! Just because she kept her thoughts to herself and was mostly quiet in front of people, people generally did not pay much attention to her. Most people, including her children, all took her for granted. Nobody may be except my father, ever had any idea about how badly my mother was hurt by the death of her youngest child.

She never had spoken about it to anybody. But I don't know why or how, it came to me almost like a revelation. I just suddenly sensed it one day soon after my mother's death. She suffered hideously with her severe breathing troubles and all its associated illness since the death of my brother till the very last moment of her conscious life before being engulfed by her last fatal coma. She did not come out of that coma. She died in the coma.

My mother did not loose any of her other children. Although she was long suffering health wise, she was quite attentive and interested in her family and friends. She was not at all a selfish person. She struck me as very impartial, generous and kind.

I took her for granted and paid very little attention to her. She was always in the background. I do not think I was aware of the space she was filling in my background until she was actually gone from this world. I have a feeling my mother never knew anybody can be anything but total tolerant of other people's mean and unkind utterances. However, she was not used to unjust personal humiliation and insult. It would deeply shatter her inner peace of mind. It would be unbearable for her quiet mind and she would be badly disturbed! Some unkind and thoughtless people sometimes did not realise the limit of the boundary of their unkindness, because she was so gentle and tolerant so often with so many people. My mother was fundamentally a dignified and sincere person. It was really not so easy to insult her even if one wished to try!

She was the product of her time in India. The values and virtues of her mother and their generation found solid expression in her life. She followed what she believed and she did it totally. My mother was one of a dying breed. One does not see many of her kind! I do miss her now that she is gone!

My mother was very religious in Indian sense. She was a strong ritualistic too. For her religion meant a complete faith, a total acceptance. Asking any question or being selective in the field of her spiritual activities was absolutely beyond her honest comprehension. But she never tried to impose any of her faith on anybody. Her faith was her personal affair. She attended to it as best as she could. She might have thought all of us will benefit from her good deed.

None of us took her seriously. We went along with her so as not to upset her in any way. Neither my father nor I had much faith in any traditional ritual activities. We took it as some form of enjoyment. We associated it with Indian feasts and festivals but not much with spiritual being.

Foreigners call typical natives of India as Hindus. Perhaps the term refers to the indigenous way of living. Frequently they identify it as a particular religion. I do not know if they are correct in doing so. Even if Hinduism is a religion it is not quite similar to the other religions of the world in religious characteristics. It is not organised. Also it is the cultural melting pot of various facets and aspects of spiritual aspiration of the ancient people of India and her geographical surroundings.

The main message of this apparently confused conglomerate of ideas always pointed to the fact that any spiritual enlightenment or progress of an individual lies, within one's own inner self. Above all one is free to seek salvation in any way one can and able.

Strictly speaking it is really the question of attaining true peace with one's own inner conscience and one's entire world and beyond. One should follow sincerely whichever way one understands best or, maybe, whichever way is open to one. There is no room for pretence, falsehood or even boastfulness of any kind. No one is perfect! No one has the ultimate truth. There is always room for improvement, and there is still plenty of new ways asking questions about the same thing.

Energetic and truthful people by nature, try their best to find a way which is meaningful to them, and which gives meaning to their life and spirit.

Mystery of life mystified all mankind. It is a void which lies within ourselves, and we try to fill it in whatever way seems most suitable to us!

The core of Indian religion is Indian philosophy and Indian metaphysics. It grew naturally to the people close to nature.

Racism is simply fear of other cultures and creeds. Is not it high time we all should come out of the arrogance of the logic of our premature historic mind! Should we not now be able to shed off the inability to accept the maturity and flexibility of mind to understand the need and freedom of man to express himself in any form or shape, he likes.

What does it matter if a man projects his mind's creativity in a way which is pleasing to him or gives him some kind of comfort! In any case none of us can go beyond the limitation of our mind! Can one really!

We all suffer in some form or other! Suffering may be ugly for some people, but out of all ugly hardship comes beauty and big things we want to be proud of one day!

Original ancient people of Indo-Germanic stock were against all forms of idol and image worship. Maybe this very same thought-form and idea raised its head too many times through the ages of history in the name of various and different religions.

Basically it may be nothing but sticking to the tradition. Maybe it is no more than simply a prejudice. All people like doing what they have always been doing. It is just human nature! Indigenous Indian Hindus developed a very strong and lively love of worshiping anything and everything their fanciful imagination took them over many centuries ago. They do usually feel religious devotion towards many forms. They naturally are respectful for theirs and others' devotional objects and objectives.

Hindus do not object worshiping Christ or any other Christian or otherwise god together with their own. As long as they are able to devote themselves to their own form of devotion; they will happily add everybody else's devotion to their own.

But if you ask them or force them to leave theirs and take up with only yours, they will not do so. They will reject yours completely. They will consider it against their spiritual ethics and react violently opposing it.

Maybe the Hindus are in some way quite mature in their subconscious mind about spiritual sensibility. Maybe they know it all too clearly that yours is as rubbish as theirs. So why should they take up with some one else's rubbish at the expense of their own! They would rather stick to their own as they are brought up with it. It may bring them some comfort and happiness of a kind or other! At least it is only humane for them to be hopeful or apprehensive or may be just conditioned at that!

Powerful races or nations are not necessarily wise, resilient or thoughtful enough.

They probably think of themselves as strong, self-important and all powerful----capable of doing anything anyway anywhere on this earth.

They practise their acceptable code of conduct and almost absolute loyalty amongst their own race or at least amongst their own countrymen. But they appear to feel that they owe little or no loyalty to other men, should it benefit their own side!

If they consider it is necessary they would not think twice to use absolute brutality towards other people. They can be very proud of their excessive base aggression and ruthless nature so long it is practised on people who belonged to other nations.

For a few centuries it worked for them to their advantage. They managed to keep power in their own hand and used the entire world and its resources for their own self-righteous and self-important purposes.

In other words they have really never been anything but selfishly self-fulfilling. They were quite convincing in their role of play-acting omnipotent rogue.

They may have given to believe that the progress and the salvation of the whole world is their responsibility. They are used to think that they know best. Whatever way they perform their duty must be right for everybody.

It is very interesting though that the qualities they admire so much amongst themselves, is a total repugnant if it is found in anybody else who does not belong to their own race and creed. Then it would be regarded as too base for human; and must be stopped at any cost.

The power they enjoyed so much must not be shared with anyone else. However, the tragedy is that other people have their eyes too. They can see clearly what has worked so nicely for these people for so long, and are now too envious of them.

Everybody is now more or less used to looking at things through the eyes of powerful people and desperately longing to be just like them one day as soon as circumstances permit it.

This is perhaps, how the world gets populated by rogues of different colour and nationality. Almost everyone's life-ambition seems somehow to become self-righteous of some description and feel so very much fulfilled.

The master-race has succeeded in imprinting their code of conduct amongst people of not so-called master races. The powerful masters and all other imitative counterparts now make the entire earth a perfect hell, or may be nearly an ideal inferno for ordinary people!

Perhaps the master race thinks that the world is so wretched because the total power is not entirely in their hand anymore! In their opinion other people are in no way capable or competent enough to use power in rightful or correct manner; and so they are to blame for all the unfortunate, unpleasant, immoral and corrupt incidents and accidents.

Feeling of superiority and confidence is a very powerful force. Once it is set in the mind and gives some comfort and beneficial experience, is not very easy to shed it off suddenly and forget it all altogether. It takes a very long time to fade away and looses its grip from the mind!

However it does eventually get lost though. Strictly speaking the world is really nobody's oyster for too long! In spite of all too clever tactics and strategic manoeuvring things do not stay the same for ever and everything gets changed somehow. One day powers and privileges too wear themselves off. People find them in a different world which does not work the way it did before.

Western Power and Western Culture may have seemed irreplaceable and certain to be everywhere for ever! But I bet it too will run out of time one day just the same. Somehow it will be out of charm and fashion just like all others before it! Something else from some where will take its place with no problem at all for sure!

Something always gets forgotten and something else comes up on the stage! Evolution in every respect must be the name of the game!

I think sometimes it is a folly to be wise when ignorance may be, a bliss; everything on earth has its time and place. Each seems magically powerful for a time; but each looses its magnificently powerful potent charm after a time all the same. There is never a shortage of something else taking up its place, as if it was just waiting in the wing to take up its rightful place right in time!

Life goes on; but nothing is permanent and nothing lasts for ever. It is in the nature of all things to change, perhaps to suit the changing world. Whether we like it or not, no one can hang on to the same thing or same idea for eternity.

Everything gets stale and then lost or thrown out. You cannot live in vacuum. You must have something; and something does come up! This is how the world goes on as long as it would!


When we cry, we only cry for ourselves. We shed tears for the pain we bear in our inner-self somewhere! Why we do so I do not know---but we do---maybe we are programmed to do so to release something out of our system. This may help us to manage with our lives and living. This may be just a survival mechanism we inherited as a living organism!

I was always too meek---far too meek indeed. I wish I was a bit bolder and took some real part in life. I never did take any proper part in real living. This is what makes me now so sad and depressed sometimes.

The world is not at your beck and call to please you if you want the whole world to feel sorry for you. The world will never do that. It is your own duty to do whatever you can for the world. The world will take it and may even be pleased sometimes. You are then pleased too. But one cannot buy the world, or bring everybody over to your side by any misery in our life, not even by our good deeds, self-sacrifice or self-pity or whatever.

The world goes by with you or without you. You are not that important, but you can make yourself feel good by doing something you consider good. That is all!

If you want to be good and kind---you do try to become one for your own sake. Do not kid yourself by the idea that you will have everybody grateful to you for that. Even if they are a little sometime, you would find the idea not that much nice when you think about it seriously enough!

Feeling sorry for yourself, does not do any body any good ever! We all are here today and gone tomorrow! The world does not really depend on anybody in the total sense.

The world produces its own saviour when needed! One of the children of this world one day can surprise us all.

At different stages of our life different things make us sad. We all feel sorry for ourselves at times. We simply cannot help it. I often wonder, where does this sadness, come from. It is probably created by the chemical imbalance in the brain.

Whatever may be the cause, it is often there for me in my brain. I feel I always follow my life from long, long way behind! I consider that is the tragedy of my life!

Many of us may often think of the life we have left behind and remember the feelings and thoughts we used to have then with great nostalgia.

Things do not always turn up the way we expect them to. Maybe they never can. Life has to have its surprises, pleasant or otherwise! Still, that is how it is!

Life is so full of nice things to fill up one's heart with joy and happiness. Often it seems though that none of them has come in our way. Anyway, that is how it strikes us on many occasions which are not particularly happy.

In our very private moments we may sometimes feel a tinge of intense sadness in our inner soul. Sometimes it can be very hard to shift or bear. Still, life is what life is! It does turn up as it does turn up. Beginning is always unknown but the end is already old!

When life is almost lived through, no amount of wishful longing is going to make much difference. Life has brought us where we are---we know not why! Like it or not, this is our life; and this is the life we usually live.

In my own case there is not much of my life left now. There is no way I can really now go back to the start and make any change.

It is probably only humane to feel unsatisfied now and then, and also regret quite a few things when you already lived major portion of your life. Nobody's life is all that perfect. We should be just glad that we managed to go through most of our life in whatever manner we were able to.

It does not really matter that much, how many things we could not do but wanted to do in our life. Some one else will do them after us if they need to be done for sure.

When everything is said and done, there still remains, your personal feelings for your own personal life and emotion. There you are absolutely alone to face up to it.

I know I am only a poor old woman. I like sometimes wearing some jewellery only to look a little beautiful and attractive but definitely not to show off my wealth. I like to look nice but I do not particularly want to look rich! Money is not that important to me!

I wish I have some joy in my life which I could cherish. I wish I could spend my life in some sort of creative activity. Life is so short and so hard! There is nothing in this world one can keep for oneself for ever. It feels good to give all for others.

As I am born and went through the sorrows and pains of life, it would seem to me worthwhile if I could use my life successfully for the betterment of other people.

I have not been too idle. I have spent my life for others to some extent. I have tried to teach my pupils to the best of my ability. I have spent the best years of my life to teach young people in England. But I always felt that English people do not really want me. They could not care less if they could get rid off me.

I must say, I often wonder what the hell I am doing here! Why I am here? Doing a hard and serious job, for the country who does not want me---who constantly look down on me!

It is not the ordinary people of the country. It is not even the people I work with or for. Otherwise I could not have survived this long. They are very nice to me most of the time. Also most of them have always been unusually respectful and appreciative towards me.

However, it is the authority, who frankly would not give a damn, about me, ever! Nothing can really improve their opinion of me. In their eyes I am expendable and that must be it. I feel they do not think I am worth bothering about; except looking for faults in my work if they could.

After so many years working here I now swallow my pride, accept my humiliation and continue to work at the same place. I cannot escape this second rate existence; and it surely makes me very small right inside me.

This brings out such a low self-esteem. No one respects helpless people. No body really lifts a finger to shield insecure people. People, who are at a disadvantage, are always alone!

Everybody loves to boss, find fault in and patronise disadvantaged people. It is so easy it feels right and righteous to hurt people who are not defended!

No body would admit what an insecure person is made to put up with and neither would anybody believe what exactly such a person is forced to go through. But it goes on all the same.

There is so much injustice in this world! It is truly incredible! No one pays much importance to it. No body knows about it much either, unless one is somehow involved in it or at the receiving end of the matter.

Even when you are at the receiving end, you still cannot believe it to be true. You feel quite numb and stupid---you feel you deserve all what comes to you hurtful or no hurtful. Besides, you cannot prove anything to anybody.

You live with a lump in your throat. You only cry out in your inner conscience and ask yourself why is there so much pain in your life!

People, who did not experience pain, would not know what pain is. They can be high and mighty. Underneath of all the refined sophistication, pride and high culture, there may exist nothing more than callous insensitivity which simply does not feel for others. There is nothing one can do about it.

People who are mostly fortunate and privileged, do not always know what it is to be helpless and at a disadvantage. Superiority often makes one smug. It can breed contempt for less fortunate people.

People, born in luckier circumstances, can grow up to be brute, ruthless and cruel. People, who are fortunate to be at an advantage, often want to exploit and use those who are not at advantageous position.

Hardly anyone really practices or feels true compassion towards less fortunate. If they do, it is quite often only a pretence and usually with some ulterior motives.

I am not saying that there are no exceptions what so ever. Certainly there are. But they are very few and far between. They are just exceptions and not a norm. One cannot take them for granted. Also, it is perhaps wise not to depend on them either. Because most of them are some sort of pretext, if not hoax.

As far as I am concerned I have lived and worked with racism all around me. I simply got used to it. It happened to me when my self esteem was rather low. So it seemed to me quite alright---I thought this was the norm and it happened to everybody.

I have always been invisible to people when they did not need me. And when they wanted me to do something for them, they just told me to do so.

If I have done the work well, it was no surprise to anybody and it was supposed to be done well. If something has gone the way which was not quite satisfactory---it was no surprise either. It was almost half expected of me. I was never really been seen to be competent in people's eyes. I felt that in their opinion it might well have been better if I was not there to do that particular job. A sad sense of inferiority was forced to grow within me. I fought with the feeling all the time inside me. I learned to live with indifference and lack of warmth and appreciation. I never expected anything else.

Lot of faults lie with me, I am far too passive. I often felt hurt within me by unfair discrimination. I knew I was being discriminated. It felt so hurtful, sad and helpless at times. Yet I always kept it to myself. I never fought against the injustice of it all. I just do not know how to fight effectively. I felt I must put up with it or else perish.

There certainly have been many prolonged periods of utter isolation and painful existence. On many occasions my life seemed such a failure, it was definitely not worth living.

In spite of it all I somehow managed to keep going. But I never fought and I never complained the way it could matter. I always hated going head to head with anyone. Confrontations were never my cup of tea. And I do not feel proud of it. I survived but never lived happily.

Interestingly, half the time I thought nothing of it was true. It was all my imagination---just the product of my over sensitive mind! Everything was as it should be. No one was really unfair; and there was no injustice anywhere unduly. People are as fair as people can be.

I often thought: I myself am simply suffering from some inadequacy of my inner personal being. It happens to people who are not fulfilled in their personal life.

I tried to think that my personal life is the cause of all these dissatisfactions and unhappy happenings; and not the other way round. I tried not to feel that the distress, disappointment and isolation might have ruined me and bereft me of my personal fulfilment.

No body can be absolutely certain about whose fault is what; and why some people feel the way they do. Maybe it is, really my fault and my fault alone!

No one asked me to come over here and spend my life as a stranger amongst the people who could not care less about me. I chose to come on my own accord and did not go away. So I only am responsible for everything whatever has happened to me and my life.

In any case, once again it is no use to be sorry for one's own life. Besides it is too late for that as well. No one is totally satisfied with one's life anyway.

In many respect I am quite highly successful really. As in my circumstances I had to be twice as good as others just to survive; and I did survive.

If I were not good enough at my work, people would have been far too unforgiving and would not give a second thought to get rid off me at the first instance. They were not able to do so and that surely proves something indeed! Maybe I should congratulate myself for being alive and also for having gone through my whole working life. Not that it matters though all that much!

I do not know what to think and make of it all. Maybe no body really knows the root of one's unhappy feelings. Maybe everybody is bound to feel sad about one's own unfulfilled potentiality. Things could have been but did not! The reason for lack of achievement and discontent may be not that simple.

Still we do find some reason and something to blame in our mind. It may not do us any good, but it keeps us sane; even though it may be all pure imagination on our part. However, all this imagination must be simply because of insecurity and lack of confidence generated by isolation and loneliness.

It is possible though that at some point somehow some member of some society may have managed to brain-wash me in deeper level. Maybe I began to believe subconsciously that I am not regarded here quite as equal to the others. I felt I was often invisible, ignored and over looked. But it did not feel too unbearable.

I was able to accept everything that came to my way without too much fuss and fight, no matter how unfair may have it all seemed. In other words, I might have been damaged in my make up, strength of mind and morality as well.

Maybe it is the price one has to pay for one's lone existence amongst people to whom one does not really belong.

Maybe some people are strong and well equipped to make the best of all possible situations. Nothing can harm them and nothing makes them suffer any loss. Some, on the other hand, are over sensitive and cannot cope with adverse atmosphere. They do not survive successfully without proper support, encouragement and appreciation.

I worked all my life. Most of my working life I worked as somebody who looked different from the rest of the community I worked for. I happened to be a stranger in a strange country.

I worked hard and quite well. I produced good result from the start. But I never got any promotion. True I never asked for any either. I had a strong feeling I will not be given any; and it will only cause more humiliation and further frustration if I try. Also it may make situation more untenable for me.

I was well qualified. I even taught some members of the staff. One member of staff I taught became the principal in charge of my section. He passed the subjects I taught, at his first attempt, but needed more go to clear all the rest. He was one of their favourites; and was promoted happily without any hesitation.

I was never thought of one of them, I suppose. There never was a whisper of any kind to the effect that I may deserve any promotion. I never complained as I felt I will never be listened fairly. I was overpowered with the negative thought that I was without any muscle power against the indifferent authority.

I never tried actively to change my position at work. I behaved harmlessly and was too meek. To the authority I must have been totally invisible always. I caused no trouble for them and so it was very easy to ignore me.

I made their life quite easy. I even spared them from the trouble of having to say no.

Maybe I did not deserve to have any promotion of any kind. Maybe I should not need to be praised or appreciated in any way when I did well and even above expected standard. Maybe I should be doing well and that was the purpose of my job anyway.

Also, maybe in the opinion of the authority I was too lucky to be where I was. Even though it is inconceivable to think that I was posted in my position simply out of charity.

I did not start my job at the bottom and then climb up the ladder. I came in the middle position and remained there until the end. There was no progress for me. I started and finished at the same position exactly.

It would be interesting to know what exactly the authority thought of me. I do not even know if they thought about me at all. Maybe they considered I could always go back where I came from, if I am not satisfied with my luck of draw. Maybe I should have if I have any speck of self-respect in my vein.

As I was not very happy, why did I not go away and start some where else a-fresh. I do not know why. All I can say now is that circumstances simply did not permit me to do so.

At the beginning one is full of courage and strength. But after a while things are no longer the same. Your mental strength seems gone away and you are in a tight corner.

I must have lost all my courage to start anew again. I became a coward and was doomed to whatever my luck brought to me. Personal misfortune wiped out the last shred of optimism. Nothing seemed to work in my favour any more. Only disappointment after disappointment at every level came in my way.

I was brave no more. Eventually the easiest escape for me was to resign to my fate and take no action to change anything. What one can do when one is young, is no longer so easy when one is not so young any more!

As I was unable to change my destiny, so I stayed where I was almost from the start to finish. Life was empty and without inspiration. Never the less I lived the life I felt I had to.

I know it is far too late to reflect on thoughts about what could have been and did not. I have finished at my job now for good.

I know very well it is best not to think of the past too much. It is surely wise to bury the past for good.

Still, memories of pain and desolation come back to haunt me over and over again. I feel I would feel better if I confide in somebody. There is, however, no-body for me to confide.

So I thought the next best thing for me must be to put it down in writing. This might give some relief to my mind! I just want to get it out of my system.

I know same thought is going round and round in my mind. As I try to express it in writing, I may be writing the same thing over and over again without much variation and content.

To my surprise it does feel nice to be able to express myself open. Whether it is profound or not so profound that does not really matter too much. It is my blocked out emotion and it must be good getting them out of my mind and body.

I do not see any virtue or benefit in keeping them locked up deep inside my mind and taking them to my grave with me in the end. For better or worse I just want to write them down! It makes me feel a kind of happy in a strange sort of way!

Poor countries of this world do not need charity or sympathy from anyone. Only thing they really need is the freedom to sell their own produce as they please or, to their best advantage possible. If they can sell their excess goods what they produce with their toil and sweat, they will soon be rich enough to defend their dignity and self-respect. But without this opportunity, and freedom, with no-string attached, poor remains poor. Nothing changes for better. There are always some strings attached, and some mischievous and crafty traps to corrupt some people within the society.

They do not improve. They remain without progress; and they then produce contempt and pity in others. Their confidence in themselves gets worse. They become unable to protect their self-interest, and fall easy prey of more exploitation to foreign interest.

British people talk about people starving in India. Have they ever truly tried to stop Indians from starving?

They never mention the fact that Indians really started to starve, since Britain actually occupied the country and made it a colony for the British.

Affluent people of the west are sometimes so smug and arrogant it is very difficult to forgive them. Do they ever ponder on the fact that they were not always so rich and all that mighty. Behind their prosperity and abundance there lies a lot of sacrifice and contribution by many poorer nations of the world.

Well-off British often have such an air of superiority about them, it can be quite annoying. Perhaps they think they are created by the very special hand of the divine power. They feel they are so special; they deserve all the good things of the world. They are frequently so high and mighty!

Poor India and Indian poverty is so repugnant to the wealthy people of England as if it is a dirty infliction brought on by one's own sinful act. Maybe the rich is repelled by it because they think it is immoral to be poor.

Nobody can argue that it is very sad and a terrible misfortune for anyone to be desperately poor. However, no one has any right to make the poor Indians feel ashamed of their poverty. Platitude does not create a moral being in anybody neither does it help anyone in real sense.

Besides all these western sympathies, seem far too superficial and quite empty. The way they talk about their concern in this matter makes you feel as if the phenomenon of extreme poverty or starvation is something inherent in India. Maybe it is. Maybe it is not. Nevertheless the question comes in one's mind is, since when the British or the Western power did anything honestly to stop starvation in India.

If they were not so busy making use of India for themselves, India may not be starving to-day. India was a colony of British power for several centuries.

Directly and indirectly British boast so much about their rights and records of running the colonies. They make you to feel as if they did all these only for the good of the people of the colonies out of the goodness of their own heart. They were the most superior people of the world. They used to say: 'it is the White man's burden to rule the world'.

They try to make you believe that they sacrificed their own interests and comforts for the benefits of all these backward countries. They want to say as if they felt it was their sacred duty to spread civilisation amongst all these uncivilised primitive people. They themselves were very civilised and righteous indeed! They felt they were compelled to make it known to the other people of the world!

It is all very impressive and clear, no doubt. But I do not know who exactly do they really want to fool? They might be thinking of themselves so high and powerful still! Perhaps they can not help feeling that everybody must take it for granted whatever they may utter!

They may like their words to be taken as gospel truth! But it is just a wishful thinking on their part. It has definitely very little to do with the actual truth.

The truth, in reality, is quite mean and simple. British must have managed to acquire all these colonies for the sole purpose of using them for their own benefit and usage. They must have found it very profitable indeed, at least at the beginning of the imperial colonial history. The greed and opportunity must have set fire in their imagination. It was a life and death struggle amongst European powers at the time. In some way they were lucky to win their success.

They found it easy to exploit all these lands and populations without any mercy or consideration. The natives are not from their own stocks; so they did not really count as human or even near human at all.

As soon as they managed to establish their power and authority over these vast lands of backward people, their aim must have been to enrich themselves and their own country at the expense of the others. They started to bleed these places bone dry and continued to do so as long as they could do without having to face much difficulties and resistances.

All the big talks about the goodness of their good heart for others came much later. It must have been the invention of the clever manoeuvre when ruthless exploitation, endless pillage, spoils and open plunder became not so easy and without some backlash. It may have been a kind of British PR exercise!

It helped them to feel good and justified in doing what they wanted to do most.

As the opposition grew more and more powerful, they needed some lawful and legal rights to help them. To dominate and over power all these unfortunate countries and their people under their domination they quite successfully invented, this clever tricks of the trade.

They systematically brain-washed all the population believing that they are inferior and British are the most superior people on earth. They made it absolutely clear to everybody that God has given them the right to rule the earth. In their opinion it was almost blasphemy to oppose their divine right to rule. This trick worked quite well for sometime and to some great extent.

They managed to break down people's self-respect, pride and faith in themselves. They were quite good in enslaving people who did feel that they truly have the right to rule them. This alone made an immeasurable damage in breaking down people's backbone and morality.

It helped the British to do whatever they wanted to for a long time without much danger or opposition to themselves. People believed they are the Masters and so they can do whatever they wish to. This incredible invention of divine right earned the British a fantastic power and privilege for a very long time. Within that time and space they themselves grew into the idea. They became bold and believing in their own conviction. It became part of them and their history.

Over the years they pacified people and put a legalised coating on their activities to control people with big and powerful moralistic terms and words.

Perhaps these gestures were really nothing much. Maybe they were as empty and meaningless as anybody's imagination. However, these gestures were made with one motivation in the mind. These were to justify and enrich themselves and themselves alone, and no-one else!

They did not use any "jokery-pokery" technique to improve the people or bring them to their own level. Instead they knew how to divide the people and rule to their own advantage. They were very busy in causing fractions amongst people and were perhaps great expert in setting one fraction against another. Maybe they learnt this technique from the Roman Empire!

Under British rule all over the world all communities became fragmented. All the hostilities and differences between the fragments came to the surface and set in motion in self-destroying fighting amongst each other. While all these self-opposing fragments served their British ruler without much question as their protector and master. Fractional differences were so much magnified. Hostilities and intense hatred were built on these differences. No value emphasis was made on the immense similarities between the groups. No one made much point on the vast gain which was possible if animosities were not pursued so vigorously! No one seemed to like thinking that they are practically the same people. How could those little differences make them such a foe and not a friend! It is strange indeed! But implanting seditious hate in the unsophisticated simple mind by clever sophisticated people is always a very powerful weapon. It runs its own course; and it does its own damage!

Once the genie of jealousy and hatred amongst the fragments of the population of the natives was out of the bottle, no one needed to do anything anymore. Self-destroying power engulfed everything. Some kind of evil force grew out of all proportion and was hell-bent to destroy each other to the end. Nothing can stop them.

They are still fighting each other long after the British left them to their own devices. None of the fractions perhaps knew well how exactly they were playing as Pawns in some one else's game!

If colonial rule was so divine and righteous, how come none of the ex-colonial countries became self-supporting, prosperous or well grown; they are termed as developing countries. Why were they, not developed during the long period of Imperial rule; if that was so beneficial and civilising for the people of all these vast regions?

Only those countries where the British and the Europeans themselves settled down to live for ever, are different. It was tragic for the Natives of these counties though. They were massacred almost whole-sale in order to make room for the white-race.

Once the white people established themselves on the lands, they did not put up with any colonial rule for long. They came out of the colonial shackle quickly and grew well in no time. Maybe it was possible for these people to successfully resist and oppose colonial rule because they belong to the same race, and was able to understand and so stand up to all the tricks and treats of both sides.

Anyway, long time has gone by; the world has changed a little too. Even so the Western world is still the most powerful in the whole world. They still play a big role in the fate and future of the little people of the rest of this earth. Technologically most advanced and materially very rich, the west even to-day is very proud, able and possesses the key-role to control the power-struggle of the world.

All the riches and possessions alone do not make anybody truly happy. The general public in the west is not happy. They have a lot of problem in their lives. Many family lives are becoming up-side-down, not functioning properly, and incurably problem-ridden.

Some of them have come to realise now that the time to play with other people's fate and feel big may be over. It is at present the high time they should play with their own fate and discover that they are not so big after all!

Quality of life in the West drives some to suicide. The life in the East exhausts some in the process of living. None is great and none is a winner; but there is a difference.

The empty feeling in the inner soul can be self destroying for some. The numb feeling and the resignation to harsh fate force most people in the poorer country to go through the task of simple living without a choice to absolute nothingness.

I am Indian. I talk about India far too often. Maybe I should not. Maybe it is very boring for anybody to hear me talking about the same subject over and over again. But I cannot help it. Maybe I am beginning to sound like a record that has got stuck. But that is alright in some ways. It helps me.

I am not really complaining about anyone or anything. I am just facing the facts. I am trying to explain to myself why India is what India is to-day.

One cannot change the history. I am neither kidding myself in thinking that India could have been able to escape colonial exploitation altogether, nor

I am imagining that India would have stepped into the modern age without some form of foreign domination.

If the British did not or could not help India to themselves some other force would, definitely have done.

When the British came to India, India was in a very sorry state. Mogul Empire was on the decline, in fact at the very last stage of collapse. Entire indigenous population was completely and utterly indifferent about who rules or does not rule India.

At this time Europe was bursting with power and energy. For European it was high time to expand and take over any place anywhere and anything they could lay their hands on. They scoured, explored the whole world, and took possession of everything possible.

Amongst the European powers British turned out to be the foremost. So it was almost inevitable that India got in the clutches of the British. In any case if the British did not have India, some other power surely would have. That might have been even worse! No one can be certain about that now! One way or other Europe took hold of the entire world. India could not possibly escape. If somehow she could have managed to avoid it for a little while, history might have taken some form of even more cruel revenge in some other way. No non European country could possibly come to the present century without being dominated and thoroughly exploited by some European foreign power.

So the British would come to India and start their empire there, is no surprise to anybody. It is simply an inevitable step in the history. There is nothing now to gain by quarrelling over it.

It only gets under my skin if or when people try to imply that British came to India out of goodness in their heart. No one came to anywhere out of anything in their heart except profit and greed.

Britannia was the greatest colonial power, the most, shrewd sophisticated capitalist institution. India was their market place to sell their industrial produce, collect revenue, and obtain raw material as cheap as next to nothing.

Some people do like talking big and high. It would be too foolish to trust whole heartedly all of the high-minded talks of some people. For example when some proclaim that all men are equal; what may not have been made clear that they mean all men are equal amongst their own equals. It is usually the aristocrats or the people who control power, are regarded as equal to some extent. It is always well understood everywhere that some are more equal than others.

All talks must therefore be judged by people's action in conjunction with their intentions.  One can talk, but it is quite another thing to be believed. Also it is simply not possible to deceive all the people all the time!

# Chapter Seven

Feudalism was too much established in the world; and it was so for a very long time. Its roots were so firmly rooted in the social soil all over the world, it seemed absolutely permanent.

To uproot this, was a very difficult job. It caused too much upheaval. The amount of massacre, bloodshed and suffering was needed to make room for a change, is now difficult to comprehend.

For the suppressed people to come up in the world, the world needed a great deal of bloodshed and violent up-rising. Established power does not give up its hold easily to the mass. Down-trodden, illiterate, poor mass is never well-equipped to take over power from their powerful masters. It had been a long and hard battle. It still is in some parts of the society and in the world.

The fight often ends up handing power in the hands of dictators which only makes thing much worse; and a much harder and bloodier struggle starts all over again in earnest.

To come up to a fair and well-meaning democratic rule every society has to go through a long-drawn and ever-vigilant battle. It is really a never ending struggle. Some societies are more successful than others. Some are at various stages of the struggle; and some have a long way to go still.

World-wars were really class-wars. Upper class people used ordinary people without any restrain for their own power-struggle.

Nine millions supposed to have died in the First World War. Who counted those died just outside the direct link of the war! No one can really estimate the true effects of a big war. One war produces millions of inhuman ready for another.

Cruelty and desperate dehumanisation experienced in the first-world-war, must have prepared, the Germans for the second-world-war.

They were ready then with unbelievable cruelty and unheard of beastliness. They killed millions with their innovative gas-chambers and concentration-camps. Powerful races carried out mass-murder many a time whenever they wanted to get rid of helpless people.

This idea of killing innocent women and children, as long as they belong to a different race, was not a moral problem. This was done many times before without any serious consequence on their racial superiority.

However, the Germans had gone too far in the Second World War. They thought they were Master race! Good looks, good physiques, well-dressed and polished appearances with love of refined music, good food and whatever alone, do not enhance the measure of quality of anybody's humanity amongst any race; and without humanity what is a human being! Master race or no master race, who really cares!

Even though one may consider that the first world-war experience was responsible for and consequently led to the second world-war. Nevertheless the Germans have proved capable of darkest possible inhuman qualities within their race. Besides they lost the war. If they were the winners, who knows how they might have been able to justify all of their beastly actions in some form of approval!

Americans wiped out quite a few million Japanese people in a flash with their invention of atom bombs. No body would dare to put any blame on them. They are the winners. People think it is somehow justified because, otherwise the war would have been dragged on and more American lives would have been lost. As if American lives are more precious than Japanese ones.

No one even dream of considering this as racist. Killing Japanese to save Americans is supposed to be just the right thing to do. To annihilate the racially inferior Japanese in millions is nothing of great consequence. If by doing so a few valuable Americans or the Westerns could be saved, is obviously very admirable thing to do in Western eyes.

Maybe it is so. But if the situation were in reverse and if the bombs were in Japanese hands, where would then the ideology go! Would it have justified the Japanese to save their lives at the expense of the millions of the Westerns! Or should the logic take different colour in order to fit the benefit of a race!

Asian life, most probably, does not have much value in the Western calculation. But Asia and Asians were mercilessly used for their wars. During second-world-war the British were losing at the hands of the Japanese in the Eastern front. They were much shaken and worried of losing their empire.

Without much thought or, making appropriate provision for the local people, the British removed the food stuff and destroyed the granary. So that it was out of reach for the enemy.

In the process, there were, grave shortage of food-grain. Many died of severe starvation. Millions dropped dead in the street like flies.

Starving people cried at the door, begging not for a scrap of food because there would be none. They were begging: "Ma fan"; they were begging for the excess water people throw away of their boiled rice.

My mother told me about this tragic cry. I think I can faintly remember it even though I was just a child. I do not know how but I can visualise the disastrous calamity. It often haunts me, particularly when I am sad and alone. It breaks my heart. I cannot help crying by myself for such a dreadful tragedy amongst my people.

No body, none of the British ruling authority said sorry for the death of so many people, caught in someone else's war. No one took any responsibility for them. I do not think anyone ever even acknowledge the event. It was most probably just a non-event necessary for the cause of powerful British Empire. As an Indian, it is very hard for me to forgive the British and forget the event though.

No body took care of my people. There was no infrastructure for the benefit of my country: no aids, no soup-kitchen, no safety-measure of any kind, for the natives of India at the time. People simply died and it was, as if, of no consequence. But the British were ruling India and they were the masters of the people.

There were very little food-grains left in the country sides. On top of that there was a crop failure as well due to some natural mishap. The price rocketed sky-high and became completely out of reach for most people. A great number came to the cities in the vain hope of finding food there. But there was none for them anywhere. And there was no relief either.

Consequently a vast number of people just starved and died a painful death. Skeletal bodies were everywhere.

The ruling power of the day did not seem to have cared. After all, these were only Indians. Maybe it did not matter that much to the rulers!

The British are great diplomats. But diplomacy and clever-smooth talk is one thing, real care and genuine generosity is quite another; in truth diplomacy is simply another name for sophisticated efficiency in deceit or deceiving skill when necessary.

India has not got over this misfortune since. The black cloud of starving population in some form or other is still hanging on over India. I do not know if she will ever be able to feed all her people properly.

Top people are corrupt and deceitful. Many are exceedingly callous, selfish and insensitive towards the sufferings of their poor brothers and sisters. They did have good teachers!

Livelihood of poor population is still very shaky. Hoards of people still come to the cities from rural areas in desperate hope of finding some form of livelihood which is not there.

The image of moral India is no longer present. It has gone. Poor India seems for ever poor. Lot of her people still do not have enough to eat.

India's poets had always been singing about their motherland; she was supposed to be full of green pasture land, fertile and plentiful. She was like a graceful mother with everything for the well-being of all her children.

What made them sing so! If she was really like this, what happened to her! Where has she gone and why! Will she ever be back!

India was never a land of famine, death and grave destruction, at least not before the British came. There is no clear record or evidence for any such thing.

India had a lot of foreign invasions. There must have been great many killing and some destruction in the wake of each invasion. But they were only short lived and regional. After each event India must have recovered quite quickly and prospered rapidly. Since the ancient time the people who invaded India, usually settled down amongst her population and contributed for her prosperity in some form or other.

Only the colonial age was very different. Its aim and purpose were altogether, completely new phenomena. India may never be able to overcome her prolonged colonial experience. Nobody really knows how long or if ever she will take to come out a new.

In spite of all the tragedies, misfortunes and injustices the mind of man is evolving all the time. Human understanding is moving on more and more. Mankind comprehends things which were beyond comprehension before.

Collective knowledge builds up with time. Things do not stay the same. The mind changes and so does the man.

Feudal age was a very long period. 1900 may be regarded as People's century. It is the age of hope for common people. It is the century of despair, destruction and hope. Immense hope for common people has arrived. Innumerable loss of lives and long-drawn vicious struggle with all its bitter consequences was for this precious objective.

Next people's century 2000 could be called hopefully the age of wisdom.

Maybe this will herald centuries of enlightenment, understanding and endurance for mankind.

Maybe people will learn how to be tolerant and be able to co-exist with mutual benefit, respect and regard.

Whether or not this euphoric age for mankind will truly come about on this earth, only time will be able to tell!

So far, man has wasted so much of her energy and resources just to destroy each other! Nations employed all his ingenious efforts and might only to exploit, kill and annihilate other nations. It is really incredible and difficult to apprehend, how absolutely huge is man's killing industries almost everywhere!

It does not make much sense! This culture and age-old tradition of animosity towards others is very expensive and self-destroying in the long run!

Given the same amount of energy and resourcefulness if engaged for the common benefit of all men, an enormous savings in lives and prosperity can easily be achieved. If people can trust each other, and nations can depend on other nations then, the fighting machineries become devalued and redundant; may be a kind of heavenly bliss can almost become a reality! Maybe it will never happen; and maybe it is only a pipe dream. However, let us hope that the evolution of demonic qualities of human mind has at last exhausted itself, and it is now time for the turn of more noble aspects of aspiration.

Education is our only true vehicle for the modification and improvement of mental faculties. Our mind is our life. With our mind we persuade the secrets of life and beyond!

I read sometime somewhere a mother asked her child never to be mean, never to be cruel and never to be selfish. It must be the priceless words of wisdom, if there is any such thing at all!

It struck in accord with my heart! No one can really gain much in the long run by being one without a soul! Every bad act of cruelty and meanness eventually catches up one somehow either outwardly or inwardly. It is almost impossible to escape from the bad and degrading aura of one's own immoral action. It applies equally to individuals and even to nations as well.

Collective guilt is known to crush national spirit and nation's forward progress in history.

People may think it is clever to deprive or cheat other people who are not powerful enough to stop them at the time. But the power of morality is universal. It does come to haunt and take revenge in some strange way or other. This must be the ultimate wisdom of all the religion of the world.

Racial differences are facts of life, but racism is not necessary. Western people often seem arrogant. In some superfluous way they appear to look down on us, the people of the poorer nations of the world.

I do not know if they really feel in their mind that we do not count as much as themselves. I, on my part, do not care what they think. It is not that important.

We do count. We count just as much as anybody else. I personally come from India. My country is huge; and the people of my country are enormously versatile.

I am certain that my country is a country with great and bright future. I am very pleased and also greatly proud of it. I wish my nation all well and all the best of every prospect of this world. Surely she deserves it without a doubt.

English people are proud. England is a country with great history. It is very nice no doubt. But it is not the same. My people too come from a long line of ancient civilisation.

Left free, independent and non-interfered by outside power, who can say that India will not catch up with the rest of the world in terms of prosperity and power one day not too far away!

Indian people have a lot to be proud of. India produced Gautama Buddha amongst other things. He came to the scene when the rest of the world was in dirk ages. He gave the world the most matured spiritual thoughts which even now people perhaps cannot quite fathom it clearly! These thoughts were part of Indian conscience five hundred years before Jesus Christ was born.

Even in recent time India gave the world Mahatma Gandhi----Gandhi was incredible too. He challenged the Western Power in an unbelievable way. The world never knew anything of this nature before. The West never met anything like him and did not know how to deal with him.

He forced the Imperialist Britain to look at themselves and noticed for the first time, how fatally inadequate and immoral they were to rule Indians in India. Their imaginary authority of Colonial Power was nothing but a sinful act against humanity. In reality they were simply playing the part of a savage race in someone else's country.

Gandhi was truly fantastic. He was simply unbelievable. It is very difficult to grasp how he came to be there in the British dominated India. Nevertheless India did produce him. And I am very proud of this fact!

British were bent to destroy India as thoroughly as they could. They really wanted India to become a very obedient and obliging slave country instead, in their own image!

Gandhi spoiled their dream. He was determined to make India proud of herself and remain as whole a country as possible! He therefore was totally against the British interest.

So the British could not possibly let Gandhi stay alive intact. Somehow they had to destroy and discredit him and his influence in the country as far as it was possible for them. And they somehow managed to do a very good job at that.

Fate, fortune and hard work favoured them greatly; they became a great power. But in that transformation there were a great deal of contribution and sacrifice from other people who became insignificant in their superior egoistic eyes. It was the riches, the man-power and the vast market of India, what was a major factor to help them to become a great powerful nation.

It is quite easy to understand that they should feel proud. But they clearly forgot that they did not come to India as a benevolent godly nation for the sole purpose of saving India from the sins and ills of the world. They came to India for helping themselves; and they did it very well indeed. So the only thing, hurts us poor Indians, is their total lack of acknowledgement of this fact. They learnt to use the Indians, but never had much love for them. In their eyes Indians remain inferior and nothing much to be grateful or respectful for! Of course this is quite human and ordinary, and nothing to be too surprised by. People always despise the people they use for their own benefit. Indians in India, Negroes in America, never quite managed to be equal in their master's eye. All these are therefore only too natural!

It is no wonder that British always look back to their past. Everybody knows they had a powerful past. Of course it is quite natural for them to be very nostalgic to their history. But is it really very good for them to get so hooked in their past glory!

In any case, if their past was so wonderful and exhilarating, why have they lost it! And why are they quite out of steps in quite a few respects with some other advanced parts of the world! They are now regarded as comparatively quite backward in the modern world!

They had a great opportunity to dominate the world when the world was not developed enough. They did that for sometime. They deprived, exploited and disposed a lot of people who were not able to protect their own interest. If they want to be proud of that, good luck to them, of course!

But no thanks to them, the world suffered and worked hard to get improved and stronger. The world is no longer a child. By being treated rough and bad by the world's shrewdest people at the time, the world is now, perhaps more grown up, and able, to look more straight, at the clever nation's eyes! The poor nations can now see through quite a lot more clearly than before in many situations. So it is not so easy to bluff away and cheat as it was used to be.

Thus a new era is now dawned. The survival of the people is now depend on how one can truly compete and worked hard amongst people who are more or less equal and not culturally disadvantaged.

Everybody is now more or less grown up. Knowledge is no longer the secret weapon in the hand of rich nations only. Ability of a nation now is real ability to produce, supply and make things in more honest and competitive way.

In this hard and fast competition, it is remained to be seen who is the powerful and who is not! It is no good just to look back. It is simply urgent and essential to look forward into the future.

Past is past! It is gone and gone forever! Every dog has his day as the sayings go, all people have history: some maybe comparatively more impressive than others. But all are related. Poor nations helped to build richer nations in more ways than one. Who is to say who is more important than whom!

Without the poor people there will be no richer people at all. One existed at the expense of the others, only until the other can take care of the situation and rebuild their life to take charge and improve themselves.

When people in the east were more innocent, unsuspecting, unprepared and undeveloped, the west came, made them their slaves and misused them to their heart's content.

This ability to rule over the lives of the eastern people made the west big, big-headed, high and mighty in their approach towards the world in general.

But the world changes; the slaves come out of their shackles and start to think for themselves. Eventually, even they learn how to manage their affairs better.

The west then has to compete with these not too unprepared people of the world. Now comes therefore the time for the West to prove to the world how really clever and masterful they are in comparison to everybody else!

Historical Buddha of India had his realisation of ultimate truth: Life cannot reveal what is beyond this natural world. And compassion for the fellow beings is the only thing to achieve satisfaction in life. It is unlikely ever to surpass the truth of his profound wisdom. Also Gandhi's proclamation of non-violence helped the poor India to survive to some extent against the ruthless suppression of the super power.

However, none of these is enough for India now to exist in this modern world. India needs to modernise and grow industrially, technologically and sociologically if she is going to exist in this world. Morality and fairness for all people should be her message for the world we live in.

# Chapter Eight

There is perhaps a difference between Eastern and Western spiritualism. Eastern aspiration in this field is basically to promote peace and happiness in the inner development of individual mind. This is not at all a matter of proving great or small in any body's eyes.

However, the western religious history seems to be an unending aspiration and struggle of one group to overpower another. Also they seem to feel that it is the most important part of their religion to impose it on others. They use it very skilfully and ruthlessly. It is in their hand a powerful and dangerous political weapon.

They must fight to the end and kill if necessary to erase all other ideas and people with different spiritual conviction. They actually feel very religious and spiritually uplifted if they can manage to destroy a community with a different discipline and establish their own in its place. They honestly seem to think, this is what God wants them to do and feel, very much fulfilled, in God's eye.

For some reason Western philosophy always seems to end up in disaster for other cultures and countries. The Western mind is so arrogant, aggressive and brutal in their approach to other people they do not leave any room for others to survive in any shape or form of their own. Identity must go and go for ever!

The Western culture became powerful. They became used to having an upper hand in any circumstances any where. They do not think they need to go deep in their search for solution for other people's problem. People do not realise the West is in reality very superficial in their understanding of other people's need and true progress. They may even be simply callous and could not care less if some of their activities are going to hurt others or not.

In spite of their high and mighty talk of concern for the world and its progress, the truth may be that they are quite insular and only can think about their own short term benefit and interest. Everything else is just pretence and simple hype in disguise!

For a long time they wanted to believe that the people in the West are not much less than God Himself! At least they are the God's chosen agent on earth. They therefore feel that they must have been bestowed with all-knowing, all-understanding and all-powerful attributes of God, the almighty. And so they do not need to seek anybody's approval. They should do whatever they feel right or want to feel right about. In any case, it must be right if they feel it to be right!

People are people everywhere. But in terms of world power and world politics things do take on a particular shape and colour. It brings up definite sufferings and hardship on groups in places. However, it may be a great folly to expect the rich nations to help the poor nations in real sense.

I often think, it is a great irony that the land of Buddha and Gandhi had to go through the hostility and total bitterness of religious intolerance. The land which gave the world the philosophy of peaceful co-existence in nature with every living thing can no longer live side by side with people who have different way of expressing their religious ideas.

This is really an incredible blow inflicted by the foreign overlord who was our master for a couple of centuries and tried to eradicate our cultural views and tradition for the sole purpose of preserving their own interest and power. And maybe we were not strong enough to have a clear vision in the matter. We simply allowed ourselves to be played in their hand for the destruction of our own land, unity, fate, lives and living.

We then helped to set an example of communal intolerance and hatred for the whole world to see. And the world seems to judge it as a natural consequence of backward and uncivilised social existence.

Gandhi wanted unity. He knew India's strength and future lay in unity and unity alone. British knew their danger and destruction lay in Indian unity. They did all they could to spoil and prevent it. Eventually, by hook or crook, somehow they managed to break India up on the basis of religious differences; and directly or indirectly achieved their intended goal.

Gandhi was shattered. His dream of saving India was lost for ever, at least for a long time to come.

Under British rule Indian unity was nothing but a very fragile thing. From the start British wanted to break it up. The future of their empire rested on the break down of Indian unity. Divide and rule was always the ultimate British policy for preserving their empire. They learnt this from Roman Empire.

And dividing a country on religious ground is something British was an expert of. This is one thing they knew a great deal about. They had long and solid experience in this matter. Their whole culture is really based on the power of religious differences in the society. They knew exactly how to use it to their best advantage and exact aspiration. They were terribly astute to develop this as a highly successful political power for their entire empire.

It is probably very difficult to imagine now, how they actually played with the fate of our lives and pretended to be the lord of the land. To play with the lives of somebody else's country and also have misplaced authority in the games of politics is wrong and should not have happened at all! But who was to stop it. We were not strong enough to prevent it. So it happened alright. Our country was broken down to pieces. Millions of lives were shattered and lost in vain. No one accepted the responsibility, and no one said sorry either.

With all the goodness of Gandhi's heart, he did not succeed; the Indian unity was broken. The peace of India did not hold. In spite of all efforts and wishes things did not work. The hard and crooked conspiracy, the absolutely determined political doggedness worked against India. India was broken in the end. Gandhi was defeated and forced to fail for the good of India. As far as India was concerned, her hope to stay as united India was never to come, that entity was cleverly and cruelly killed off, perhaps for ever.

I heard in the Television that Churchill hated the Indians. He thought Indians are an abominable and foul race. He would have liked to obliterate them if he could spare the time and effort. Anyway he hated the Welsh as well. Perhaps he hated anybody and everybody who did not fit to his interest.

He thought Gandhi was a naked fakir; more trouble than anything else. In his opinion Gandhi was nothing but an utter nuisance.

Maybe Margaret Thatcher in the later time has the same opinion too, as she is a great admirer of Churchill. Maybe all old Britons used to think in the same line. I am sorry we can not oblige them in any other way. Maybe they would like to use us as their target practice!

They seem extraordinarily arrogant and have very poor opinion of everybody except only of themselves. It must therefore have been India's great misfortune to be ruled by these people for so long. They must have despised

Indians all these years. They must have killed and ruined everything and anything what was truly regarded as real India. All the originality and unique creative perspectives of Indian world and identity must have been thoroughly discouraged, ignored and neglected under their patronage.

Maybe everybody needs their education. Maybe it is high time the British to be educated in somebody else's culture and values. On the other hand it is no longer of much importance. It does not matter anymore what the British think of other people. They now need to be careful about what the other people think of the British themselves.

In any case no one cares much until one manages to take care of oneself. No one ever have done anything much for us. We, the poor people of the world, always worked for the others, the rich people and the rich nations of the world. It has always been so easy to exploit us and work us hard to death.

We never had much muscle to use against the clever and powerful rich. We never even had much intelligence to work out clearly how we are really being used up for other people's interest.

The rich managed to form collusion with the local demagogues and tyrants. They first subjugated the local and regional powers and then used them for their own self interest. Using collaborators is a highly successful technique in the management of empire.

We in India were lucky in one way and unlucky in another. If we uprose against the British in arms, the British would have tried to wipe us out with their high power and might without any mercy at all. They would have a huge excuse to do so and the whole world would have sympathised with them in pleasure. In any case the powers of the world at the time really had only the interest of the British in their hearts.

Use of religious differences to incite detrimental monstrous hatred amongst one community against another was absolutely foreign in Indian culture; because Indian basic belief always believes in the individual differences in their approach towards spiritual development. There are hundreds of different variations in Indian religious sphere. It never was a cause of too much trouble in Indian mind. Manifestation of human adoration towards spiritual goal is supposed to be manifold according to Indian philosophy. It is supposed to be natural and expected. There was never been the conflicts of organised religion in earlier India so to speak of.

But the Western power has always been an expert to use religion as a tool of hatred, destruction and annihilation. This tactics played an important role in their entire history of development.

For some time Gandhi was able to save India with the civil movement. He wanted to raise people's conscience, strength and determination against foreign domination. British were unable to crush India to dust even though they tried their best.

Gandhi was far too sincere and superior politician of great moral values. It was not very easy for the British to overthrow his strategy, plan and success. They had great difficulty to overcome his moral strength and powerful principle.

Maybe because of this strong obstacle, British in the end went in for far more mischievous way to ruin him and his India. They resolved to find a way to create an un-surmountable wedge of hostility between the two main fractions of the society in India. It was never been their intention to leave India in peace and intact. With their clever hand and superior intelligence they succeeded to engulf India with a gigantic blood bath of social frictions and destructions which is going to last for a long time, perhaps for an unforeseeable future.

A vast country with enormous poverty and ignorance was under foreign power. Leaders of different fractions might have been tempted with all sorts of promises of personal gains and privileges. God only knows what they were promised and what they understood to gain. In any case, under the circumstances once hostility started, there was nobody to stop it. The game was up. India was lost, may be for ever!

The secret weapon of bitter hatred implanted with care and nurtured with vigour, proved to be impassable obstacle for India to acquire any peaceful history anymore with or without the British as her overlord. India now has to suffer from this social and political wound of horrific dimension for a long time to come. Maybe it will never fade away. Maybe with proper progress and prosperity, with real education and understanding, population one day with a bit of luck, may be able to see the futility of this self-destroying hostility amongst our own people.

Variation is really the very essence of life. I hope everybody will come to understand this. Hopefully one day everybody would realise and appreciate this fact of life; and also all futile attempt of uniformity and lack of differences, will stop.

Only thing is important that people should be aware of what is in existence and what is available. People should be educated and given the opportunity to know and find out for themselves.

All we should hope for that people will have strong, bold and well-developed mind to choose, assess and analyse. They must have proper sense of morality. They must know right from wrong, in their choice.

Whatever appeals to our mind, need and aspiration, we should be able to explore and persuade. There is really no right or wrong in true sense---it is only a question of living our lives to the best for ourselves and also for the others. We are all social beings. If we do something to hurt others, they will do the same to us.

If we do not respect others, others will not respect us either. No one is going to get their own selfish way all the time. Unfair ways brings backlash which is hard to bear and causes much more destruction and unhappiness on its way.

If people come to know and understand all the facts of nature, they will automatically learn to curtail their evil ways; as they will know it is not possible to get away with unjust thing for long.

Powerful people always wish to draw the entire attention of the world to themselves. They wish to occupy the whole arena. Yet, contrary to this desire, the evolution of life towards better prospect perhaps lies in the mystery of the differences around and not in any monotonous aspect. Out of diversity, always borne things, which are greater and better than ever before, in life! Yet every effort is made to keep things always plain and narrow every where in the history of mankind!

Maybe people just love to live under patriarchal domination. They do not want any change. Maybe demagogic arrogance is simply the natural consequence of this. They are afraid of change, and the possibility of any change happening.

Ethnic ideas are being treated as marginal. Ethnic culture is a source of great suspicion. It is simply pushed to the margin.

If the poor are not so poor any more, the world would be quite a better place to live in. At the moment though, poor are poor not without a reason. It may be so that the better-off people can be better-off. And the better-off people want to keep it that way.

The rich make their money, but the poor cannot get theirs. It may not be straight forward stealing from the poor. Nevertheless, the money is not there for the poor to have. So stealing and making money may not be all that different in the stricter sense.

When everything is said and done, one thing we all should understand that justice cannot be kept down for ever. It cannot be tricked or bluffed off for long. It will always come up. In spite of all the tricks and power it will catch one up in one way or other. Somehow it always will triumph over in the end.

Educating human spirit and encouraging fair-minded people will always benefit society. Depth of wisdom and honest foresight is absolutely essential for human progress.

The Chinese genius Confucius said, in the wisdom of the past lies the hope of the future. However, in the popular culture of today everybody knows the best!

As the saying goes, curiosity kills the cat! And maybe superiority kills the race too!! Yet some people think they are doing their race a great service by trying to make it feel superior. By ill-judged gestures, silly actions and by being cruel and indifferent to the well being of others, they try to achieve superior status. This does not help anymore. It will never make any body any happier.

We need education and enlightenment of our soul. When we achieve that we become wise and a credit to all of our people. Unfortunately, not many of us are capable of getting it at all. For most pretend superiority is just a game! It makes some feel good!

If and when the poorer parts of the world get developed and become well-off, I wonder what will happen to a lot of high opinionated Western do-gooders. Maybe the suicide rate will get much higher. They will have a lot less to make them feel so superior and self-important amongst their fellow people.

For some reason they feel very righteous and smug inside. God only knows what exactly they and their countries are actually doing for others to give them such highness in their head and mind. This high-flown, highness may be the product of their imagination. They feel very important and perhaps this is the expression of their self importance.

However, they have not changed the world much. They themselves may have gained from their activities. They are happy with themselves. Other people do not seem to have a great deal to show for as their progress or prosperity.

Selfishness does not produce anything to be too proud and happy about. It is a negative product of our subconscious mind. Manifestation of developed mind is usually more positive and productive. Institutionalised racism will not glorify any race or anyone in the long run.

All these charities and aids, what does it all mean! The rich feel good and proud, the poor feel nothing. The destitute and desperate remain the same.

Aid is always in the news. The rich nations giving so much in aids to the poor nations; by now the poor nations should be all too rich with all these aids all the time. But no such luck! Poor nations do not seem to know much about these magic aids. So much news from this end and hardly any news ever of the end result. It is a mystery no doubt!

Maybe aid is a sort of bribe to the crooked cronies of the Western powers in the third world. These pet dogs in the third world in return do or buy the things these powers want them to as a favour. So aids perhaps do more harm than good! Perhaps aid is a technique to manipulate and exploit the third world much too ruthlessly than it is generally known.

Maybe powerful people are naturally selfish! They got away with their own ways for so long; they become more and more, greedy over the years. Unless something forces them to change their ways, they are not suddenly going to change their methods and make-ups. They remain important, deceitful and self-satisfying as ever.

With their powerful ways and means they know exactly how and where to lay their hands on. They are very enthusiastic and full of energy and inspiration. They are dying to lay their energetic hands on everything or may be, at least as many things as possible. They were, once upon a time, quite good in plundering other people's things without much squirm.

Later, when they had finished taking away as much of the things as possible, they started a popular myth that they would not touch other people's property even if they could; and in any case there were nothing to take. Whatever they had taken, they deserved it and were given or earned for their good services! In any case that is the idea people would like to believe!

They were very good to start a smear campaign against the people they managed to subjugate over the years. They had discredited these people of their culture, heritage and almost everything they had possessed. They discouraged, demoralised and turned these people to slaves. They thoroughly used these demoted mass of people for their own benefit and glorification.

These rich and powerful nations nearly succeeded in making everybody believed that whatever they themselves own and have, are the best in the world. In their high and mighty opinion, all other people are simply inferior and whatever these other people have is not worth having. They were extremely thorough and successful in making these unfortunate poor mass of many nations clearly and absolutely inferior in every respect. They made no bones about it at all.

For the rich confidence soared, moral boosted; they became more and more clever. Eventually they became too clever and shrewd to be put at a disadvantage by anybody anywhere in any circumstances. However, they did not think it safe to send everyman to the devil in his, own free way. It was important for them to organise in an air-tight way.

The British learned to play with laws for a long time, at least perhaps, since Henry the 8th's time. They came to know how to use law as it suited them. It is regarded almost as sacred as divine to them. It helps them to shake off their conscience and makes them free to do whatever is to their advantage at the drop of a hat if necessary, but within their laws, of course.

They discarded God and made themselves the god for all reasonable purposes. The law became a convenient tool in their hands to be used for their convenience.

However, nothing stays the same for ever. What is permanent in this world! Perhaps spiritual energy! Perhaps the universal natural whatever! Who knows!

Anyway, one can ignore the ordinary common people of this world for long only at one's own peril. It has been proved over and over in history; but people still do not acknowledge this truth.

Ordinary people are the salt of this world. They are plain and honest. They contain the truth of this world---that is, as much truth as possibly be contained in human beings!

They are not glamorous. They are not dressed up in much fancy clothing. They do not have much to exaggerate anything artificial or otherwise. Many people do not think it is worthwhile to show consideration to these simple uncomplicated people of the world. They are the down trodden neglected people on earth. It is quite easy to ignore them to start with. But it is a grave mistake and a very unfortunate one for that matter too.

People, even the very poor people, do one day grow up to face the fact of life and take charge. Human resilience is incredible!

The depth and dignity of Indian soul is no less than anyone else's on earth! Some people may imagine so because they want to feel that way and it may give them some sort of self comfort. But there is no truth in this false ego, just the same.

When every thing is finished and done for then, all that matters, is who can take us as we are! Everything else is of no consequence at all!

It is not just the colonial Powers are ruthless, damaging and soul-destroying influence in their colonies. Kings and queens of politics or politicians behave and talk exactly in the same way all over the world. It must be the privilege they enjoy which makes them seem polite, sophisticated. They are always patronising, empty, and full of rhetoric and pretence.

Maybe nobody wishes to loose their perks and privileges. They want to keep everything for themselves. Maybe that interest makes them careful and sets them the way they talk, think and behave.

At the moment the people who are getting to the position of top-power in almost in every country, seem to be all very hard headed and strong. All these hard headed people at the top are very conceited, rigid, big-headed and power-mad. These people are not always right; they can loose their head. They are bound to make mistakes in taking their decisions against each other. That would surely make them angry and aggressive. They do have their rivals.

Out of these frictions and frivolities there may come, their defeat and down-fall! And may be after that there will come, the opportunity for the common people. The poor may gain confidence in their own merits and values. The ordinary poor people will then have the courage and determination to achieve strength which will help them to stand up on their own feet. Anything can go wrong though!

Frivolous personal whim can make a pretender! But the benefit for the common people from him is always a bit thin on the ground! To expect real help for humanity from any self-important ruler is in itself nothing short of flippant frivolity! You have got to be joking if you think such a thing is ever possible. The power and the powerful, frankly do not give a damn. Although the poor always look out for a benevolent saviour in their ruler!

Sincerity, honesty and strength of mind together in the mind of a man can produce miracle! It is the most important thing in the world of people.

Unfair competition makes people resentful. Deception, intolerance and harmful patronage eventually make people handicapped. Diplomacy is no blessing to this world. It is simply a political word for deception and nothing much else!

No doubt life in the third world is not heavenly. But the quality of life in the West is not that glorious either. Man in the east is exhausted in the mundane act of living; life in the west on the other hand, is driven almost suicidal. None seems great; but that is, what it is like at the moment.

In a way we are all victims of time and place. Depending on where we are and when, we go through the experiences of our lives. We have to endure or perish.

All the time we fall victim to many predators waiting in the wing. The history of human life is the history of predators prowling to pounce upon the victims.

This is always going to be for some people, unless their society and country can safeguard their safety and security from any possible predators.

We need to understand other people and learn from them. The world is now a small place. Nothing can be hidden for long any more. The more we know the better we will be.

Differences are the source of vitality. No need to look down on one's neighbours just because they do not belong to the same culture.

Societies can be withering away from within for lack of adventure, excitement and from sheer boredom. Differences and variations can bring vitality.

Maybe it is because of the differences in the American society, America has the vitality and lively growth. For lack of acceptance of the ethnic differences in the main-stream in Britain, United Kingdom seems like back water and not so full of vitality any more. The bits of spark it has on occasion may have a lot to do with the forces of minority culture and its activity trying to exert itself.

People will never be all angels. There will always be human conflicts. But as long as there are more fair-minded people, there is a greater chance of peaceful co-existence amongst more people.

Life is so short and time goes by too fast! One must make the most of one's life; and that is the end of that really! Life will not wait for anyone!

People do get old, rigid, fussy, fastidious, futile and foolish. It just cannot be helped. This is simply in the nature of things. But to an individual human being it is still perceived as sad and mournful. People do not like the final passing of anything in their life. But it happens and people talk about it with great regrets and sadness.

I often wonder, when exactly people are supposed to enjoy their life! When someone is young, the time is spent mostly in constant worry about what to do, how to do and when to do things which seem very important at the time. This is the period of anxiety, doubts, restless thoughts and unsure feelings about everything in life. Definitely no peace of mind for one to enjoy!

On the other hand, when one is old, things are then all left behind. One is only sad about not being young anymore. One is not happy at all to have to leave everything behind. Life is about to finish at any time for ever: the thought is very rarely welcomed by human mind. It always mars the time of life still left for one in the world before the final curtain drops: so no exaltation of mind is there then either!

Therefore the only time I can think for peace to have, is when one is dead. Life is finally over, finished and done for. There is nothing more for one to do, think or feel. Absolute end, deadly quiet peace and final certainty, is at last to last for ever. Is it possible then that in death people enjoy life! Or maybe it is far too strange to consider anyway!

Human beings are funny in many ways! They like fiddling with the images of those who are gone for good or are not available anymore. But they could not care all that much when those departed ones were alive and nearby.

Ancestor worship is one very good example of human emotion. Putting decorations and flowers on the graves and on the pictures of their departed friends and relatives help them greatly to relieve their emotion in the depth of their nature.

Anyway, life is never simple! The more you get, the more you want. The more you get spoilt, the less or worse your life becomes!

In spite of all these failings, the quest for wisdom is very humane indeed.

Human beings always acknowledged the feeling that he, who carries the true seeing eyes in his head, is the real lord of the human kind. No matter how poor he may otherwise be, he is the leader to lead people to their destiny!

We have to hold our horses, and forget the contemporary values, we need foresight. Without it we are not going to improve ourselves much.

Plan and preparation for the well being of our fellow beings can never be given the short shift. It deserves all our wisdom and the true love and respect for the entire human kind. Life is a gift and we can only try our best to make the most of it.

Perhaps some people are just fools. They go through their life with some sort of sadness without any apparent reason. Maybe they are simply born that way. They are born to feel tragic. Tragedy is in their mental make up!

Most probably I am one of these people. I always feel I never have achieved my destiny. I do not know why I feel this way. It makes me sad and forlorn. But it passes, and some other time I do not even think about it at all.

I feel I have ended up as such a failure! Who would have thought it could be so! I never did. The world must be full of many failures like me. Some are perhaps greater tragedy than others. No one really bothers about it that much. People always proclaim that this is life! And yet it is so painful. It is hard to bear for the person who has to live through it.

Maybe I have a passion for feeling sorry for myself. I feel sorry for my country and sorry for everything as well. In my life pies are always in the sky!

Some people boast of their mean civilisation. They are proud of their ruthlessness. They seem to enjoy a lot to kick someone around. They look like natural bully to me. They seem to have some kind of meaner and bitter social sense. It is hard to live amongst them. They would make me loose faith in myself. It would be very easy for them to find a stick to beat me with.

Some western public sometime look down on India and the Indians. But what do they know about India! They only measure it on their own term. India may seem so ordinary and unimportant in their arrogance and assumed superiority. But they are basically ignorant.

No amount of all knowing, all powerful, self-important and self-righteous pomposity could hide the fact that they know very little indeed. They enjoy being pompous smug. The complex air of superiority is not going to make them happy for long.

I have a feeling that in due course India will surpass them all. One day India may be looking down on them for their short comings. I feel quite strongly about it. And I wish people everywhere to mark my word!

Another thing I have noticed is that lots of people marry for wrong reason. I am specially thinking of the Western women marrying Eastern men.

I suspect that these women perhaps have a deeper need and wish to be treated as a queen. They perhaps think that the Eastern man comes from a background which in their eyes nothing of any particular value or importance. So, even though these women themselves do not come from a background of any special culture, education or any particularly rich environment, they in their head feel bold and proud. They are very ambitious to fulfil the role of a queen in the eyes of their husband whom they consider to have no standard to measure or judge them by.

They take everything from these men and give very little in return. Their life often drifts apart and the men are usually drowned in misery. If it suits them and if the time is right, the women can leave their men and make a different life for themselves.

Going back to me and my feeling of sorry for myself and my country, I often get quite indignant with people's hypocrisy. No one is perfect; neither me, nor my country. We all have our faults and short comings.

I know India is poor, poverty stricken and very hard up. But nobody is going to do anything about it and nobody ever had. Hopefully India will grow and is growing from within.

British kept India under their thump; the more backward she stayed the better it was for them and their capitalist interest. They used India and her vast market as the dumping ground of their human debris and capitalist goods for many, many years.

They did not encourage any industrial progress in India. All they had there was for their full-proof colonial future as long as they could possibly hang on. India was a great opportunity for them; and the times like that were obviously very far and few in between for them. It is quite simple to understand. But what is not so clear to me is why they always try to pretend their concern for India.

They never loved India and they never will. They do not need to either. But they always make so much noise with their make-believe love for India and for Indians. It makes my blood boil and my hair stand on end. Do they really think, we are all half-wit; do they really think we do not understand their game! Or, it may be a smoke-screen for something else!

None of the Western power ever cared much for India. Their love for India is love without respect or any real concern whatsoever! They want to use India; they always did. They are over zealous about it. It is still quite lucrative for them.

Over the recent past, India is no longer the usual dumping ground of their human debris. The rich British families used to supply a large number of administrators and experts especially trained for India and Indian civil service. Also a huge number of old British patriots were desperately needed for top-class soldiering in India. They are not needed anymore. The dumping grounds of all these human debris from the West are diminished.

The West is now at the receiving end for human debris. They need cheap-labour and so must act as the necessary dumping ground of human debris from the East. It is no good being neurotic about it. You cannot have it in both ways. If you want cheap-labour, you will have to have the cheap people.

They probably have more than they bargain for. But you cannot win every time. They are not really great lover of foreign people. The prospect of foreign people living peacefully amongst them in their own country may not be very attractive to them. It may even make cold shudder runs up and down their spine! But it is not easy to change the scene now. Maybe it is not worth the bother.

The world is changed a great deal. In this changed world it is very difficult to walk too freely as it was once used to be for some. We all owe respect for the living world; and it is no good to be too determined to turn the ways on their heads. If we try uncaringly it may turn round and hurts us.

We all have to hold peace in this new world whether we like it or not. Also we all have to learn to care more honestly for people far and near, and not try to plot behind the back of some or other.

When I think of India and her historic division, I can not help feeling very sad indeed. I know it is useless to blame anybody for anything if one cannot prevent the misdeed or mishap in any positive way.

However, it does interest me to try and understand the historic perspective of this massive tragedy and destruction.

If a country is mismanaged, mishandled and manipulated by a very shrewd foreign or outside power, it is possibly impossible to stop anything happening to the country. Also it must be absolutely unreasonable to expect guiding and controlling the country successfully and contrary to the opposing foreign authorities and their self-interest. Such a country can rarely escape from being doomed for ever, if not at least for a long time.

This is perhaps what exactly had happened to India. India was a British imperial colony for a long time. Occupying interest at the time was to keep India subdued and subservient to its rule. British authority and interests were paramount. But the interests of the Indians and India in general took a much lesser role in the hearts of the ruling power.

Indians became disheartened and disillusioned with their masters. They started to have clashes with the power.

Imperial authority enjoyed their position in India; and hated to loose it. Indigenous natives, on the other hand, did not like it anymore and started to oppose it seriously. Obviously the foreign authority was no longer welcomed in India. Britain must have been greatly incensed.

Authoritative powerful personality like Churchill was supposed to have hated vehemently all Indians, Indian cultures and anything identified as Indian. Hindus, the Hindu-race, culture and religion, aroused severe disgust in him. He was supposed to have remarked: Hindus are a despicable people with despicable habits and despicable religion. I know I have mentioned this before. It made a big impact on me. He, perhaps, would not have minded to do or use any technique or policy to give these abominable Hindus a hard-hit lesson. He might actually have master minded one such blow. No one is going to tell us now about it, or exactly what action he managed to take against India in the end.

However, the British perfected their extraordinary lethal-policy of divide and rule. It never failed them in the entire history of their colonial rule almost all over the world. It helped them a great deal to prolong their rule in India and damage India in the process.

At some stage, the occupying foreign interest and power might have colluded with some of the internal subversive and selfish sub-groups of the population. These fractional groups might have been motivated by internal hatred and lure of easy power. One cannot be absolutely certain about the actual history behind all these intrigues. But it did manage quite easily to damage and cause an untold amount of destruction in India. India is ruined for a long time to come, if not for ever.

One might ask who really ruined India; and how actually did they do it. The answer is of no great consequence now. It is done and it is too late. One may still enquire, who, were they!

Somebody or some vested interest must have done it. And they did it with sure collaboration of like-minded interest. Indians were poor, stupid and backward. It could not have been very difficult to manipulate them and made them act according to some shrewd, sophisticated, political hand.

It is obviously no use now to know exactly who did what; but whoever might have done what that certainly was not for the benefit of the Indians in general. One can mention it once again that India is ruined and perhaps will stay ruined for a long time still to come.

It is a great misfortune for India that India was not clever enough to save herself from the severe destructive force which acted against her fate. Maybe it is not ever possible for a colonial serfdom to save itself from the pitfalls and abysses of internal stripes and mutilations.

Everybody knows, it is no good blaming anybody now. It is all a simple history now. But India is still living through this history. And Indians are paying the price for their misfortune and unfortunate history.

India needed reform, modification, modernisation and improvement, but she still got desperate destitution and large-scaled destructions instead.

It was quite some time ago in my young days I wrote a few things which were personal in nature. They were not really of much importance; but they seem interesting to me now at my mature age.

In January 1971 I do not remember why I wrote as follows:

Oh well! I am not exactly a pauper or a destitute! I am not a queen either. In any case, I may not be a princess; but what do I care for a princess! Aim in my life has never been any such thing.

I came from an ordinary family. My parents were honest, brave and possessed a kind of personal dignity and kindness which I value most.

I know many Indian women may value a great deal of their personal possession of great many expensive Saries and a lot of jewelleries. They are not that different from many women in anywhere else. But I do not feel like having too much of too many unnecessary goods. It makes me feel too heavy and uncomfortable!

I like my pride to come from, my believe that, I possess a fine, warm mind of my own. I hope it is quite sincere and at the same time sophisticated in many ways! The thought that I can survive anywhere in the world and I can communicate with anyone of any nation, makes me feel quite happy and satisfied to some extent!

I know, I can make a reasonable living anywhere in the world. Also I never really feel too poor in the ordinary personal sense. But I do not forget that I belong to a poor nation. The knowledge that millions of my county-men and women live in extreme hardship touches my heart; it humiliates me in my deepest soul.

I sincerely look forward to some days when I will be able to do something worthwhile as my contribution to the wellbeing of my nation. I hope this is not just a little self-righteous hype to make me feel better momentarily.

I seriously believe that there is no reason why my people, one day, should not stand up firmly on their own feet. I do not believe my nation is potentially any more stupid than any other. My simple logic tells me that potential strength and ingenuity of a nation bound to come out strongly as the nation faces an enormous crisis and humiliation at large.

I am only a poor Indian. I did not learn to exploit the love of God in the

European Sense. Somehow, I only believe in the greatness of man. If the man is made in the great image of the Great God then, the man must be able to be great as well without any kind of reservation for anyone in anywhere.

If a man, in one corner of the world, succeeds in improving himself to a considerable degree; this tells me that the others can do the same. The other men in other corners of the world should also be capable of doing themselves just as much good if they put their minds in doing so.

I honestly fail to see how a man in Asia or in Africa could be a lesser man than one in Europe or in America. He may be poor and backward at present; because he has been exploited for centuries by ruthless colonial powers. Indeed he may as yet be ignorant of many things due to lack of education, opportunity and proper development. He may even be ugly and repulsive; as things necessary to enhance his appearance and well being, are well out of reach of his impoverished hand.

All the same he is still a human; and one could not possibly ignore his identity as a human being. One could not be certain why one day he would not be able to gain a little bit of material standard of living and thereby will acquire all the gloss and charms of comfortable life and living. In the end, we Asians and Africans may not be as impotent as the Western popular myth might like us to believe.

I do not wish to be rude or unkind to the Western outlook in general. Many of this people are very clever and also extraordinarily skilled technologists. But some of them do make me a bit sad. They can be quite narrow-minded about other people.

Sometimes they are too mean to share even a little bit of their good fortune with the less fortunate nations. Also there is nothing they would not do for their own interest. They can always make up an instant philosophy of their own, justifying thoroughly and solidly all of their action. They seem too fond of preaching their self-righteousness.

The Western popular opinion is quite obsessed with a kind of belief that God and His blessings are almost the monopoly of the white-skin race of the world. Whatever they do to the other races, is supposed to be simply God's wish! They feel that God speaks and works through their mind!

It is very convenient indeed for them. Obviously, in their mind poor God has no other business but to mind the interest of the rich nations only!

It is extraordinary! It puzzles me enormously. How could a human mind give so much importance to their own racial interest and be so lack of respect towards others. Maybe they are somehow brainwashed to some extent!

The world does not belong to just one race though. All races exist. The existence of the people with different skin-colour does not depend on the opinion of any particular race or nation or culture.

The British wished to sell arms and ammunitions to the white South-African government; they did not see why we, the Africans and the Asians were not very happy about it!

Why indeed! It was surely a very good business prospect for the British. So why shouldn't they do it! Maybe quite difficult for them to understand how anybody on earth could possibly dare to stop them!

We are only poor, destitute nations of the world. We have no wealth. We are not even Christians and do not even share the same God with them. So we should be totally powerless.

Maybe we do not have much. Perhaps we have absolutely nothing except, may be, a little bit of soul in one small corner of our little mind; and we do not wish to sell it. We do not wish to be a nation without a head and a soul as well.

It must be difficult for a powerful nation to face up to the fact that they cannot always buy the poor. The conscience of the poor may be quite strong, and not for sale. Just because the rich people have been used to doing whatever they wish, it may still be wrong and should be stopped.

The Christian British may be proud of their righteous behaviour, but they do often sell and provide arms and dangerous items to the wrong hands.

They believe in God; and it is quite alright if they themselves sell arms to the devils; as God must be strong enough to take care of them, and also be always loving ,them all the same.

Their God is a loving God; and He can't help loving the nations with white skin only! That is His job! So it must be a poor little God! He has no choice of His own! Has He though!

No body or no nation is perfect. But the poorer nations haven't been able to do as much mischief as the rich ones so far. That is perhaps all one can say! Given half a chance one is probably just as bad as others! No one can be absolutely certain about it yet!

Maybe as the East becomes more able, the West becomes more rational and understanding!

In 1970, towards the end of that year, I must have been infuriated with some people for something. I cannot remember what it was; but I found some of my writings and statements on a piece of paper. They run as follows:

It makes my blood almost boiled to find how strongly and excessively the British public underestimate the Indian people in general. They try not to say much if they can help it; but in the depth of their mind they seem to believe it as an infallible truth that the Indians are nothing but a stupid bunch of primitive people.

According to their notion Indians are poor simply because they are too lazy; and they die of starvation because they are not Christian enough.

Maybe the powerful nations are astonishingly ignorant of the poor ones. They perhaps could not care less about the existence and culture of the people who do not belong to them. It still seems incredible to me, how they could possibly think of themselves so high and ignore the others so completely! Wouldn't respect for oneself automatically teach one to respect the others as well! Do they really believe that one is big if one just says so! I should have thought that the big is he when everybody else thinks so!

Not that I should really bother too much about what the British people think of my nation and my country. I guess they are not all that special either. They are after all only human. The education and the opportunity available to them, help them well to earn their living. They are materially quite well off so they perhaps, cannot help being a bit big-headed too.

The technology gives people a lot of material improvement and comfort, but it may not necessarily make anybody better and wise. Just because someone is born in a country which is technologically behind at the moment, and is unable to buy a good earning, it does not immediately make him a lesser man. There is surely a lot more in life than just money.

Technology, education and good standard of living are important; but given half a chance, every country should be able to achieve them alright.

Also I often wonder, why on earth so many good western conscience, are so keen to share their Heaven with the heathens. If only we, the heathens of the world, would throw away our cultures, customs and way of life, they would be so very happy and feel that they have saved us from hell and hellish inferno!

If they could somehow manage to make us feel that all the cultural contributions of our forefathers are just rubbish, they would be overjoyed. No matter why it must all be rubbish, but as long as we can accept it to be so, and are willing to copy their culture in return without any question then, the good conscience of the west seems triumphantly happy. Their aesthetic sense is satisfied by their good deeds!

They reassure all the converted ones that they will persuade their merciful God to make little bit of room for these poor ones as well in their wonderful everlasting Heaven!

They are too eager to make room for us in heaven but nothing much in this world. It does not make us rich or powerful, and so the contempt for the poor still goes on.

The power of material culture is overpowering. No one is willing to share this power with us on this earth. Even the very sight of any of us too close to themselves on their own soil, often seems to make the spring of all their love and compassion disappear.

To help us truly and honestly with ordinary things, is simply much more expensive than giving us a part of the Heaven! Not even the greatness of Great-Britain can really afford that! After all, the great British business-mind knows it quite clearly that it is never a good time to play with interest. Also big fishes must live on small fishes. That is the game of the world!

Besides who are we to the big powers! They will happily go on using us as long as we allow them to use us for their own benefit and interest. Hopefully it does not sound sarcastic. I am only trying to amuse myself a little, when I am really sad.

As for one's own interest is concern, I do not think, one has any hope of any help from anyone else. If we wish to build ourselves, we must do it ourselves.

If it were the interest of the western power to help us, they would have done so centuries ago. In fact, it is a plain truth that their interest in some ways lies on us, not getting any real help from anywhere at all. The longer they can exploit us, is obviously better for their interest. The chance for us to use them for our benefit is in practice far too remote.

Still we cannot allow it to go on like this for ever, if we wish to live with dignity and self-respect. We must do something to change our misery. And why shouldn't we do something to improve ourselves? We cannot remain foolish for ever!

British interest might benefit from us behaving as fools; because they want us to be fools. But that is not a good reason for us to remain so. In any case who are they really? We must think for ourselves.

A shrewd sense of reality and a true break through of our crippling serfdom of the selfish world power is absolutely urgent for our progress. The world has kept us intoxicated and silly with wrong ideas for far too long. This is high time at last for us to try to stand on our own feet.

The basic knowledge of technology, science and all its achievement is no longer the personal property of any nation. It is available to anyone whoever is in a position to make good use of them.

There is simply no need any more to be discouraged. The internal and the external discouragement is something every nation must overcome if they wish to get anywhere at all. The discouragement of any nature is mostly based on falsehood of some kind. It is usually just fear of change; and a kind of reaction to anything unknown or untried. These are all very ordinary natural reflexes of human mind in human society.

So if anybody says that India cannot change, there is no need for India to stop changing. On no account India should let herself to be played in the hand of any crafty old power of any sort. In the natural things of any matter, things always change naturally. So everything is going to change in time, whether we like it or not.

India and the Indians are part of nature; and therefore change or evolution cannot be escaped even for them! Thanks to the exploitation, hardship and all the handicaps of colonization, India started at the bottom; and hence she can only go up.

I don't know why I always write about India, and inevitably about my reactionary thoughts in connection with some stereotyped British institutional ideology.

I may or may not be right about anything; but I cannot help thinking about them. As I live long, long way from India, it is always in my mind in someway or other. It may not be the present-day India as it truly is at the moment, it may be something what I imagine India in my mind.

Also, as I live in England I often feel too free to criticize Britain, British culture and British power. Again it may be mostly imaginary and not strictly backed by absolute fact. British people probably would hate me bitterly. But, interestingly, Indian people hate me as well. Every time I go to India, I criticize India very freely indeed. I feel I am Indian; and if I can not criticize India, who can!

But the Indians, themselves misunderstand me completely; they think I am trying to show off, just because I do not live there. And also I have no right to be analytical about anything in India, as I do not share their daily-life there!

According to them I am far too privileged, comfortable and spoiled in a society far away from them, and hence I could not possibly have the know-how of anything over there.

In a way it is really quite sad for me. I do not belong to anybody, anywhere or anything. Still I dare to think thoughts. Whether I have any right or not I just cannot help thinking about things which are close to my heart or which come to my head; I cannot or do not claim anything to be absolutely right or wrong. They are simply my personal thoughts. And now and then, I like writing or talking about them. I feel they are just my personal and private property, I do not really expect anything from anyone. As long as no one is chopping off my head, I am quite happy and grateful. It must be so nice to know what is right and what is wrong. I wonder if everybody knows it really!

I do not seem to know anything about it. Whatever I consider right turns out to be wrong for me in the long run.

I wish I had the power and the courage to go through my life as it would have suited me and made me feel happy. As it happened, I only had those notions and ability which made my life thoroughly unbearable at times.

I often wonder, are there many like me! Or am I the rare mockery of nature! I made my life such a misery for myself!

Everybody has children of their own. Everyone seems to have husband to share the life with. I wish I had the same too; but I have none of it. I wonder why not! Was there no chance of happiness for me in my life! Perhaps there was! Maybe that I just did not know how to take it and make it real!

Anyway, it has all gone wrong. It is almost all over now. Life is coming to an end absolutely dry and empty. Maybe it is all for my good, or for someone's good! Maybe living a natural life is not supposed to be for me! And so it is after all for the best somehow!

At least that is how I should try to think of it. Otherwise it is quite difficult for me to live through my life at times. Often, my life seems unliveable, odd and very different from everyone else's life.

Nevertheless, I should try to keep myself sane until I really cease to exist. In this natural world of ours, we all have to live whether we like it or not. So it may be wise to do as best as we can! To keep one's own peace of mind is all one can do.

I found out a good cry can sometimes make one feel a little calmer inside, after a strong sorrowful emotional experience. It can really help in one's lonely helpless heart in one's own lone privacy!

I wish I could make peace with myself. I just crippled myself with a strange sense of guilt and regret. I can not overcome it. I suppose it can only get worse and worse.

Life is perhaps just something to grin and bear it. There is, in fact, no choice whatsoever. One can be intensely unhappy at times; but it will pass only if one can bear it at the time!

Some other times, strangely enough, it does not seem so bad after all. Another time it can even be quite enjoyable if one's mind is ready to enjoy it. It is all far too mysterious for me!

I can look back and see how unhappy I was with my life at times. However, it seems all so unnecessary now. Long time passed over. I feel that may be I was a bit overdramatic. Or, perhaps I wanted to feel tragic and important. I just do not know or understand for sure!

Things are not as simple as it seems. Everybody has to work hard to get anything worthwhile. Maybe some people do it quite naturally; and so it may seem that all the good fortunes are poured over these people without any effort on their part. But it may not be so in truth.

Some people, on the other hand, may not put their heart into the right action and hence, even though they may appear to do work hard, nothing seems to work for them. They seem to be the unfortunates of this world without any reason. The reason, however, is that they do not somehow work up to it. That is, perhaps there is to it all! Fault may lie, in ourselves only and not in the outer world after all!

I often wonder why nobody loved me, I mean really truly. The answer may be in the fact that I never loved anybody either. And you do not get anything in this life without having to earn it first. I did not give anybody anything and so I cannot get anything in return from anybody.

It is probably quite a simple arithmetic! Everybody creates their own loneliness. They may or may not know it; but that is a different matter! The truth is always simple; but people may not want to see on the face of it!

I do not know why I cry so bitterly inside and feel sad about myself. After all, when I think of it seriously, I do have a long life. Somehow I managed to live it through. Everybody will die one day. Life must come to an end; it cannot go on forever. Whoever it is, will have to stop at one day.

I did not probably enjoy a lot in my life. For some reason I lived a kind of lonely life. However, it did not feel too bad then; because I was of high spirit and used to feel one day I should surely have better time. I used to feel the air was full of promises; but better time never came. Not a single real wish of mine ever came true.

I always hope in vain. Nothing good ever happens to me. I still go on living on hope. All these fragile hopes never can last long. Yet my desperate heart cannot do without them. One after one, my hopes shattered in front of my own eyes. Even then, I always refused to give up my hopes. It is a sad story, but that is what it is. There is perhaps no use crying over it!

I oscillate between two kinds of moods. One is a feeling of desperate depression: an acknowledgement of my whole life passing me by, and nothing very much to show for it; and I know I have not made a very good job of my life. Another feeling is that of no feeling at all; a kind of numbness. Maybe it is just human nature.

Human mind cannot sustain one kind of feeling for long, be it happiness or be it a great sadness. I am sad---very sad at times. Often a guilty feeling overcomes my mind. I feel so guilty. I have not made much good use of my life, neither for myself nor for anybody else. I have simply let it slip away for nothing! I really know not why though. It seems such a waste and without a reason.

This feeling of sadness gives way to a state of mind with no feeling at all. This is probably only a pause before my sadness comes over me all over again. During these short pauses my mind does not have any strong feeling; but there is always a slight expectation that everything will be alright after all in the long run, which never proves to be true though. This is only a short-lived illusion which helps me to keep going in spite of all the odds against any possibility of any remote happiness in my life.

The more I am growing older, the better I am getting to tolerate and accept my life. I become a lot more and more, calmer to bear all the disappointments of my life.

But earlier I was much worse. All the things I wrote during 1980's, sounds much more painful and intensely sorrowful. I remember in 1981, I scribbled down a few lines as follows:

I lost my faith in my life, I lost my hope too; and my mind is numb. I feel I am drained of all my inner strength. I am sure I am a hopeless creature without any future or prospect in sight. I just do not understand why or how do I come to be in such a state! I never thought I could possibly end up like this!

During the same period, on another day I expressed very much the same and similar sentiment:

Somehow I lost my balance---the peace of my mind is gone. Either I live in a kind of fantasy which is a sort of unreal state of mind, or I live through quite a strong depression.

Anything, a very trivial matter, or even a most insignificant affair of any kind, could easily set me off to a state of depression. I never feel any joy. Neither do I feel like doing or creating anything. My mind simply goes off to a kind of isolation. Loneliness seems impenetrable.

People's pride and self-respect always do something for them. But my pride seems to be always destroying me somehow. I do not know why it does not do anything for me! It is supposed to be good for everybody; but strangely enough, it appears to be just bad for me.

It looks as though, because of my pride in myself I ended up to a life without hope and very little happiness indeed. People's boldness and confidence is always so good for them. It always helps them greatly in their life. I truly envy them! Why everything is so different and disappointing for me! I probably will never know!

Quite sometime ago in 1960's, I was a student in the British University. The young people I used to meet there were different. At least that is how I used to feel. They seemed to me, were kind, generous and very willing to do good deeds towards their fellow human beings who were not as privileged as themselves.

I found them very friendly and warm hearted. I thought they wanted to play fair with the world's affair in general.

Quite a few year later things have changed a lot. By contrast, the young people now-a-days strike me as changed to some extent in their attitude towards others. They seem hard and too worked up about their own welfare. They could not care less about other people's interest. They just do not have time for anyone.

The lack of security around them, less chance of getting a job for themselves made them more keen in their own material well being and indifferent towards other people wherever they may be.

Perhaps they no longer think that it is their duty to try to be fair towards people who are not too fortunate in some respect. They seem a bit insensitive towards less fortunate people. They do not seem to have a great deal of dignity any more, and are no longer too ashamed to behave in some cruel manner if it helps them in personal benefit.

They lost the euphoria of helping the poor. They no longer think that they are the people to save the world. They feel that it is important for them to save themselves, even if it is at the expense of somebody else. The people, who cannot defend themselves, do not deserve to be saved.

In their eyes, the weaker section of the community is perhaps not much of a value. Maybe it should be got rid off in order to make more room for the well being of the more valuable members of the community.

Suddenly, all the brutality, hatred and anti feelings of all kinds against any people who do not belong to them are present and too visible in their minds and deeds.

Maybe it was always so to some extent. Also, maybe not all young people think and act in this way. However, some obviously do; and it seems that the whole society is quite radically changed for the worse.

For some reason or other, there seems more racism now than before. Maybe it was just the same, but definitely it was not so clearly exposed and violent amongst certain section of the society then. Some feelings of hostility are often coming to the boil. There must be a reason for all these explosions. I do not know what though. However, for some reason or other, some people somehow appear to be a bit changed! Also one single wrong act always seems so overpowering!

Maybe the real truth is that the things are just the same as before. But there is perhaps less pretence now than before. Maybe people in general became more honest and straight forward. And the pretence of the do-gooder is no longer too fashionable any more in the society. Everything is now simply transparent for everyone.

Once people know the real truth, there will come about a better understanding of reality and reason. Eventually, perhaps things will truly improve for the better. No more bluff or make-belief, we all need real changes.

The old sentiment is gone. The old-fashioned superiority of some is now quite out of date ideology. It no longer brings much comfort to most people. It is high-time for everyone to modernise their thinking process.

Until the present time, the men in power all over the world as ever played too much with the lives and feelings of ordinary people. I do hope there will come the day at not too distant time, when these powerful people will no longer be in position to play good so much any more for the common mass anywhere.

People always talk about God. Who or, what is God! I wonder! Maybe God is both the understanding and the non-understanding of the secret of nature by human mind. Thus whatever a mind is capable of creating is really the reflection of one's own God. God is supposed to be creative and the Father of Nature!

Whatever we honestly project from our inner soul is appreciation, awe, and admiration of our natural world and beyond, must be a kind of manifestation of our God. There could not possibly be a right or wrong God. In any case who is to know about it!

Intellectually speaking, one's own God depends on one's capacity of grasping the abstract as well as the non-abstract aspect of one's entire world. This cannot be exactly the same for any two people.

However, if a group of people decide to follow a certain faith and feel happy and content in the pursuit that is entirely a different matter. It is simply a question of community spirit and culture. Different communities are naturally likely to produce different faiths and cultures in its course of nature and tradition. This is perhaps how religions came into existence!

Powerful people feel self-righteous. They enjoy thinking that they are right and other people must be wrong. For example, the British played with this concept for quite a few centuries. There was no body strong enough to put a stop to this. So they happily brought about world wide havoc amongst many poor nations of this world.

Maybe English are somewhat quite prudish. I do not know if it is simply natural for them. Maybe they have actually imposed it artificially on themselves for some valued reason like religion, patriotism or something else. This was definitely self motivated. They were very careful to serve the interest of their nation. It was clearly not based on any intellectual ground.

Interestingly English is so strong and powerful outwardly, especially away from their home-front. But they are not so strong in their domestic world. They seem quite weak at home. Their home is usually run by their dominant women folks.

English man's home is a castle. It is in fact a closed world. They like to do what they always did. Women do not like any change in their home; and men are quite happy to follow their women there.

Perhaps English people are usually used to live in their familiar customary domestic atmosphere. Maybe it is a kind of closed world! Maybe they do not feel, it is a bit worthwhile even to peep through other people's customs and habits. They seem to feel absolutely certain that it is of no use whatsoever. They are most probably conditioned to believe that the others are surely too primitive and worthless. They do not think that they have any reason to change. So they contentedly like to follow their life-style as they always did.

However, the younger generation seems not so closed up. They appear to be not that happy to stay the same for ever. Somehow, they seem trying to break through their self-comforting blanket of self-glory and self-satisfaction. The young ones look like beginning to discover the excitement and exhilaration of the wider world-culture. The colour and exaltation of other people's life appear to be no longer too much unattractive to them. Some of the new generation British seem quite fascinated by the idea and value of living a much more, fuller, richer and open life in a more international light. It looks quite worthwhile to them after all.

Powerful people are always proud. People of powerful nations are generally quite smug and very complacent. They are lucky no doubt; but they are not of that importance. The world will not come to an end without them!

They are well-fed and of good health mostly. But they are not all with good brain and special intellect. They do not necessarily all posses power of quality thinking and reasoning.

In fact, they are not really as much of an intellectual giant as they would like to believe. Most people are most ordinary everywhere. Not that I am blaming them for it. In truth, I am glad to acknowledge that people are simply people anywhere. Also, I do not know why, it gives me hope, if not anything else.

Roughly speaking, one may be able to say that the people in the west were trying to grow strong and bold during 15th and 16th centuries. They had to struggle hard to survive. Through out this period they had to go through severe hardship and harsh existence. They learned how to survive and exist well. Some of them became tough, clever, inventive and ingenious.

During the next two centuries the west grew far too strong and powerful in relation to the rest of the world. They acquired strength, tact and cunning unsurpassable in the entire world. They soon became very competent in using the whole world for their own interest, satisfaction and greed.

In no time this power and skill went straight to their head. The conceit and courage became too much. They started to have a very high opinion of themselves. They began to think that they could do anything and everything.

In course of time, the misuse of their power seemed the right thing to do as it suited their interest. They under estimated and misjudged the people of the world, as they were no match for themselves.

The western power did not care for the weaker people. A great many people were a lot less developed in material and skill. They did not grow up in power at the same time the west was growing its strength and might.

The powerful people of the west thought, these less powerful people will remain stupid and at their mercy for ever.

The popular myth must have been that there was something inherently wrong with these poor and meek people of this world. There was no way these people could possibly ever change.

So it was very safe for the west to do with these people whatever they liked or wanted. They thought, they would never be held responsible for their action, and also they would never be asked to answer for their deeds. The world belonged to might, and therefore the might was entitled to do whatever made it happy. They had their mighty empire; and so they never could imagine, it would ever end.

The 19th and the 20th centuries continued to tell the story of power misuse, corruption, injustice and unfair play in world wide scale all over the world. This was the period of play-God acting by sheer ungodly people.

In playing these plays they were planting the seeds of their own downfall. The ruthless injustices forced the immature and weak people of the world to grow up and grow up fast.

The western power thought the people of the middle-east and some people of Islamic faith were the slowest of all. They did not hesitate slightest or, they did not think of anything at all to use middle-east to their own advantage.

They even snatched up a part of middle-east and made it to be the state of Israel as an easy solution of a problem of their own creation.

By doing this they were planting a time-bomb which is causing an enormous amount of destruction and disharmony amongst a wider circle of population. The west never thought it would cause them any headache. This was beyond their comprehension. It was simply too impossible for them to realise that even the Arabs could grow up and would hold them responsible for their action.

Power game is of highly complex in nature. Even the self-made gods of the western world could not keep it exclusively for themselves for ever.

Because of misuse and misunderstanding of power-game, power may be about to change hand at last at the end of 20th century. Who knows who will eventually have the upper hand in the world affairs after all! Things can never be fixed for all eternity anyway!

# Chapter Nine

Once upon a time, people of Great Britain must have been quite simple, straight forward and disorganised. However, the country was occupied by the Romans for a very long period of time.

Maybe the British were trained and became matured by this experience of the Roman occupation. The cruelty and the undue injustices of the foreign rule might have scarred their mind, united their spirit and made them developed in a much faster rate.

Their political development achieved an astonishing maturity in the understanding of the world. They became an expert in using the world for their own gains and interests. Perhaps they had gained an exceptionally advanced training in how to control and have power over the land conquered by an outside authority.

So when the British came to rule India, they were not at all ignorant of the tact and tactics of controlling and ruling other people.

On the other hand the Indians had no such development or training at all before they were muted and overpowered by a series of foreign invasions. They were engulfed and very busy in putting their values and faiths on self enlightenment for spiritual satisfaction. They thought non-violence, peaceful co-existence, renouncing of worldly goods for the service of humanity and for the fulfilment of higher conscience, were the only goals to pursue in life. Any hint of useful political awareness was totally in non-existence in the country at the time.

The subjugation of the entire India by the mighty European desire of power over other people and lands might have proved to be almost a piece of cake. Besides, the whole India was already enslaved, demoralised and on the way of accepting degraded life by the over-run of Muslim invasion and cruelty. Almost all of India was quite subdued, fatalistic and in a state of humiliation, insult and inferior existence when the British appeared in the scene. Also, when I say India I do not mean the Muslim over strata in India at the time, I do only mean the indigenous natives of India with Indian values and culture.

Now the Indians have experienced the bitter hardship and humiliation of foreign rule for a very long period of time.

They still do not seem to have matured much in political sense. They are still disorganised, disunited and fragmented. But they seem to have totally forgotten their earlier culture and values. Now they are overwhelmed by the overpowering attraction of the Western culture and values. They feel that the only worthwhile thing to do in life is to follow this foreign lifestyle.

Many Indians are in earnest trying to copy Western values with quite a bit of thoroughness. Many are completely engulfed in corruption, selfishness and desire to benefit for personal gains at the expense of anybody or anything. Service to humanity and higher spiritual conscience are now quite meaningless ideas. Hardly anybody is interested in any such thing anymore.

Interestingly enough, the Western societies now organised themselves. What they did and still do with other people, they do not do the same with their own people. They learnt that life does not pay enough if the mass is kept under served and unprivileged in their own country. They found out that to survive well and fully they should work for their own people, and they do. They call it civilized society.

No such luck for the people of India yet. People there do not feel the urge of doing anything much for their fellow beings. They are still too busy to acquire material comfort for their own self only, and could not care less about anyone else in the community or in the country. But majority is too poor and unable to do anything even for themselves. It is only the few who are in power, they can misuse their power; and they do for their personal gains and goals

Maybe they are going through a phase. Perhaps they are in a state in which they can only value the feelings like an animal. Intoxication of power has gone in their head. The country as a whole is still far too undeveloped to put an effective end for the misuse of personal power.

So the only thing for the powerful people of India now is to do everything they could do for personal power and benefit, nothing else what so ever. This seems to be their aim and glory in life, even if the country goes to the dogs. But a poor, exploited country like India with high degree of illiteracy cannot really help without depending badly on their leaders, even though they may be the wrong ones.

Whether the leaders of India in time will overcome their selfish values and look for, something really noble in actual values; nobody really knows at this moment. I hope they will.

If India with her long forgotten ideas and values does once again break through, comes back to the collective conscience and produces any new original activities which could be called as something Indian and not a cheap copy of something else in this world, that should make everyone happy and proud. But at this stage of the sorry state of Indian society and people, no one could be sure if it could possibly happen one day or not.

However, collective mind and people's conscience cannot be destroyed for good. It might come back from obscure forgotten memory and who knows what.

Phoenix always arises from ashes. No one really knows how and why it happens. But it does happen, and that is the main thing. Maybe it is simply a natural progress. And this cannot be stopped. What human mind grasped once, can be kept hidden in obscurity; but it does not die out for good. It comes alive with new strength, vitality and purpose in life.

There is no dignity in slavery. Human spirit does not really get any true pleasure in imitating or mimicking other people.

Creating something new and original somehow satisfies the spirit of human ego and aspiration. The noble activities as recognised by the higher senses give a greater, deeper joy and satisfaction for human mind.

Maybe this is the true nature of human being. Cruelty, injustice and baseness towards fellow beings never give peace in the mind. In the end people are ashamed of all these baseness. It makes them in some direct and indirect way, most unhappy, dispirited, and depraved. It can only take them to the path of self-ruin and death of self respect. No one gets joy and happiness from all these negative attributes of mankind.

This is perhaps how the man is made. Anything wrong done to the others always comes back to haunt. There is no escape from it for anyone. This is probably the human destiny. There is no real freedom from one's own ill deeds.

Anyway, after all is said and done, I hope India once again attains her high mindedness, high moral and honesty, so that she can hold her head high in the world for everyone to look up to it.

Roman Empire trained the British for better things to come. The British Empire so far does not seem to have produced much good results for the Indians. But who knows, it may still come one day in the future. Maybe everybody has to go through a long period of chaos and confusion before any real development is possible. Even the English did not grow so powerful in a single day. They had their prolong period of dark days. They went through their civil war. They killed each other amongst themselves quite earnestly, just for the minor differences in their religion.

Even now the British people are quite busy in killing one another for the same old reason in one part of their country, Northern Ireland. Maybe they stopped their battles to some extent recently. They had their agony, depravation, dreadful internal strife before they were able to establish their power, colonies and high position in the world. Their poorer and working people had a very long period of suffering.

In spite of their vast colonies and mighty monopolies of enormous free hand in the resources of the world, their internal strife did go on and on. They continued to have their social evolution, clashes of power and deadly serious conflicts with other world powers.

They were responsible for huge and unprecedented loss of lives, hideous destruction and desolation in large scale in their own country and all over the world.

Maybe no nation is supposed to have peace, at least, not for too long. Perhaps all men are naturally programmed to get bored with peace; and start mischief, shameful activities and destruction just for a kind of excitement and change. Who knows, maybe one day man will kill himself for fun!

Anyway, before the western nations can be too proud of their prosperities and achievements, they should take a good look at themselves! They might notice a few things amongst themselves, and may not feel all that proud any longer.

Western nations are all rich and powerful. They control trades, industries and power in the world. They dominate rest of the world quite ruthlessly and safeguard their interests with total vigour.

In spite of all the power and affluence the dignity and grace of the Western nations do not seem to be increasing. They have everything they could possibly want and use in their life. But with all these wealth, glamour and power, they are still not really happier in their personal life or in their own community!

Too many moral degradations and quite a lot of social sickness are getting more apparent everyday. Besides, the meanness and the base motives of some of the actions of some Western powers are being exposed quite clearly. They are not so successful now in hiding the true nature of their activities from other people's eyes. Maybe this is a sign that they are becoming a less effective force in the world. Maybe they are no longer in command of their wish and action.

The Western powers are seen to make more and more empty noises and too many blunders. These in turn are bound to undermine their confidence and other people's faith in their infallibility, as well as in their solid and sound judgement. So they are in reality becoming more like everybody else.

The high and mighty attitude of the Western power may be full of hypocrisy. Maybe it has a kind of ill motives of their own selfish reason and interest. I just wonder!

In the television, in the news and in the media, one always hears about so much concern and such a lot of western aids for the poor nations. I just cannot help wondering that if it is truly so then, how come hardly any change is noticeable to us, the poor people of the world!

I just do not understand, what does it all, really mean! What do these aids actually do! Where exactly all these generous aids from all these kind western nations go! So many charitable bodies and organisations of the powerful countries are supposed to be trying so hard for the unfortunate poor nations. It is simply too strange that the poor are still there and may even be poorer. I wish some one could kindly explain something about it to me!

I am not sure if the whole world is still stupid enough not to realise that something is missing somewhere! The third world is mostly poor and not powerful. It does not have much muscle, and it does not really count much in the western eye.

After so many years of deprivation, injustice and exploitation, should the poor third world still be in sleep and not wake up to understand what is going on! I do hope that they do not. They should now be in a position to see through all the pretend concern of the west. They really should be able to call it a bluff and prepare themselves to stand on their own feet. No one is going to help them unless they help themselves. I understand very well that it is easier said than done!

Maybe the helping hand of the west should not to be trusted. The west never helps anybody if it does not help them profitably and profusely. Also anything that profits the powerful nations may not be profitable for the poor of the third world in real term.

The west has been getting away with their deception and cunning tactics for so long that they probably believe it as a kind of divine right for themselves. This is now regarded as almost part of nature or natural law in their eyes.

So far there was hardly anyone in the third world who could successfully challenge the west. Also the west did not wish to admit any wrong doing of their past. They always identified themselves with the rights and the righteous power of the world. With this image of superiority they were able to gain a lot of courage, support and impetuous force to promote their interest further.

However, things have changed to some extent; and they are going to face more and more embargoes against them. They will most probably have a lot more difficulty to keep hidden any selfish and greedy nature of their action from other people.

If it gets exposed once, things may all go against them. Their mask and image may be destroyed, and they may loose the universal trust for ever. Also if their activities are identified as wrong and unfair, they are going to be caught up in their own game. They may loose the will and courage to protect their self interest so ruthlessly. In fact they may become truly more humane.

Anyway, to be too greedy and selfish may be only natural for anyone and any nation. Perhaps it is not at all practical to blame anyone for it. However, we cannot forget that it does not help the poor people; it cheated, deceived and robbed the poor nations. The western nations and the United States of America are together in most things, as far as the rest of the world is concerned.

America is now the most powerful country of the world. People there are mostly very rich indeed. They are generally the envy of the whole world.

Unfortunately though they maybe too rich and powerful to feel genuinely for the poor people or the poor nations; maybe in their eyes it is quite natural not to count the unfortunate people of the world the same as their own. Maybe they just cannot help feeling different and distant.

In spite of all the pretences and make belief talks, Americans are usually quite bolshy, arrogant and insensitive in their dealings and understandings with other nations, particularly the third world. Individually one might be very kind, warm and philanthropic, but the political power of the country is quite a different matter. The country's rights and wrongs defy widely when it comes to deal with the poor or less powerful countries.

Although they are rich, wealthy and possessed a great deal, they still wish to have the upper hand in every aspect of the whole world; they are determined to dominate and use the people without enough muscle of their own. Sadly to seek help from America is a sure way to invite disaster without fail. In fact America cannot help anybody but themselves. Where ever they go to help, when ever they are supposed to take side, every thing gets wrong, ruined and troubled. Somehow the other side always ends up as the looser.

They went to help Vietnam and it ended up inflamed; great destruction and dreadful loss of lives and everything followed all the way to the end.

They were supposed to be in friendship with Iran at the time of Shah and Iran has ended up facing great tragedy and dreadful time of restless upheaval.

They had terrible rivalry with the Russians. They and the entire Western power together were absolutely determined to stop Russian influence any-where. So they offered their kind hand to stop Russian power in Afghanistan. And that country is now totally destroyed and severely ruined. No one now cares that much, if it will ever come out of the nightmare and live again in peace.

Thank God that they were not too keen on India. From the start they did not quite like or trust her for some reason. But they were very fond of Pakistan. From the beginning lots of help in the form of military aids and other form of aids flowed in Pakistan. All these aids seem quite sinister to me. Why these helps and what are they supposed to do! Pakistan remained mostly undemocratic, the society is mainly feudalistic and the poorer section of the community is kept primitive, ignorant, uneducated and desperately poor. The leading people are thriving; the power, wealth and privilege are in their hands. Many of these top rich families now live mainly in the West and America. A section of the common people is always engaged in killing and fighting against another section. Another section of public is vigorously busy in constant conspiratorial trouble making against India. One just cannot help wondering about what the Western aids are really for!

Similar curious situation also seems apparent in Bangladesh. Two cut-out bits of India, one in the Northwest and one in the East, seem to draw a lot of interest and attention from almost all the countries of the Western power. Their aids do nothing for the common people, the country seems as backward as ever, and the same injustice, desperate poverty and insecurities ravishing the ordinary public without any check as before, if not more than before. In my opinion, one must therefore be forgiven for being suspicious about all these aids.

The Western morality might except the principle of divide and rule as acceptable; the West might feel superior just because they are rich and well connected. But all lives are sacred and injustice is always unjust. Also in the end no one can come out unscathed from the consequence of ill act anywhere on anybody.

As far as I am concerned the division of India in the bits, is a sore point. It bleeds a raw wound in the depth of my heart.

I am in fact at the receiving end of the deadly consequence of the act. I lost my birth place. The land and the home I should have grown to love, is no longer mine. It is now called Bangladesh and no part of me anymore.

But it was taken from me and from the people to whom I belong racially, culturally and traditionally. I consider the whole deed unfair, unjust, immoral and criminally wrong.

How come it was decided to be the right thing that I should be thrown out of my home land, just because there were a few more people of Islamic faith living there than my people. I simply fail to see any logic or decent human conscience in this. I am told that the British found out that Muslim population was 51% and non Muslim population 49%. That gave them the power to divide East Bengal in two parts: Mostly East Pakistan, belonging to Pakistan, and the rest to West Bengal, belonging to India. However, the Muslim population there are mostly from the original people of India though. Just because of different faith does not give anyone the right to divide the country. In any case the people there could not live with the Pakistan even though they share the same faith. Also how could anyone trust the infallibility of statistics in 51% and 49% in a country of too much mess, ignorance and corruption!

I rather feel that there must have been a great deal of conspiratory mean hands and secret unholy activities behind the affairs.

I will never understand how the world's most powerful at the time and supposed civilised nation could agree to legalise such inhuman deed. No matter what if they were truly well wishers of India as a whole, they could not possibly have done this.

How a small selfish and reactionary minority group could actually persuade them to enforce such a murderous idea; if they themselves did not have a kind of their own sinister consent in the matter.

Maybe it helped them to take some sort of revenge against India as they were no longer able to keep India for their own gains and interests. I do not know the answer; and I suppose no one is likely to tell me the real reason either. But I am sure one day in the distant future the story will come out in the open.

Somehow it was agreed as a sound proposal to carve out two pieces of India, one in the north and one in the far away end in the east, to be separated for the Muslims only, without any due care and consideration for the other people there. These other people there, were in reality sentenced to absolute death, desolation and destitution with no fault of their own and just because they happened not to have the same faith as the Muslims.

But millions of Muslims live all over in India. No serious consideration or thought was given for their protection either. My problem is that I do not understand why or how those minorities who happened to be the majorities at the two far away ends of India, could become so special that they must have their own special home land, a separate country, from where they would in no delay, almost immediately, chuck out all the people they thought different from themselves in terms of faith.

How did they possibly earn such special favour in the heart of the colonial power in India; it is truly a very grave mystery to me! Why were these Muslims so important and powerful that they could have anything they wanted even at the severe detriment of all others! India is now the second highest Muslim population in the world. Why the Muslims in India are less important than those Muslims in the separate lands! And why no precautions, or any security of population exchange was there at the time of hostile division of India! Millions of innocent people were perished in terrible inhumane communal riots and struggles. No body cared a tiny bits bother at this loss!

For some strange reason the colonial rule on the verge of leaving India, seemed all out bent to make the militant Muslim leaders happy and satisfied with everything they wanted. Apart from the British archives kept in secret, perhaps God only knows the reason why they had to do so.

Maybe the British knew and understood the rich and wealthy Muslims in the northern India well. Many of them might have been the descendants of the Muslim rulers of India when the British first came to India. So the British really took over power from the hands of their forefathers. They must have always had a kind of connection and knowledge of these people as they still possessed a considerable wealth and power in the region. Also these were the people the British always kept the first hand contact and through these people they usually conducted the rule and administration of the land area.

The British probably never knew much of the indigenous people of the land. They did not really need to. The majority population was always in the background, subdued, suppressed and almost invisible, as far as the British were concerned, at least at the beginning of their power in India. So it is quite possible that they were naturally indifferent to these people.

But it must have been very different for the rich minority Muslims. The British knew them well; and maybe they felt that they aught to do them some favour, or give them a farewell gift, before they depart from India. After all these are the people from whose hands they snatched the power of India. Maybe they felt sorry for the Muslims, and did not want to leave them at the mercy of the Indians as a whole. Maybe the British felt more strongly about them, as they were once the ruler of India.

Another factor was that these rich descendants of the past rulers of India, perhaps never felt really Indian themselves. They did not quite belong to India in spirit. Culturally they perhaps followed different notions and ideas; and more than that they still loved to rule and have some power in their hand if possible.

So obviously they initiated lots of internal strife. They also succeeded in creating hostile and divisive atmosphere to convince the sympathetic ruling authority to their cause and interest.

They knew very well that the whole of India was no use to them. It would not serve their purpose at all. So they cleverly wanted the next best thing for themselves. They demanded two portions in their care, and called it to be named as Pakistan. And in a kind of indirect way it might have served the interest of the foreign power of the world as well.

My own profound curiosity in the matter is that why no one was able to expose it. Why the actual truth was never out. How did they justify themselves as so special and important without any due regard for the whole of the Muslim community in India at the time. Without settling the question of the Muslims in India as a whole separate people if they were and if there was anything to settle at all, why should only a portion of the Muslim community, should have a separate land for them!

If many millions of the Muslims had to live in India without any choice, why then those leaders and their followers could not or were not able to do the same! The reason, the purpose and the formation of Pakistan, all seem unforgiving and sinister work of deceitful politics indeed to me.

People in power in the Muslim world of India at the time, had their wish come true. But millions from both communities lost their lives; huge amount of blood was spilt. Too much suffering was endured by people.

Most probably the history is not going to stop there. The selfish and short sighted leaders might have thought that they won. But they might have in fact done a great disservice to themselves and their people. Who knows what can happen in the future! The facts already pointing in the wrong direction!

The collective memory never dies; too much hurt and too much injustice always come back to haunt! There are too many examples of this fact in the world. The leaders with selfish interest and short sighted outlook never help anybody. They only nurture nightmare, disaster and devastation for future.

Another question of mine is that, what does this religion prove really in the real world? Within a few years one part of Pakistan was at the throat of the other part. After inflicting an incredible amount of killing, cruelty and beastliness on the subdued part of this kingdom, Pakistan the pure land of Islam was divided again; Bangladesh was born as a separate country. Having the same religion of Islam was no use for living together in peace.

In both of these countries the wealthy people still own and rule the poor. The poverty, ignorance, corruption and internal strife are all very much alive and thriving in both of them. But they continue to believe that they could not live as part of India on any account. Do they really know why not? I wish they could tell me what difference would it have made if they did live in united India! India is after all a secular country. Quite recently the president of India was a Muslim; and at present the prime minister of India is a well known Sikh person. Religion should not make any difference in that country. Also India is supposed to be a fully democratic republic; still the West does not appear to be a great friend of India in real terms.

Most interesting of all these are that Pakistan from the start and Bangladesh afterwards became quite favourite places for the Western countries. Too much international concerns and lot of devotion are given to these two small off-shoots of India.

In spite of all the fond attentions from the Western nations, desperately poor people of these countries are still in desperate poverty. Hardly any change in their social or political circumstances is noticeable. In fact things in almost every respect, is much worse than ever.

The rich people of these countries are quite a bit westernised and a big percentage of them live in the West. The poor section of the society, on the other hand are severely forced to live by the Koran and the Islamic rule, whatever that may mean. Also they are mainly governed by the military rule. On the whole the poor are still living in feudalistic state and very much tribal in outlook and practice.

One naturally wonders what the aids and charity workers are really doing there. The foreign concern seems quite unconcerned about it. But they are very much concerned that India still has not given away the state of Kashmir to Pakistan.

They are absolutely oblivious of the fact that Pakistan has from the start occupied the major part of Kashmir in the north by force. No one talks about it, or perhaps no one knows about it at all.

No one has ever wished to know how those Kashmiri people doing in the occupied Pakistani part! Are they still alive, are they happy or have they been wiped off altogether! No one cared to find out anything about them. Should not it be right to know if they are glad to be in Pakistan!

International watchdogs for peace are not bothered about the part of Kashmir invaded and occupied by Pakistan. They never uttered a single word about it or the welfare of the people there. But their sense of fair play seems outraged as India continues to resist Pakistan having the rest of Kashmir under its fold.

One may ask why? Perhaps it is because the majority of Kashmir is supposed to be of Muslim religion. Once again is the same old game of religion.

Islam seems to excuse Pakistan doing anything against India. Why does not Pakistan go in and occupy the Islamic parts of China or of Russia? Would those parts wish to live under Pakistan?

But Pakistan cannot keep peace amongst its own people even though they are all of the same religion. Internal conflicts and violence between different sectors are continuously raging through the country.

It seems very peculiar and awfully strange that the Western opinion finds it all quite acceptable. Maybe there is a very good reason for it. It just serves their interest. Pakistan probably a very useful ally and also a profitable base for them! Furthermore, it is most probably needed to keep an eye over India and Russia for the world power. Maybe Pakistan has always been used as an effective thorn and a poison chalice for India. Pakistan might have been originally created for this purpose specially. We do not really know the actual truth.

Because of the division of India and all the retaliatory struggles involved in it, the Muslims lost their lives and homes as well. But it was mainly their own doing; their leaders were greatly responsible for it. In any case the loss on the other side is almost incomprehensible.

If the Muslim leaders and their followers did not want India to be divided; and if they were all ready to live in peace with the rest of the Indians in India, none of the upheavals and massacres would have happened.

The Indians had nothing to gain by division. They did not want it to be divided. They were never against sharing the land with the Muslims and the people of other religions. In reality India is doing so today as always.

Somehow, or for some reason, the Muslims got it in their head that they did not want to live with the Indians. They must have a separate land for themselves. The huge number of Muslims all over India did not seem to be counted; only the special ones in special parts are to be taken care off.

They caused and created lots of communal riots, an awful lot of disturbances, in order to prove that it was not safe or possible for them to live in peace in India.

But if you give rise to trouble, you have to live and suffer trouble too. Whoever thought it was profitable to fight for a separate land for the Muslims, might have been politically played on and encouraged by some other hands. There must have been too many interesting parties to profit from it. Indian's worst misfortune is that the people are poor, simple ignorant and it is really very easy to exploit them. Religion is nothing but the ultimate weapon to destroy them.

India used to be the land of peace and peaceful contemplation. Who has driven her to such fanaticism and self-destruction! Who has taught her so much corruption and cruelty! One just cannot but wonder about why and how such misfortune really did fall on India!

For centuries India was made bone dry with poverty, lack of education and no progress or prosperity. The British never bothered about any land reform, social reform, or anything which could help the Indians in their daily life. It was no interest to them. In fact to keep India as backward as possible was very useful for the imperialism. It helped them to use and exploit the people as much as they wished. And why ever should they not! That really was the purpose and aim of colonialism! It was simply India's bad luck that she had fallen in the trap!

Imperialism by nature is supposed to have a country for the use and glory of the Imperialist power. It is not for the salvation of the colony. If at any stage the power is unable to have and use the land then, no one else should be able to have it either. It would be left unfit for everyone all together.

This happened to be the legacy of colonial imperialism. The whole world bears the example.

If ever the world will be able to overcome it and come out of it at all, no one yet knows the answer.

Pakistan is poor. Bangladesh is poor. India is poor. All of these countries are poverty stricken, corrupt and full of misfortune. In all of these countries the well-off people could not care less for their worse-off compatriots. So the poor people of Bangladesh and Pakistan might have been just as badly off in India if they lived there.

But there are some subtle differences. India is no paradise by any means. Nevertheless different voices can be heard there, and it may be difficult to handle India exactly in one's own way for long. India has a lot of potential, and is trying hard to come out on the surface. She is suffering from too many problems and disadvantages.

Fanaticism is oppressing India for a long time. It is pushing her too far. Perhaps it will in the end produce similar extremist views in the Indian mind. Maybe the Indian psyche is forced to alter for the worse. That is indeed a great pity.

No one will benefit from it. Maybe the fanatics will learn their lesson; and so one good thing might come out of it!

India's social reform was long overdue. Lots of her social problems and social injustices were rooted deeply in the past. With proper reforms and determined efforts everything could have been sorted out. It could have been so much better.

In spite of all the drawbacks, misgivings and misdeeds in the past, the leaders of the moth-eaten independent India tried very hard to appease and reassuring all the people, particularly the minorities. India became secular in constitution.

The Muslim minorities are given special privileges and dispensations under Indian legal system. But none of this is enough. The age-old distrust and deep hatred for each other is still strong and alive. The separation from their fellow Muslims in Pakistan makes the Muslims in India very awkward. They cannot help feeling close and pro Pakistan.

In return they become very vulnerable. It is easy for Pakistan to use them for subversive activities in India. It makes even more, harder for India to have peace in the land.

Because of Pakistan some odd ones from the minority communities may occasionally work as traitors in India. That puts the whole of those sections in black spots, and jeopardizes the safety and the security of the entire country. It simply opens up the dark and dangerous life for everyone in India.

Pakistan might think that this continuous hostility would force India to give up her claim in Kashmir. But it is a misconception. India's total honour and integrity are bogged down in the claim. If she is pushed too far, it could easily bring down total calamity on both the countries.

The basic hostility between them will never go away. It is perhaps a kind of fight until death would do them apart or something even worse. Besides there are still too many outsiders, who have a lot of vested interest in encouraging Pakistan tirelessly to keep at it!

At one time it was perhaps not very difficult for the shrewd British to notice the differences between the Indian people with different faith. It took them no time to stoke and ignite diligently the smouldering fire of hostility between these people. After all they had a lot of experience in the matter. They always used it as a great device to divide and rule everywhere. It worked for them every time.

During the later part of the British rule in India this hostility took up the life of its own and became completely out of control for everybody. It has already succeeded in great devastation and destruction of enormous degree. But it is still no where near any end. The division of India has not stopped. Maybe it requires a far more, greater tragedy yet! The interested international bodies seem quite enthusiastic to keep the fight going, even though they pretend otherwise.

For a while there were two world superpowers, Russia and America. After independence India declared to be non-aligned, not part of any of the two power blocs. But Pakistan and later Bangladesh both went in the Western bloc.

India was immediately put in the black book by the West. America and the British never trusted her, and were not ever very fond of her either.

On the other hand, Pakistan and Bangladesh both became very handy and useful for the Western superpower. Both of these two countries draw quite a bit of attention from the West. There are many aids and charities given to them in one form or other. Although what they exactly do or do not do, that might be a different story altogether.

There used to be hard competition between the two superpowers. But Russia now lost her power and international influence quite a bit. That made America and the West all in all. UNO, UNESCO, IMF and all now mainly serve the interest of the United States of America in real term. There is no one to check it in any way whatsoever.

America became all in all as a superpower in the world. The more she becomes powerful, the stronger she desires to keep it that way at any expense. The West always has double standard, one for themselves and another for the people they use and manipulate for their own benefit. Their business interest and the ways to keep their profit high, know no bounds.

The United Nations and other aid agencies perhaps work for the same purpose. Innumerable spies, extensive spy networks probably cover the whole world and work for the CIA as well as other Western bodies, all in the same power bloc. So many charity organisations, voluntary services overseas agencies and many more well meaning bodies, all working so hard for the welfare of the poor old third world, may well be just the perfect cover for the same thing; who can be absolutely sure! Pakistan, Bangladesh, all along the border-states, and areas, of India must be, especially significant for their work!

Anyway, it may or may not be true. But I just cannot help expressing my opinion. As most people are unsure of what exactly is going on! One does not see any noticeable improvement of welfare amongst the common people of all these countries, where so many agencies are supposed to be helping the poor so hard. At the same time, those countries which are closed to foreign aids or other activities show some kind of change and positive improvement in progress. One does not know what to think!

America is a very powerful country and wants to stay that way. But nothing in this world remains the same for ever!

Every nation needs the wisdom and moral courage of its leaders. Through the wise, intelligent and farsighted leadership a country can progress and protect itself from decline and deterioration. The lack of rightful, righteous and careful leaders, always bring downfall, disharmony and degradation on it!

All over the world people seem to become too greedy in almost every respect. They want to have and keep everything for themselves. Material is all they desire. Materialism is really their ultimate religion. But they want God and religion on their side too, in case any such thing exists. They would definitely like the heaven and all heavenly powers to look after them and fulfil all their desires in this life if possible.

The well-off people with comfortable life do not ever wish to die! They would like to use the whole world of medicine to make their life long lasting. They really do not want to miss anything. With a view that there may be some benefit to have, they would not hesitate practising anything known to them as the Eastern virtues or something. They would practise yoga, meditation, vegetarianism, special nutritional diet and lot more, hoping it might make them immortal!

They would not like to work too hard. They do not want to go too deep. They do not wish to sacrifice anything. But they would love to have everything for themselves.

The rich, self-satisfying Western public seem to produce quite a lot of arrogant and dogmatic leaders amongst them. They might feel very superior, and maybe they think that some of their right-winged views are justified.

In the absence of a second super power for any possible check, the world could easily come close to a disaster. The West does not have much sincere feeling or understanding for the poor nations. The poor people are mostly regarded as inferior by the rich. There is no one really to supervise any wrong doing or rigid manipulation.

This could in time bring about some kind of unbalanced power setup which might badly upset the world peace!

People are naturally proud of themselves. Everybody thinks, they are superior to others. Maybe they are in some respect. But nobody is perfect in this world. Each and everyone have a lot to learn for the better.

The English are supposed to be the most superior race. However, as an Indian I am very proud of my heritage too.

As a matter of fact one does come across a few things about the British. From the history and the stories of the British India certain truth comes to light. It was generally understood that the British enjoyed the freedom to plunder India. In the earlier days they took freely anything they liked and they could lay their hands on. They took all that caught their eyes and with both hands.

They used the Indians whenever they needed them. They used those particular Indians who became dependent on them and also those who somehow developed a kind of fondness for them. They knew exactly how to turn them as collaborators. Also there were some Indians who felt friendly and attached to the particular British person for some reason or other. They often had a lot of good luck to get substantial help from such people.

But the British themselves never really felt any true love or compassion even for those Indians who gave their lives for them. They always managed to preserve their detachment from all Indians in general. They remained very true and absolutely stuck to their own kind.

Maybe there were exceptions. But the British did not acknowledge them. They did not wish the posterity to know about them. So we do not know.

This attitude may explain certain aspect of their general psychological make up. Over glorification of one's own history is a natural human tendency. Every nation wishes to remember their heroes and the glories, but not their cowards, cowardice or any mean treachery. Besides, no one wishes to acknowledge that lot of their success is in fact based on a lot of their mean and very rotten act. Obviously it is not very flattering for any one to admit that a lot of deception, unjust, unlawful and wrong doing on their part was really the building block of their empire.

The Western Countries still wish to push forward their policy of aggressive nature, and self-gratifying principle in the international field. The Western elders and leaders think they can bluff their way off as they did before. But their own siblings and the younger generation do not have the same convictions. They have some change of heart, and they have a bit of clear understanding of the world affairs. Also they have enough intelligence to catch up with the old tactics and politics of their fathers' generation. Some of the newer generations do not like it.

In spite of the corporate following of aggressive policies and high profitability popular choice is changing to some extent. Institutional choice of violence against others is not so popular any more. Some individual conscience and some peace loving people are trying to bring about a world of change for peaceful coexistence.

People are beginning to realise that selfishness destroys one's own innermost soul. Brutality breeds brutality. It is becoming understood that the industrial nations will help the poor nations, only when helping seems to be the most profitable option left to them. They are beginning to wake up to the fact that just helping themselves and owning more and more for themselves may not necessarily the good policy for them.

The amount of evil, it produces in one's own life, is very detrimental. Left to the temptation itself, they probably destroy the entire existence of the quality of their own life. This realisation and this realisation alone would make them think hard and think differently.

They are about to appreciate the fact that the desire to help the others is a noble feeling, and it brings richness in their life beyond values which cannot be bought with money. This brings real happiness and true well being. It opens up other ways to improve quality of life altogether.

Genuine goodness is far more valuable in a man than any of his bravery.

All men are brave when desperate. Some do not need to prove it, because they are fortunate enough not to have any desperate situation in their life. Some, on the other hand, are desperately unfortunate to have to prove them very brave for the whole world to admire. They would perhaps rather live an ordinary human life they were born to. Peace and happiness is almost all, most people long for. Lack of these vital necessities would always drive anyone to become brave.

I never met a good man. If I have, I have not recognised him to be so. Anyway, I always wanted to meet one in my life. It might have changed me a good person too.

I ask myself why I have never really lived and why don't I have any quest in my life!

I always seem to have been a miserable silly fool, never ever made the most of my life! Maybe that is a peculiarity I possess and cannot help it. I was always a bit different from my sisters. We used to get pleasure from different things.

My sisters used to help my father with the practical things he needed. For example, if he needed a button to be sewn on, they would just do that happily. I was no good at anything like that. I would rather provide him with the news of the wide world outside our home and neighbourhood; and I would derive quite a lot of pleasure in doing so.

I always make too many mistakes. We all make mistakes, some more than the others. Some of us pay for our mistakes with our lives. Some perhaps can get away with their mistakes, without too much repercussion.

Nothing goes right for me. I always seem to have problem. Everything is a problem for me. Even the most simple thing in the world would turn out to be a problem in my case. If there is no problem I would probably invent one!

I lived mostly a lonely life. Maybe I will die a lonely death too. It makes me feel sad and full of sorrow most of the time; but I do not know why I do feel so. I never had a better choice. I always wished I could choose something better, but I was not lucky enough to have any. So there was never anything else for me to do. Still I feel a sort of grief for the things which never happened to me. Isn't it strange!

Maybe most people live a lonely life in their soul. And most people are sorry for their loneliness. Maybe this is in human nature. Very few people can really escape this fate; but all wish that they could. This is life and perhaps, this is how life is lived in general in the natural world.

I always felt somewhat vulnerable and hopeless. I was useless to draw attention to myself. I thought I was invisible to other people. I never knew how to secure one's own security and gain personal fulfilment or happiness.

I do not know how other people manage it. Everybody except I, seems to possess some kind of special power. Nothing ever gets in their way.

Maybe I was too proud and this got in my way. But how come, the same self pride works for others. Isn't it supposed to be good for you! Or, is it because the others have some sort of special magical power and I don't!

Everybody seems to attract other people by their action. Maybe no matter what they do, or do not do, people simply get attracted by them. Their proud appearance is no handicap. Perhaps they are extraordinarily charming!

Maybe people never liked me seriously because I am not charming enough. Perhaps people find me arrogant. Perhaps my proud and detached attitude, detract them from me. I do not know. I do not mean to be arrogant. I do not wish to repel people from my side. I need friends just as much as everyone else.

But, maybe that is how I appear to other people. They do not really get to know me any other way. So they can't help not liking me enough and keeping themselves away from me.

I wonder if there is something wrong with me. I wish I knew what exactly it is. I would have liked it. However I never found it out and never had the chance to remedy my fault. I am not a lucky person.

Maybe, being Indian might have something to do with my peculiarity. I might have developed it as a kind of some safeguard against a host of things I wanted to resist.

For a long time women in India became just a kind of simple breeding machine. The strange thing is that the women themselves want now to remain so to some extent. The people of India want them to remain so as well.

The women seem to live in the past, and they like to bring up their children according to the rules and ideas of the past. Hardly any Indian would marry a woman because she is beautiful, clever, educated or skilled to do a clever job. They usually marry a woman according to the amount of money or wealth her father has in his possession.

The idea is, perhaps quite silly and childish no doubt, as very few Indians do really possess much in real terms. Maybe it is just a tradition left over from the past that women should be weighed up according to the weight of her father's pocket.

There is hardly any way she can increase her worth in other people's eye. She is valued if her family is valued and especially if her father is a valuable man.

Generally speaking, women's beauty, skill, education and intelligence are regarded as just a few added bonuses, but are not of much value by themselves.

The value of a woman is not in what she does but more in what she does not do.  Usually people do not like women to do any job to earn money.  In majority cases they like their women educated only as a kind of status symbol, but not for any use in real life situation.

In a country of half-starved people, it seems quite a mystery that ordinary people should still hang on to this out of date middle class concept.  It is truly incredible how they could possibly put so much value on a few miserable Rupees in a dirty-old torn pocket of a father, and not to a well-educated or skilled woman.  She could well earn plenty of Rupees to support her family and be a growing vital force as well as a loving companion to her husband.

It is quite extraordinary that the men live a life of hardship and misery, but still do not like their women to go out to work.  It seems they regard it as a blow to their ego and manliness.  To let or train their women earn a living, is in their mind to admit a lack of virility.  And virility in India is of course, highly valued.  They love their women as breeding machine.  Maybe the tradition generated because of some trouble in security for women out of door in the country.  After all India was occupied for about twelve hundred years by people coming from outside.  Who knows life might have been too dangerous to go out at any time!

Now amongst some educated young people things are changing but still somewhat slowly and sporadically.  Hopefully things will one day change for the better.  I am sure nothing teaches you faster than hardship and injustices!

When I was a child I used to think I will do a lot of good for people.  I thought I will be able to help the unprivileged people of the world, once I am grown up.  It was an idea very dear to my heart.  It was the purpose of my life.

I did grow up; but I did nothing for anybody so far.  In fact I grew up as useless as one can be for everybody including myself.

I feel I have done nothing in this world; and I am a total failure in true sense of the world.  This sense of failure to do my duty is my grief to bear.  I still wish I have done something for the people, I would like to care.

Sadly enough, I do not even have a child of my own through whom I might have been able to try a little to fulfil my wishful thinking.

I am just left with all my unaccomplished wishes.  Everything in my life seems to be left in the dream land.  I have not been able to live a fuller life.  My life is absolutely empty, unfulfilled, and all in void; that is all there is to it!

One can live any life.  But one cannot live an unfulfilled life; can one!  It is really and honestly unliveable!

At long last, perhaps I understand life a little.  I know now what is the matter with me, I knew something was wrong; but could not quite see it clearly.  Now everything is clear to me.

Maybe I am simply the victim of boredom.  I am sure I am going to be killed by my boring life. I always desired lots of excitement in my life. Instead I have only got absolutely dull, plain and boring living all round me and all throughout my life.

I have hoped and hoped that someday something is bound to happen; and that will make a change and bring some excitement in my life. However, that has never happened. The more days go by, the more cornered I have become by my boredom, the more desperately I wished for a miracle.

I really needed a miracle to save me from my lonely life. It must have been against all natural laws to exist such a miracle, because no such miracle saved me yet. Also at last I came to my senses too. I see now, there is nothing worthwhile in my life, and there will never be any such thing in my life either.

To live a life like this is simply a hopeless waste of time. Even though it seems to go on, I do not really know why or what for! I have no idea how I am to bear this headache without a head!

In spite of all my disappointment, disillusion and boredom I still wish I could use my life for other people.

About thirty years or so ago, one day I was quite fed up and wrote a few lines in a kind of some annoyance:

People always ask me what is my plan and I wonder what kind of Plan! Well, the plan of my future? Actually I doubt very much if I have any future! Still, I suppose one can always have a plan for the future. Future or no future, I guess there is no harm in making or talking about a plan for one.

People only ask as a matter of course, just to make a conversation. I know that, but it is a sore point in my heart. So to counter act it I have decided to have more than one plan for my future. To be precise, it is in fact one thousand and one! Now which one in particular people would wish me to tell them! Or have they got any special preference to any special kind of plan for my future! I simply wonder in despair!

Another question I am asked far too often is, what do I, do in the weekend; I know very well it is a harmless question and is really meant to be quite well-meaning. But it does not help me and it does not make me happy at all. And I do not know why, but I do feel like answering them back something severely outrageous.

How about saying that I meditate all weekend! Or I just sit still, shut my eyes and use a rosary! I practise yoga! No, I think I should say something much worse; like I pray that the whole world should go to hell and the entire mankind ought to fall in the fire of eternal damnation!

But to my utter dissatisfaction I do not manage to say any of these. Instead I simply say nothing. Perhaps this is the best way to irritate people who irritate me. Anyway what can I say? I do not know the answer. And I ponder badly if I ever will!

All I wish is that I could use my life for other people. But people do not seem to need me. Perhaps it would give me some satisfaction and purpose in my life.

My life seems such an empty and purposeless life. I often wonder why I was born in this world. I have done absolutely nothing with my life. It feels so sad and wasteful. Should a life be like this! Wouldn't it be much better if I could offer myself for my fellow human!

Maybe it has turned up like this for me, because I am a negative sort of person. I can cry, talk and feel for this lack of fulfilment in my life; but I can never do anything positive, and actually offer myself for anyone.

I am sure, only the positive people are capable of doing things for others. They are warm, kind and a sort of selfless, so able to use their own life for the joy of others. Only the negative people keep themselves to themselves and live a rotten miserable life.

To give is positive and you get joy in return. But to keep things to yourself is negative, and you get nothing for it; and the thing you are keeping, is soon to become a burden to your soul. A useless life with all its treasures around it is really like a pain in the neck.

Maybe life is to live it through without feeling too much sorry for oneself. And this cannot be done without giving yourself up for somebody or something. This way one can at least occupy one's mind and time. One can feel that the life does have a meaning of a kind, and maybe it was worth coming to be born in this world. Time, perhaps would pass busy and easy, and surely not as a drag.

Maybe my life has something to do with me being an Indian. Perhaps Indians teach their people to stop living long before it is absolutely necessary. The Western philosophy on the other hand trains their people to try to live until the very possible end.

# Chapter Ten

Long time ago, soon after I came to England I wrote a few lines about religion. I do not remember why. Maybe I was annoyed for some reason. So in 1964 I tried to express my feelings:

No, I do not believe in religion and definitely not in any organised one. I am quite anti religion. I think it is stupid, harmful and horribly silly attitude of mankind towards the humble truth that no one can know everything; and no ultimate truth has ever been revealed to any silly man anywhere!

I don't want the protection of any kind of set idea in the field of very sensitive want of my mind. It is after all my very personal mind. My belief is my ability, my capacity and my quality of understanding of my reason for physics and beyond. If I failed I don't want any other reason except that I am not able.

But I will never forget that even if I am not able, even then I have the right to try and it is only me who can understand for me and nobody else. If I want the truth of life, I shouldn't want it for the sake of anything except the truth itself.

Also I believe, if there is any God, He must be clever enough to understand that all people everywhere mean to worship Him, Him alone and nobody else. Although people of different background use different way of worship, does it matter at all at that! God must know what they actually mean and why. After all God is supposed to have created all men, and not any man is to have invented God! So why shouldn't He understand what is going on in the mind of His poor man!

After so many million years of creating mankind on this earth God shouldn't have any excuse for not understanding His man! He must have enough time and enough interest in these millions of poor but potentially individual souls on earth wishing to express their prayer in their potentially individual ways.

I simply guess God is quite fond of differences. Otherwise He would not have created different things. So He must be happy about different people calling Him by different names in different ways, and in different rituals; if He is bothered at all about how and whether people call Him or not!

At least I should like to feel that God enjoys individuality in every possible respect; and I should think there lies His greatness. I cannot even imagine God is mean enough not to allow the fullest aspects of individual status for His creation. Why does He then create individuals with the full potential of being individuals! If different minds with different ways are not His wish then, He must be a terribly crooked Thing; and I do not think He should bother to be so. In any case if individuality is wrong then, God Himself is wrong but not His creation.

Besides I must have enough respect for myself. I must recognise my own ability, the potentiality of myself to become as great as I like. I myself must try to be an example. I must look at me, at the very personal mind of myself. I am supposed to be a part of God. If there is any God, I am surely included in Him and so are all other beings and things, even all the bits of important and unimportant corners of this world as well. He is all the seen and the unseen universe, everything is in Him, nothing left out and nothing forgotten anywhere whatsoever!

I cannot make my soul as sinful; there is no special sin in myself! I am neither sinful nor virtuous. I am everything, good and bad, sin and virtue. I am a sort of creator too. I create my mind and that create my sin and virtue! Mind changes and so changes everything.

So I must know me, the mind linked inside and outside of myself, which really includes everything and that is my God! If I love myself, I love everybody and then, I love God too. If I hate, I hate God as well. Love and hate all are in me!

If I wanted to know Him, it is not for any safety or security, not for any interest, not even for any reason at all; but it is because I want to!

But I don't understand religion. I want to leave it alone. It is not my kind of scene at all. I do not know much about it. Long time ago I do not know why I wrote a few lines about religion though:

Religion is in reality a military term originally invented by the Jews in the Middle East. It is perhaps developed out of the perpetual instinct which desperately wish, to dominate the ideological world of other people.

In Roman hands and subsequently it became a great political weapon. As a matter of fact it is nothing but a very shrewd technique to conquer the ins and outs of other minds, which is naturally a strong desire felt by all conceited minds in all times. It is probably a very good controlling power!

In old times material world, perhaps wasn't a matter of great interest; because maybe it wasn't too difficult to achieve success in that respect. In those days, conquering a land or a country, didn't effect a great deal in reality, the life on the ground. Maybe it wasn't therefore too much satisfying either. And hence there was so much concentration over how to conquer the minds of the people.

The invention of religion was perhaps primarily to bring under control a huge collection of mass-mind. It was not very easy to do this job, as human mind is naturally very personal; and a personal mind is usually not very open to other people unless it is highly tempted or convinced to gain something somehow in exchange.

Obviously it needed hard work. It seemed impossible at first; but it attracted many, aroused great emotion and gave a feeling of immense satisfaction in the subconscious mind.

Some people in greatly privileged position could sometime be quite confident and conceited in many respects. In some circumstances they could quite happily love to impose themselves and their own notions on other people, especially on the less privileged or dependent ones.

To do this successfully one ought to feel a great inner urge and a strong compulsion in their head for their dutiful work. Without this the inner conflicts and other complications would stop it to be fulfilled. In a very special way the material gains in immaterial context always seem to have a great appeal for the powerful nations.

From the Jews it was taken first by the Romans, the then power, and it was used to keep control over their empire. The more people come in touch with the idea, the more they try to spread it. So it spreads naturally in one way or other, for conscious or subconscious political purposes.

Later, after the fall of the Jews by the Romans, the Middle Eastern minds under the leadership of Mohammed the prophet or the God's messenger, wanted to recover their freedom, and once again recognised the full scale military use of religion. Since then the conflicts between religions and its far-reaching consequent implications are all very well known facts of the world. It has worked and perceived as an intoxicating power in the mind.

I do not believe in religion. Personally I think it is nothing but some kind of ploy to dominate the world. I believe in the spirit of the world; and if there is any truth or anything in any religion, it should then be the part of human knowledge which should belong to everybody.

When I came to live in Bristol, one day I went to visit a nearby church. Afterwards I wrote about it:

On my way to the post office or, to shopping I pass by a Bartholomew church. It is a small old church at one corner of the Saint Andrews Park. I am living quite near it at the moment. I see people coming out of the church on Sunday morning after service.

I wondered once or twice about what it is like inside! Yesterday I went to see the flower arrangement in the church; and today is 18 May 1969. I went inside with my land-lady and her daughter.

I wrote, so I was inside the church after all! I was not really that impressed or, anything of that sort! It was quite ordinary and of the usual kind. I was just following the people looking at one thing or other. Also there weren't too many people, but there were some; mostly older people.

Being a foreigner living in a foreign land, I know I am always being observed. I am young and always wearing Indian Sari. No matter where, or how, I am certain that some eyes are somehow observing me with some curiosity.

However, soon after I went inside the church, I suddenly became relaxed and much less aware of people for a moment. I was quite absorbed and carefully examining the bottom part of my Sari if it was too long; because I did not want to topple over again. I had broken my ankle only quite recently and certainly I have not forgotten it yet. Once is really enough for me for the moment!

As I cast my eyes up, I suddenly caught a sight. It brought me back to my normal senses. I saw the vicar or the minister; anyway a man in black was looking at me through some strange corner of his eyes. It startled me and I jumped in my mind. I thought there we go again! I started to walk respectively.

People started to talk to me; soon the man in black came near me and was asking me questions. I never really think much of the professionally religious people; I simply don't understand them.

The man was telling me all about the church. He was showing me proudly the displays of the church silvers. He asked me what I was and if I was an Anglican! I said quite innocently I was nothing. In a second I realised, it was a wrong thing to say to a clergyman. So I could not quite control myself, and I laughed loudly with an uneasy mind. Then I said I was sorry! The poor man could not help laughing too. Did he take any offence? I hope not. I do not really know, what was the matter with me; even in my nightmare I would not dream of saying "I am nothing" to a minister in an English church. Not because it matters that much; but it is not right. I feel a kind of pity for them. Also I have no intention of challenging their faith. If their faith makes them happy and keeps them busy in their life, I have nothing against it. I wish them good luck. But I am not part of it. That is all.

I do not believe in any organised religion. I feel they do not do much good for anybody. Also I often wonder why the Western nations are so keen in preaching their religion, when very rarely they know anything about the other people's faith.

Why are the rich nations so forceful and particular for the poor to change their religion and nothing else much! If they were really sincere for the betterment of the poor, the world would have been a different place by now.

Maybe it is difficult to love the poor honestly, so the rich nations usually leave it for the God to do it. Perhaps the rich feels that poverty is due to the sin of the soul. The rich nations are often in a great evangelical zeal to save the poor from their sin. They are very passionate and determined to play with the soul of the poor nations, but nothing else.

They think it is their fervent duty to save the poor souls in their own term. But they are in no hurry to save the poor body and leave the soul to God! The poor body is not so much healthy, as the rich. Maybe it hurts them to accept the fact that their bodies and the bodies of the poor nations of the world belong to the same humanity; the difference is only in the nourishment and not in the flesh.

Perhaps it makes the rich happy to believe that they are with God and the poor are without. They never think of the poor as their equal. They do like to do the job for their God but never the job they would like to have done for themselves.

They pity the poor, mostly patronise and often misuse them. Eventually they leave the poor disorientated and deprived of their peace of mind.

The powerful nations have their bread, but they still pray to God for more bread. They feel, God is obliged to grant them their daily bread and much more.

Their faith helps them to think that it is their legitimate claim from God and they must have their share in God's wealth, as they are His chosen people. God must give them more comfort, more luxury, more and more of everything.

Need it or not they must grab and guard their share. Between them and their God their conscience concentrates on making material wealth and material well being for themselves, and themselves alone. They build their own societies more and more better off, also more and more better to live in.

For the poor nations, however they do not think in the same way. They do not pray for the daily bread for the poor. They do not help the poor to make their society any better to live or grow.

As far as the poor are concerned, the rich concentrates more on their salvation rather than their well being in this world. In this effort they often manage to confuse the poor and distract them from growing or getting more food to eat.

The powerful nations of the world would gladly help the poor to be more and more dependent on them. They would love the poor to depend on their pitiful handouts, and remain wretched as such for ever if possible. They would rather engage the wretched poor of the world to denounce the values and the cultural inheritance of their own past, and thus undermine their faith in themselves.

The western power is too eager to drown the poor of the world in the spiritual world of the rich, which does not accept the responsibility of feeding the bodies of the poor in real sense.

By alluring the poor into the spiritual world of the rich, the rich succeed in causing a total alienation of the mind and the body of the poor amongst their own people and geographical surroundings.

When foreign God, foreign values and foreign standards replace one's own familiar ones, man can easily plunge in a serious confusion of destroyed personality. Man could involuntarily become socially impotent, unproductive, immoral and incapable of creating anything original or worth creating. The root is destroyed, or at least badly damaged. The image to identify with is removed. The ideas to comfort and reconcile are made to disappear. Not much happiness could come out of it at all!

Man is not made to live and grow in vacuum. Man cannot usually make use of things he does not understand. Ideas, values, standards and even God for that matter, are the history of human mind in a social environment he is born and brought up. This is the realisation and conscience of a society, tested and grown over the ages.

Discrediting this valuable consciousness and putting an abruptly changed cultural view in its place, is like uprooting a growing tree and planting it in a strangely different soil. It is almost certain to kill the natural growth of the society and may, at best produce only some kind of a second rate social existence with a lot of artificial caring and helping from outside.

Full-fledged robust life, living and creating in an attractive, enviable style in such a circumstance, is almost beyond any realistic possibility. As a matter of fact it is, perhaps an almost certainly, to produce an inferior quality of life and living instead. Maybe this is to satisfy some kind of notion of superiority of the rich nation over the poor.

The west never really loved the East. Things they do not understand, they always try to make it look inferior, and not worth knowing. Things they do understand and admired, they take them away for themselves and pretend them to be their own.

They often invent their own theory to justify anything and everything they do or like to do. Understandably they do not live their life to glorify the East. Of course they live for themselves.

However, the East will never be able to stand on her own feet and be proud until the whole fact is well understood and properly acted upon. So that the Western powers are not able to take advantage of the blind trust, ignorance and misguided dependence of the East.

True trust and respect cannot really exist unless it is mutual. The West has never made any history of loving and caring for the East so far.

I am an Indian. I often think about India; and quite frequently I feel unhappy when I read something about India written by the non-Indians.

In August 1970 it must have been one such occasion when I wrote a few lines in some anger:

The foreigners do not know and maybe, cannot know how to look at India in true sense. What do they really know about India? To them she is nothing but a piece of land which the British once exploited enormously and enjoyed thoroughly in doing so!

Now it is just like a giant carcass whose flesh has been almost completely eaten up by vultures. Only the pitiful structure of the bones, the bare skeleton now is left on a hostile dry world, yet to be destroyed by the natural laws of nature!

There is perhaps nothing in India now to make an outsider to be much passionate about her. In truth it now represents to them only the ugly horror of complete hopelessness of a hopeless nation which they probably love to believe to be utterly stupid and capable of absolute nothing! They might occasionally feel pity for India without any genuine commitment; especially when they are feeling a bit soft but somewhat detached, particularly if it costs them nothing very much; in fact if not too many Indians try to get anything from them.

Usually they are no doubt absolutely ignorant about India or Indians, except perhaps in some very superficial facts which are quite apparent to everybody, clever and not so clever both.

However, now and then one hears the Western prophets who spent some time in India, taking some photographs which show as crudely as possible all the humiliation and degradation of a suppressed nation. Sometime one hears about someone who perhaps spent some time in India as a honoured guest of some wealthy Indian who was delighted to show him all the usual beauty spots and the well-known remains of some past glory. Or maybe some people just visited India in order to get some very special self-entertainment for their super ego. For example, they may feel that they have some words of wisdom for India.

Most of the visitors to India seem to behave as if they are almost super men; they are so super that they perhaps believe that they must have done some good to the poor Indians just by the supreme virtue of their super presence.

The Western complex of silly superiority is truly incredible. For a few days, he or she might even enjoy the holiness of their ignorance, or the greatness of the fulfilment of their desire to have a cheap holiday while teaching some ignorant Indians or, having some fun in a carefully chosen poor Indian work camp.

At home they might not have been a teacher, they might not themselves been to school very long, they might even be without any sense of their own social culture. Still, never mind! They can all claim to be anything in India!

Maybe I am too touchy, and all these make me very indignant. He or she is always superior to the Indians in all respect! Poor stupid Indians can never stand up to them! Moreover their super intellect will surely allow them to understand everything about India immediately after or even before their arrival there. A second or two must be quite enough for this purpose. The rest of their stay may happily be spent for their personal enjoyment.

Anyway to them, India, her past, present and future are no doubt as clear as a glass of their favourite beer! They understand everything; at least they understand India in the way they want to understand her. They really have nothing to loose. It is in fact quite profitable!

On their return to their own country, he or she can become quite a prophet, prophesying all about Indian affairs; everybody will listen to them as an authority on this subject, and they can enjoy their power of authority. They can even sell their article on their chosen subject, and earn a bit of money too, or they can even pretend to be a poet with some poetic feelings about India if prophetic speeches about India are no longer too fashionable, and do not pay much any longer. He or she can always decide what will be their best course of action.

But my only sorrow is that we Indians take them so seriously. We really believe that they are honest, sincere and dying to help us. We are far too gullible. We do not realise that a vulture has sharp eye, and can see if a bit of flesh is still there between the bones. And India is probably always something to make a bit of profit from.

Personally I do not think, anybody is in general any special than anyone else. However, it is an open fact that some people develop in a special way. Some are clearly more, clever than others.

Sometimes it strikes as though a particular community produces far more clever or gifted people than others; and we cannot help putting the credit of being so clever on the religion or the nationality of that particular community. But is it really true? Has race, religion or nationality really anything to do with a gift or talent in a human being? I cannot but help wondering about it a little!

Reason may find it difficult to believe it to be so in a direct sense; still, there may well be some indirect connection. Who knows!

It maybe not the nationality, not the race or the religion neither; but the actual environment to which an individual is exposed in life, is the vital connection between human beings and their gifted minds!

In other words the special development of one's mind may actually be due to something special in one's environment. Everyman has a unique environment if you analyse it in great details. Nevertheless, one always shares quite a lot of common environmental factors as well, with the others in one's own community.

So it may not be very easy to say if anything in the environment is the cause of any difficulty for not producing special talent. It is quite hard to know for sure, what exactly can trigger off the potential mind on the way of higher achievement. Also we do not know for certain why nothing helps for some people in any special way whatsoever!

Superiority of some kind and form may actually have been developed in order to maintain a sort of balance between hostility of some degree present in the environment and a vulnerably exposed individual with his potential mental courage. It may be just a form of natural selection after all!

If a vulnerable community does not produce individuals who can draw respect, fame and attention, the community is someway doomed to extinct. Man has always been growing all along in order to protect himself from the hostility of nature. Man grows still more by nature in the hostile world!

I live in England. But I am a foreigner here. In my early days here I used to feel more homesick.

I used to miss my people badly; and long to see them very much. Instead I am still living amongst the British people, and so have to see their same old faces everyday.

One day in the middle of December in 1970 I was feeling absolutely rotten and desperately home sick. To distract myself and to make myself feel a little better, I tried to write:

Oh! I don't want to look at the same old faces everyday. At the moment, the British faces do not inspire me. They are not making me feel happy either.

Not all of their women do look too attractive to me and their men are too practical. The narrowness of their utilitarian world at the moment bores me. I want a change! I want something to inspire me a bit. I do not know where I can get my inspiration. Maybe I should go away from Bristol.

I shall go to Italy in the Easter time. Perhaps I should go to East Berlin. I do not want to go to Spain. Spain does not interest me too much at the moment. I do not know why? I do not dislike the Spanish people; they are quite nice and interesting no doubt.

I do not like their bull-fighting. I feel it is distasteful. Perhaps it is their love of bull-fighting which has turned my mind away from Spain.

I will go home in the summer. I would love that very much. I just can't wait to see my home again. But will I be able to come back? I remember the first time I was coming to England. My mother cried as I was about to leave home for an uncertain period of time. I felt upset and apprehensive, but pretended as if there was no need for that sort of soft feeling!

I remember the second time I was leaving home for England. I felt an uncontrollable sobbing, coming out of my choked throat. There was no reason for it really except that I did not like to leave home any more. All the people at home and even anywhere in the country of my birth suddenly seemed so dear and precious that I did not want to live without them.

I remember the third time. The misery to leave home was still stronger. The life away from home this time was really a life without joy. A feeling of emptiness, a feeling of loneliness is still on top of my soul. I wonder if I could bear the strain of leaving home the fourth time!

Since then I left home many times and survived. I am still lonely and long for going home all the time. But I do not have a home anywhere anymore. England is the only home I am stuck to now, perhaps for ever as long as I live.

I am now resigned to this fact. But now and then I reflect on my life and on anything or everything on earth, whatever draws my attention. Maybe it is a kind of compensation for my eternal home-sickness.

I started to put down in writing whatever thoughts come in my mind. I do not quite remember when exactly I wrote about the universal fear of population explosion. I never had much sympathy for this fear. I don't know why I feel this way, but I do and so I wrote:

There has been such a great fear of population explosion. Everybody talks about it with an undertone as if it is something like plague or much, worse and there is no cure for it. Having children is now-a-days looked down almost as a crime or, maybe worse than that; it is regarded as an irresponsible dirty animal act. Especially children of the third world bring up a horror of disgust in the mind of the Western world.

They are horrified. They suffer from the nightmare of black-fear, yellow-fear and the fear of Asiatic small people breeding like rats and thereby bringing doom's day upon everybody at anytime very soon.

This breeding like pigs in the third world must be stopped at any cost. Otherwise the West will be drowned by the crawling overpopulated dirty little insects like people of the poor third insignificant world.

Sex is very important and enjoyable for the West. They would not go any where, or do anything to procure and indulge it in all possible or impossible form or shape. But that is for them only; and they themselves are not at all prepared to give up breeding at their choice in the West. Of course they must have their children in a manner which suits their ways and means as always. However, they cringe in utter disgust or maybe in awful fear when they think or talk about the people having children in the poor countries.

They mobilized all their resources and publicity stunts in order to start a battle against the population increase in the poor countries. They have mastered in preaching the gospel of population control in earnest. They do not hesitate to apply harsh and desperate measures amongst the poor and unprivileged humans of the world.

They managed very easily to create an eager atmosphere of world's popular opinion which justifies any attempt any experiment in this direction as long as it is applied in the third world. But the idea of improving the lives and the living conditions of the poor for this purpose did not gain much strength or enthusiasm.

The lackeys, the foolish intellectuals, the parasites, the pretend intelligentsia and the toy-authorities of the poor nations are very easy to be brain washed, because they do not really have much brain of their own. They really like sheep, if you lead one, the rest will follow blindly without a question.

All the middle and upper class intelligence of the third world joined up sheepishly in this Western cry of population explosion. Without a single question they accepted it as an absolute truth that their countries are poor because they have too many children. So it must be drastically reduced.

My only objection to this is that no one is taking any responsibility for their life and death. They are not at all wanted by anyone. The life of the poor is entirely uncared for. So why should their procreation alone be anybody's business! Shouldn't they at least be left alone!

Indira Gandhi's government tried too ruthlessly to curb the population of the poor Indians. It did not work and it did back fire quite badly.

For some reason I can't remember now, I was writing in February 1978 about this population control:

In last few decades people's imagination has really caught up with the idea of population control on earth as a means of solving many of the earthly problems. This flare of imagination started somewhere in the West. For quite a long time it seems to everybody that birth control is the obvious solution of all evils on earth. It became a great panacea of convenience and freedom for women from all obligation or frustration. Women at last become able to celebrate their independence. But in the Western countries all this is people's choice; they choose it for personal gain, ease and comfort. No one is forcing them to use it.

However, the Western reaction towards the population control of the poor nations seems a bit different and offensive. In Western mind, maybe most of the evil problems on earth is somehow, associated with the over population of the third world. Just because some people are poor, shouldn't they have any right or pleasure in having their children!

The third world people have always been seemed as somewhat unnecessary or unwanted by Western perception. Maybe they are a little scared or overwhelmed by the comparatively much higher population of the poor world. Perhaps the rich always see the poor as some sort of threat to themselves.

So any excuse to control this human ocean naturally favours their inherent willingness and gives the signal to justify to, go ahead with any plan which suits their subconscious motive.

The Western power was never been really interested in the welfare or well being of the third world. It is never been one of them exactly in any way whatsoever. They hardly have shown genuine concern in stopping the suffering, hardship, illness, disease, death, ignorance or poverty of the third world population. But they are extraordinarily interested in making the number smaller. Is it because the big number somehow offers them a kind of ultimate threat!

I cannot help repeating myself with the same argument once again. I wonder why the West is so uncomfortable about the size of the population of the poor, when they don't really worry too much about anything else for these countries!

The poor dies unaccounted and uncared, still the number of them alive makes the rich unhappy. If they could do something to make it smaller, maybe they would feel better and perhaps do it. All those idealistic excuses may only be a pretence which makes them feel easy.

Maybe they genuinely believe it. Maybe the idea to curb the world population is really a very good idea indeed. But I am incensed and I suspect that it is something to do with their fear of the poor as well. Maybe this fear gave them a lot of incentive and they have to invent an excuse which suits their purpose too well!

# Chapter Eleven

I get a cyclic spell of self lamentation. Maybe it is a kind of way I try to get rid off my inner conflicts and tension. Maybe it helps me to overcome all my disappointments and dissatisfaction. The year 1978 must have been one such period of me feeling very low. I put down on paper quite a lot of dispirited thoughts about myself during this time:

I am so disappointed with my life. I never thought I will grow up such a second rate woman! When I was a child I wanted to be simply great, definitely a woman of quality; never wanted money or any special worldly possession.

The thing I wanted, most of all, was to have a really great human conscience. I thought I was going to grow up smart, bright, healthy and kind with a kind generous heart. I was eager to share and help with everybody else's sorrows and miseries.

I did not think then, that my own disappointment and miseries will be one day too much for me to bear. At the moment I am quite unable to come out of the vicious circle of self-pity, depression, apathy and inability to have a creative mind.

Lack of success in almost every sphere of my life fills my heart with sadness. I do not have any idea how to overcome this sadness and try to make the most of whatever is left to do or enjoy in my life.

I feel my life is over, at any rate the best of my life is at an end now; and it did not turn out to be what I expected or wished.

Whatever is left of my life does not seem to be much of interest to me at present. This part of living cannot satisfy my unfulfilled wishes and desires. It can only experience the actual process of my physical dying and decay of my mind and body. The world surrounding my life as I used to know it is also dying and disappearing fast. The people, who were nearest and dearest to me, are passing away in an alarmingly rapid speed, leaving me all alone, empty and lonely.

The first part of one's life is a time to build up and store success, joy and happiness. If it fails then, the second half can never compensate the first in a really meaningful way. It is then simply a matter of waiting for the very end or the worst. At least that is how I feel and think about my life now.

I have not much faith in myself anymore now-a-days. I am beginning to consider myself almost a total failure, socially and also academically. I do not know why it became so.

When I was young, no one would have believed it; even I could not imagine it would be possible for me to become such a failure! Perhaps all failures are like this. Probably no failure really starts as a failure!

It seems so strange now for me to think about my earlier life and also it does not seem all that long ago either. I was quite bright, always ambitious; perhaps, too ambitious. Probably ambition is a bad thing. I still do not know what went wrong. I never ever failed in any examination which I sat in my life. Also I always scored quite high in the examinations I completed.

Once or twice I might not have sat throughout an examination, but that was not because I was afraid of failing it; it was because I desired to achieve better results. In any case I never had anything but top grades except once; that is my honours degree examination and I was not well at the time.

I used to stand first every year in the annual examination in my school days. I had a first class in, my master of science, examination. I also scored the highest marks in a few papers individually in that examination. Naturally I was very pleased with my success. I wanted to study further. I wanted to start doing research.

The idea of doing research attracted me enormously. I was very keen. I did not see anything wrong in my desire. I did not foresee anything could go wrong in this respect, provided I could find an opportunity to do it.

As far as I was concerned, everything depended on finding this opportunity. Heaven only knows how I tried to find an opening. I do not think I really ever found a right one. I tried and tried. I feel like crying bitterly even now, if I think about how seriously and desperately I wanted to do research work in my field of interest.

No one ever encouraged me. In fact everybody discouraged me. No one even explained why I should not do it. They just did their best to prevent me from trying it. I think that because of this I got an obsession, a peculiar fixation about it inside me. I went astray. I ruined my life for nothing!

I tried as many ways as I could to find an outlet to do some kind of research in my subject in my country, but I was totally unsuccessful. I became apprehensive and frustrated. I became careless as well. I was prepared to take anything. I completely lost my sense of judgement; and I lost my ground.

I left the secured, sheltered life in the loving environment I was used to. I came to England on a very thread bare hope and a hopeless illusion. It was almost a no-hope situation. I survived, but it did not do much for my ego. I never became a truly happy person.

I came to the wrong place at the wrong time of my life and faced the wrong people. I never achieved the ambition of my life. I lost an awful lot of joy and precious happiness. I made my life a shamble!

When one is young, life is glamorous on its own. The sheer presence of a young life is presumably enough to make everything glamorous irrespective of anything else. But when one is older, life is no longer so glamorous anymore.

As the days go by it gets harder and harder to keep life going in the least respectable fashion. This is perhaps why people try to build up life's securities for the old days. They need the glamour, status, money, power, one's own friends and relation. Life in old age can only be nice and worth living by virtue of all the material virtues and emotional fulfilments, but never just on its own. One has to prepare for all these supports and enrichments.

Otherwise, one looses the light and joy of joyful living; and life then would only lead them to loneliness, darkness as well as isolation.

I am so miserable and afraid of what is going to come to me in my old age. I feel life is surely to become too ugly; and I am certain, people of the world would naturally feel like getting away from such ugly old life. And who can blame them if they want to do so!

Life thus may end for me in a sheer tragedy, not for any real reason other than simple lack of careful preparation or providence for growing old gracefully. Many people probably face this in their life. Maybe this is just a nature's natural course or curse for some unfortunate people. Nevertheless it seems to me at the moment so hard and sad!

Maybe I am feeling so strongly about it, because I am now perhaps not very far from this fate! I am sure I was too stupid and thoughtless. I did not prepare myself; I did not plan for my old age. I let time go by. So I think I have now good reason to be frightened of my old age.

For me it would perhaps be a much merciful escape from this tragedy of life, if I could possibly die before my old age actually creeps in. It would simply be too wonderful if my life could end before it starts to get any uglier. But I doubt I will be that lucky. As I never was lucky in any way in my life!

When I was younger and even a few years ago, all I wanted is to go in quest of knowledge and be a kind of intellectual. I enjoy talking about politics and all the problems of the world with intense passion. Even though I do not perhaps understand any of this rightly, I never foolishly or not, have any time to talk about anything else.

But right now, my personal problems have grown too many and too big, I am overwhelmed and too tired. These have now almost taken over my life. My faiths are shattered, and hopes are all gone. My doubts are getting too big. Maybe it would be best for me now, is to retire and do nothing! I am becoming more and more pessimistic.

Love is living. It means opening the door, inviting others in and extending oneself. This is life and living. Hate, on the other hand is a kind of death. It means shutting yourself in, closing the door, burying yourself in a hole, and separating yourself from the others totally. This is really dying.

I am sure love is the language of a living soul. Throughout the ages in every society, all over the world, real people always cried hard and loud for love. People talk about love, feel love, suffer for love and sing songs after songs of love.

Maybe it is very difficult for anybody to love people who are not too attractive in their eyes. Maybe ugliness dries up the spring of love in people's heart. Most people perhaps feel that the ugly people deserve to be unloved. They may even be thinking that the unpleasing people must have done something sinful, or something wrong; and that is why they are born ugly. So ugliness is a kind of punishment from the hand of God for their sinful life. By not loving them, people are therefore only carrying out God's wishes and thereby earning some virtues for themselves. Most people most probably hate ugly people with clear conscience.

Unfortunately though, poverty breeds ugliness. Lack of privileges, hardship, hard labour, lack of education, lack of political, economical and technological muscles, all contribute to a kind of life which is difficult to look very attractive.

Poor people, poor nations, all are very unattractive, unimpressive and quite ugly in the eyes of the people who are not so poor in material sense. Rich nations do not see beauty in poverty. They do not at all identify themselves with the poor nations. Obviously it is easy to love the things we like and admire.

I do not remember which party I went to and why I was so unhappy about some people there in February 1978. But I wrote a few lines about it then:

They have no guilty feeling, no modesty or any hesitation at all. They know what is good for them; and they seem to know all the faults in other people. These people here seem to enjoy the short comings of other people and somehow know exactly how to take advantage of these other people's weaknesses. This Western world is a very hard and cruel world.

Even though I am living here, I find it too suffocating for me. I do not share their values; I do not fit in to this world.

Contrary to popular believe, the people here love gossiping, but always about the things they do not like in other people, their neighbours or anybody they do not fancy.

I am sure they just invent these ugly gossips only to please themselves; there may not be a single truth in what they say about other people. Anyway, I find it difficult to believe most of the things they say about the people I know a little.

I wonder why, do these women do this! Are they unhappy? I can see that they are definitely jealous. I never knew that people could end up like this. They compete with everybody and anybody. They enjoy when they succeed in defeating others, but hate bitterly when they are defeated.

I am sure it is not nice; it is sad. Do they not realise it? Is it not unbalanced? It is a kind of hysteria, no doubt. Many of the women seem to be too mad about men. They want men, when they do not already have a man of their own.

But they do not seem to live a lovely life with their man when they have one. Quite often they do not seem to get on all that well with their husband or, the man they are trying to live with. Also very frequently they do not seem to approve of their grown up sons specially, if the sons are already married or, living with girl-friends.

They always appear to belittle others and perhaps get some satisfaction by doing this. I seriously wonder if they really get any good feeling in this way. Talking ill of others all the time, does not make one too dried up altogether? Doesn't it dry up the entire spring of love in their heart, and in turn deprive them of having any faith in others? Surely it would drive them to desperate loneliness in their own life. Perhaps it does and that is why they seem to behave the way they behave.

Maybe I am doing exactly the same as them. Just because I happened to meet a few lonely old English widows in a party last night in their wild gossiping mood, I am simply jumping to a conclusion about all English old ladies. I am perhaps using up my racial prejudices against all Western women. Maybe talking ill of them makes me feel better, because I am lonely, lack confidence in myself and I do not have a lot of love for them.

I do not really know one thing from another. I am always confused. I should admit that I do not know what is right and what is wrong. Anyway, who knows! I am not at all sure about who does what and why! It is all in the world I live, and hence it must be what life consists of. All I know, I do not get much pleasure out of it!

1978 is not a very cheerful year for me. I feel ever so depressed. I feel I am so silly. I do not know why I have ruined my life for nothing. I foolishly aimed for things which are not available in my life.

I wanted true love, but I wanted it to come to me, rather than I should look hard for it. Nothing in this world comes out, of the blue sky suddenly and straight into anybody's life. Things never happen like that. One has to work hard and make lots of preparation for it in every step of one's life.

Maybe some people are born silly like me. They cannot help it. They are just fond of day dreaming; they dream away their whole life. But they simply never know how to go and get things, they always dream about. I wonder what makes people so peculiar!

Maybe people are naturally different. These differences are of great importance. Isn't it so! If this is what leads one to absolute deprivation and another to some degree of fulfilment in life; I wish I was a bit more practical and able to make my life better!

Maybe no one in this world is really happy. To live a truly happy life and feel really happy, perhaps is something to be actually achieved by no one. It is probably just something everybody must dream of in their own way in their own life. Perhaps it helps people to keep on living and not go insane.

I suppose it is more or less the same thing as what people in a way identify with God. Everybody must aspire towards but no one can know much about it. It remains beyond achievement for everybody always all throughout the ages. Man can only speak of it but he knows nothing about it. Possibly it does not exist in the real world, and only a product of human imagination!

This imagination or illusion is not entirely fruitless though. I think this is what gives people a kind of purpose for living their lives. It keeps them busy, occupied and always wanting to go on one step further ahead. Thus coming to the very end in the end without having a moment to reflect without any illusion is perhaps the best for human beings. To live the dismay of the disillusion is probably wise for the very last moment in life and not before! It is perhaps better not to have the knowledge that all in life is for achieving nothing and nowhere to go except to die a natural death which everybody should do if left to the natural course of living. The life in itself is hard enough to go through without further aggravation!

Today is 11 February 1978. Yesterday I was feeling very low and depressed. I was thinking what a low and degrading life I am enduring. I feel far too miserable, and I think I do not deserve it. I am facing injustice, and it is hard to bear.

Perhaps to some extent, nobody does have justice in life all the time. But I cannot speak for everybody, I can only speak for myself; and I know I have been treated in a way which is not right.

I have been in a strange and subtle way made to feel that I am not quite good in my job. Maybe I am a bit of a failure in many ways in my life; but I am absolutely sure that I am not a failure as a lecturer in my institute. I am so touchy and I get so badly hurt, when I sense that people think of me as if I am not a competent teacher.

I know people here tend to underestimate me a lot; I often am made to feel invisible. On many occasion I wondered if it is a prejudice against me, just because I have failed in some other spheres of my life. Perhaps they feel like regarding me a failure in all respect, even as a human; because I do not have a husband and a family like the others. In people's eye failure to have a successful personal life, reflects as a failure in all respects.

Maybe they are right. I do not know. But I cannot help feeling badly hurt. I feel so hurt, low, small and badly bruised I cannot even try to fight back. I feel I should accept all the dishonour, injustice, humiliation and discouragement; whatever people care to throw at my face. I should understand that my life is nothing but a waste.


The Institute's attitude towards me or my teaching as a whole is really most disheartening. It drives me mad with anger and despair. I always found it hostile. There is always a kind of pretence of friendliness; but it is too superficial. It is very easy to see that the official policy and the institutional higher authorities are all basically most unhelpful and quite mean. It is as if, they are always just waiting to catch me on the wrong side of the fence. They have always made me feel that they are simply waiting to find a suitable excuse to use against me. I have never known if it is only the departmental attitude or, the attitude of the College authority as a whole. Maybe it is really the policy of the power beyond!

I cannot say for sure if it is personal or not. It feels very personal to me. I do not know if this attitude is truly for all the Lecturers or, just anybody teaching anywhere in the country. Maybe all teachers feel this way whenever they experience any kind of difficulty in their profession. I feel unhappy and isolated. It takes all my drive out of me, and leaves me feel most miserable. However, none of my colleagues or any of my promising students ever had any problem with me.

I never seem to have any meaningful pattern in my life for some reason.

I just drift away from one place to another, but never with a real purpose or pleasure. Maybe I always live amongst the wrong people for me, and mix with the people who have no idea or wish to have any idea about me.

If this is not a lonely life, what is a lonely life! I must have been destined to live a life like this. I now wish I could find a reason for it. Loneliness with a reason may be more bearable than loneliness without one. It may well be just a fancy of my mind, as I have nourished too many fancies in my fanciful mind throughout my life.

I would really like to know where exactly one can find happiness. I do not know why people always talk about happiness. As far as I can feel, I do not seem to see any happiness anywhere in this miserable world. Life is too full of misery! There is always something sad, something painful niggling away in the secret depth of everyman's soul!

People only dream of happiness. Maybe people just talk and talk of it not because it exists, but because the thought of its mere existence produces in them some sort of intoxication which helps them to bear the unbearable miseries of their life. It is perhaps nothing but the fantasy created by the fertile imagination of human mind!

To be happy I suppose, is a kind of unreality, and yet everybody likes to suffer from this illusion of being happy in their life. It is I guess a peculiar condition of living. You have to invent something in order to counteract the harshness of life's truth!

To have one's eyes truly opened, one needs too many awesome tragedies and cruel sufferings. Even then, the usual consequence in general is to take refuge in some kind of imaginary state of mind. People attach some sort of attribute to all their miseries, and it in a kind of way helps them to uplift their feeling.

They often invent God. They build up philosophy; produce ideas after ideas---do hundred and one things simply to make them feel a bit better, when they are not really feeling better. To ease their pain they wear emotional mask and take shelter in all sorts of illusory world.

Everybody wishes to be happy. They think married life is a happy life. People in general put so much weight in the virtue of family life. In some way they want to make everybody feel that marital status is a kind of divine bliss. According to popular myth, women who marry and women who do not marry are supposed to be made up of two very different types.

Maybe they are; I do not know. But I wonder if it is not also possible that anybody's marriage is the consequence of events leading the individual life. Education, environment, health and social status all play important role in this matter.

It is after all a personal relationship between two unrelated people. We have no choice in other relationship. We have mother, father, brothers, sisters and all blood relation and family connections. We are born as a daughter or a son. We cannot choose. But we can choose whom we want to marry or not.

It is a kind of choice of mind. It is in some way like a possession which has to be acquired by choice. However, in life nothing can be gained without a price. Two people, a man and a woman usually agree to get in a mutual agreement of paying some kind of price with their lives.

Some people like to pay on a long term basis. Some on the other hand like to pay only on a short term basis. The man and the woman who enter into such long term commitment are the husband and the wife. This marital status is not free. He takes the responsibility of the family, and she takes the responsibility of the family.

He gives security and she gives security. He gives his body and his labour; she also gives her body and her labour. He pays and she pays for the relationship. The commitment is aimed on a long term prospect, preferably life long if possible.

It has certain disadvantages: husband and wife both have to put up with each other quite a considerable extent. The husband cannot get rid off his wife too easily even though he would very much wish to do so. The wife has the same problem. The wife has to oblige the husband many times in many ways even though she would not wish to do so; and same thing applies to the husband as well.

Women who enter into short term relationship with men are also paying for their choice of short-time possession. It is a different kind of payment and a different kind of return; but it is a payment alright. Maybe they pay too much and do not have much of a lasting return for their price.

Perhaps, it is like renting. You rent something; you pay for it on a day to day basis. You have to pay a bit more---a premium price for the rent. You may not possess it in the long run. You may have to return the goods back or, you may have to exchange it with another, or you may be able to keep it for good at long last. You can never be sure and you can never have the peace of mind for future security. You live a day to day basis almost. Perhaps this is what you like to choose. Perhaps you have no choice in choosing this.

Marriage on the other hand is probably like buying something with cash price. The goods are yours to enjoy; good or bad you are stuck with it. To extract benefit from it or go mad by it, is all yours to endure.

Everything in life has a price. If you don't choose, you pay the price of loneliness. Maybe it is the worst kind of price one pays in one's life. It is probably the life of rotten goods, no one buys it, or no one comes near it. You are left to rot for ever and ever without any joy or anything what so ever.

So I must be one of these rotten goods left on earth for good then. I have never taken any action to change myself. Nothing therefore has ever changed in my life. That is why my life is so stale and disappointing!

Everybody loves success, brave men and beautiful women. Yet there are so many failures, cowards and unsightly people in this world. Maybe this is the way God likes to play jokes with human race! Or what else could it be!

When I read a book or see a film or watch a television programme, everything seems so meaningful, so noble and worthwhile. But all it does for me is that it makes me feel sorry for myself.

I realise now that in the moment of our enthusiasm, some of us forget our priority in our life. As a consequence of our misplaced priority we later suffer badly from awesome loneliness in our life. We get what we deserve! Maybe life has a preordained structure and we cannot go out of it without a drastic penalty to pay!

This is perhaps the lesson of life! Maybe we cannot do whatever we wish and whenever we wish. To our utter dismay there seems something bigger than us!

There is nothing I can do now except perhaps pray. Maybe a few lines in the form of a poem might just express how I feel at the moment:

Oh God of my life! Spare me the pain, if you can
I don't wish to live any more! What is the point!
I don't know, I don't know why I ended up like this,
I really do not know why we live or maybe what is in life!
And why we do not live feeling a bit better than this—
What is the purpose of it all! And why we are here!

I wish I did know little bit of the mystery of our life!
If only! If only I had a chance to have a glimpse of it!
Oh God, whatever you are, I wish you were a bit clearer
And a tiny bit kind as well to me just for once!
Oh Lord of our Universe! Must you always be triumphant!
And full of joy only in the helpless pain of human soul!
But please, please tell me why? And why not something else!

I did with my life what I thought I ought to do. I do not know exactly why or, if there was any other reason. But I have done what I had to do. It might also have been something to do with my background. Otherwise why did I live this way?

Maybe I wanted to live like a Greek tragedy and I have managed to make my life like a Greek tragedy. I wish now something made me to stop it at the start. Now it is too late and there is no point really of talking about it any more.

This is now the end of February 1978. So another year has already ended. I still have not achieved any happiness. There is not of any hope either. The bad thing about living a life with prolonged disappointment is that the heart becomes uncharitable and unkind towards the world.

So I feel like saying, please God do not make my heart shrink too much! Let me live a life of peace and generosity.

There could have been a lot of joy and satisfaction in my life. But it has not been so. However, it could have been a lot worse. So I suppose I should thank God for saving me from a life of more despair and more disgrace!

Please let me have the strength and will to put my mind at rest; and please help me to give the world whatever goodness I am able to offer. I do not wish to be mean and unkind. I never want to live a life without a soul!

However, I do not wish to be religious and hide behind any God or rituals. This would be absolutely hypocritical for me.

I live as a foreigner amongst the British people in England. I am quite vulnerable at times. I can see that it is quite easy to laugh at other races' miseries and faults.

As a matter of fact we all do secretly and somehow feel a bit pleased when we see other people are in difficulty. If these people belong to a different race then, it is perhaps even better for our ego. We feel a bit distant. We do not feel we have any part to play in their faults.

Maybe we laugh a little at them and feel very much distant. Perhaps that is why the jokes about other races are so potent and popular anywhere amongst any race. It is really stupid but it is probably very human.

I have just seen a very fat Chinese boy in the street. Immediately I felt in my head that the Chinese are all fat because they eat too much too starchy food. Subconsciously I must have felt detached from the consequence of their fault, and quite pleased with the implication that we Indians do not have such bad eating habit. But unfortunately we do as well!

However, I have seen plenty of very slim and petite Chinese people. Also, I should know there could never be any worse eating habit than those of many Indians. Yet, I wonder if I would like to remind myself of this fact when it comes to a question of comparison between Indians and the others. I am sure it is shockingly silly indeed!

People are too quick to generalise a race by looking at some oddities of even one single person. How often one hears people saying something strange about another race!

Race is a very funny business. People become very inhuman when it comes to a matter of dealing with another race or racial interest.

For example, when the British public utter the word, immigrant population, it sounds somehow something bad and dirty. In a strange way they make it sounds like a contagious vermin---an appalling disease trying to spring on them. Perhaps they think of the black and coloured immigrants in their country as something like a pathetic little dirty parasite, trying to grow on their body, and hence to be ruthlessly pushed aside.

Most probably they think, their pure white race is going to be contaminated by the sheer presence of these strange creatures from the poor third world. They simply cannot tolerate from choice the existence of these people amongst themselves.

In a way these people perhaps disgust them and they wish to preserve their wonderful race from the indignation of having to live next door to any such neighbour in their own country. Most of the people of Western origin might be thinking more or less in the same manner. They are too proud of their racial heritage. They really consider themselves as the best beauties on earth. In their mind they see themselves as the very best there is in all respect.

Isn't it funny though how people do become blind when it comes to compare themselves with others! Their negative points are all hidden from their mind. For others the negative sides get very much emphasized.

It is probably very natural for them not to realise, how ugly they look in other people's eyes when they are seen in the horrifying light of some of their history. What do they really want to boast about!

They never have shown much compassion towards their fellow beings. Do they not think at least once about what they did to the Jews, the American natives, the Australian Aborigines, the Africans, the Negroes, the South African Blacks and many, many others all over the world? Doesn't it make them a bit ashamed of what they did and still are doing in many places?

Over the centuries they have proved to be the champion of ruthlessly cruel and selfish race ever to exist on this earth. Their greed knew no bound. They managed to plunder everything possible everywhere and successfully corrupt everybody too. Exploitation is almost a religion to them in true reality.

Is there anybody in this world who could be any worse than them? And yet they do not seem to see it this way at all. They do not think like this either. They only want to believe that they are white and therefore beautifully pure. They say to themselves that they are the sons and daughters of God, born in God's own image. They identify themselves with goodness, purity, righteousness and everything good; although nothing perhaps, could have been any further from the truth.

Anyway, how does one measure superiority; and why are these immigrants inferior? Just because one looks different and maybe is not rich either, one is not necessarily inferior or disgusting!

The British in particular, spent years meddling in someone else's affairs and plundering someone else's properties in someone else's country. They always tried hard to make it look very high and mighty for absolutely philanthropic reason. Perhaps it helps them to feel self-righteous and full of clear conscience.

But when someone else comes to do a job in their country, it is always wrong and very dirty. These outsiders come to spoil and soil their country. So the British have the right and justification to try to get rid off these people in any way they can find suitable. Their logic always is implacable and suits their purpose.

If and when they need these people for something profitable for themselves, they change their mind and logic very quickly indeed. They really are the true capitalist lackey in this world.

The society, the country, the race, the nation, the people can make you believe anything they want to. And once you start believing, it becomes the truth for you.

Today is March 12, 1978. I am wondering what is really law and order. Is it not a kind of safeguard to protect the life and property of the rich! Law does not help the poor very much to live. Law never does anything to improve the hardship of the unprivileged section of the society that much.

If the rich did not have any fear of loosing anything they possess, there may not have been any history of law and order of any kind. It is perhaps a clever invention by the rich for the rich and to keep the poor out. It is in many ways a clever device to confuse the poor for the benefit of the powerful people of the world.

It is definitely an exercise of power to make the powerful people happy and secured. Interestingly it is a very big industry to deprive the poor and to maintain the poverty of the deprived people. It provides job, money and satisfaction for the well-off section of the public. There is no compassion really behind our so called law and order.

If there was any sense of real justice behind this then it should definitely have been some kind of mechanism which would advocate distribution of wealth amongst the unfortunates and also amongst the helpless.

Anyway the world is governed by the powerful people. The power brings richness and makes them solely interested in keeping it to themselves. So law and order must be rich man's weapon to preserve and enjoy his rich life. In the concept of this law and order there is very little thought for the poor.

If the poor do get any benefit from it that is just a by-product, entirely circumstantial or accidental. The poor often have to steal survival. Law and order would not encourage that if it means the rich people have to give up a little.

Anyway who knows, I may be all wrong; and all of it maybe just my imagination. But this is how I feel, and I should be allowed to open my mind even if only to my consciousness.

Why on earth anybody should stop me talking about how I think! I do not see any reason at all. Sometime some people treat me in a bit of a strange way. I do not know why though. I just feel that I am treated as if I am a child. Often people are too patronising or, they are making some kind of allowances in a way people make allowances when dealing with handicapped person. I get the impression as though I don't need to be dealt this way. Maybe I do. Maybe a foreign person like me should be handled like this. I must not complain or feel uneasy. Maybe we Asians do appear a bit handicapped in the Western eyes.

Some Asians are doing better than others though. For example, for some times now Japan is having a kind of upper hand in the matter of International trade warfare. Japan, by his sheer hard work, discipline and determination, managed to penetrate into the foreign market.

For quite a while he enjoyed enormous success in making a big impact in the Western countries. Many of the Western industrialist companies failed to compete with Japanese counterparts. Japan has become too successful in quite a few fields of important commerce.

However, the Western power is not going to let Japan to stay in this joyful industrial paradise for too long. They are thinking hard, they are determined to find a way. They will soon corner Japan in some way or other. Their survival depends on it.

They will somehow impose too may trade restrictions of too many kinds on Japan; and thereby make his life not so fascinating, expanding, and incredibly interesting in the trade world. Japan will not be able to enjoy the life of super industrialist power amongst all the Western nations forever.

Japan may soon feel the rough and harsh pressure forced on his nation by the others and may feel quite humiliated in some way. He may be soon going to be disillusioned to some extent. He may find it a kind of injustice for his nation.

He may one day come to know his rightful place, and not so happy and proud to be hand in hand with the Western block in full spirit and venture. Japan may soon have to look elsewhere for his explorations, satisfaction and perfection. He may start to find his place in the East and amongst his Eastern neighbours, if he wants to compete effectively with the West.

Anyway nothing is absolutely black and white in this world. Everything has two sides. One side maybe important to some people, when the other side has no meaning to them what so ever! But the other side could be vital to some too.

There are too many theories of population explosion. The popular forecast is that the world is going to be destroyed by population explosion.

These alarming theories are always very colourful and quite convincing. They are naturally backed up very strongly by the usual intelligentsia of the Western world, and happily transplanted in the thought process of the third world. Everybody nowadays seems to be very earnestly determined as well as resolute to advocate and apply any desperate measure possible in order to control population in the poor countries in the world. They are too eager to use any method they like, as 'do or die' motto. The third world is often used as their guinea-pigs. The poor people are being forced to practise harsh birth control or perish.

If the world is to be saved from over population, it has to be done at the expense of the poor. The rich is never to suffer and the world always belongs to them. At least that is perhaps the way the rich nations perceive the meanings of life on earth. In their eyes the poor do not seem to have much value. They do not wish to loose out any of their privileges, and desperate to prevent any danger in that respect with any ruthless measure possible on the lives of the poor who are vulnerable or less capable to oppose it.

However, whole of the natural universe, to which our world belongs, is strangely enough, not entirely lawless. One such law, I guess maybe that one cannot just take. One has to have the responsibility in return as well. It must be just the basic law of nature. Believe it or not, it is not so easy to override. Many tried but failed and failed badly. All had to pay back severely one way or another at one stage of their life, or even much later.

China is a good example. For a long period of time Chinese people had to go through severe suffering and deprivation. Some foreign powers enjoyed fabulous feast and profit at the expense of the poor Chinese people. The British colonial power even started a fantastic opium supply business to China for an extraordinary profit and power. China could do nothing to stop it. The world thought it would go on forever.

But it did not. China somehow turned around her fate; and now became almost a world power itself. Things never stayed the same. The whole world is now too busy to form compromising co-operation and business proposition with China. China is becoming more and more powerful.

India has not done so well, at least not yet. The reason that India did not succeed in improving the wretchedly impoverished state of her economic affair is because, Indian politicians generally only understand middle class values and middle class virtues which are nowadays truly out of date.

It is sad and tragic that India did not so far produce a leader who knows the need and necessity of the people live and die for nothing. The world of Indian labour is the product of many centuries. It is the consequence of gigantic inhuman injustices carried out by the world wide capitalist exploitation spread over many centuries.

The real and true conscience, capable of understanding the real root of the nature of these vast criminal affairs of the society has not yet been brought about.

The so called political conscience of India is really now a superficial middle class affair --- born out of fascination about affluent sophisticated Western society. To bring about a real change the country may need something more than that.

Now and then, India seems to be in the news of some kind. Big powers appear to be looking at her for some reason. The picture will be clear no doubt one day not too far!

In January 1978 I wrote:

India has been in the news again. I am perhaps a bit biased and a little suspicious as well. I can't help it. My imagination gets a bigger hold on me! Big powers are looking at India. There must be something big to pray at there. They do not take notice for nothing. I wish India will grow big enough to take care of herself---strong and intelligent enough to see through the whole pretence of this patronising concern of these big wolfs---this is in fact nothing but a clever greedy hand stretched out not to help but to snatch up something good only for their advantage. The Western power has grown big perhaps too big. They never learnt to be graceful and generous. They pretend sometimes, maybe too often; but they do not know how to be truly kind to the others. In their world to be kind means to loose some opportunity to take advantage of for their own interest. They are too good and too much obsessed with an urge to use other people for their own advantage. This urge may be in the subconscious mind of the entire civilization of the Western material power.

When this power tries to help the other unprivileged people of the world, it only cripples them further but somehow always helps them. I sometimes wonder if they are really so clever to arrange thing for their own benefit which on the surface seems such a self-sacrificing act for sole benefit of the poor of the third world. Or, maybe they possess a magical power which is truly responsible for the real consequence of all their action.

Maybe this magical power is the product of the consequence of the materialistic society. In the Western society people's life is based on the conviction of the philosophy that everyman is truly for only himself and no one else. Hence everyman learns to fight for himself. In this bitter struggle for existence everyman is stripped off his emotion. People in general do not have much time for sentiments and deep feelings for one another. They do talk about these feelings but mostly they use them in words for some purpose, usually for the purpose of manipulating things for their own advantage, in the disguise of some sort of pretence, of a big generous man which again helps to satisfy their ego.

In general they do not learn to help each other. In their society the idea of helping each other is seriously looked down on. They live up to the idea of growing up big, tough and all powerful over the rest of the population of their society and others. This does not leave any room for humility, generosity or sacrifice in reality. Everyman aspires of achieving that powerful power which will help him rule over the rest of the mankind and stay in that position for ever.

In this struggle for power there can never be any time to help other. If others are helped they will soon catch up with them and they might soon go under. This perpetual fear is constantly present in their conscious or subconscious thought. They do not have a single moment to spare for others. In fact they do not have enough time even for themselves.

In this strong competitive society people do grow up mature; but this maturity is mostly in the field of materialistic faculty of mind. They grow up too mature with a mature vision to see clearly, where really lie their interests, and how to grab every opportunity, which will enrich their interest. But they see that to help others is a clear threat to their own interest and that is probably why they do not normally help others. If they were convinced that helping others would help themselves as well then, perhaps they would and could help others. Their action is governed by the desire of self preservation which is quite natural of course.

They just see the whole world is something to play with---to make use of. Their entire culture has been built up with the notion that the whole humanity outside their society simply exists in order to be used for the benefit of only them or, maybe for their society at most. They have a long history of being able to make use of the other societies for their own advantage. They have done it for so long, they became very good in deceiving other people. The people in other society are almost like children by their standard. They know just how to manipulate these societies full of children and nothing else. They know how to pretend convincingly, play act as the sole saviour of their soul, salvation and country. But all the time they are really after something for themselves---they are finding a way how to deprive these more or less stupid people of something very important and essential for life. These people are sure and confident that the poor stupid people of the third world are incapable of seeing them through. They enjoy play acting ---they love talking big. They have grown too good at pretending anything whichever suits their interest. But these are really all but empty---at least for the poor people of the world---who are nothing but pawns in their hands.

I only wish the poor of the world will grow up one day and become a right match for the rich who has wronged them for so long in so many ways.

These big people have been showing too much concern about India lately. This simply means to me that there must be something big going there. There must be a big prize for the big power there! They are little bit like vultures, can smell blood from a long distance and even before the blood being there. I just guess that is perhaps why so much sudden love and friendship for India is in the news lately. The visits of American President and British Prime minister to India can not definitely be for nothing---I am sure of that. What exactly they are up to now is not absolutely clear to me but they want something for themselves that is for sure! Would the Indians be able to stand up to them, look in their eyes and see everything through? I do hope that they do. This is about time too. How long does a nation need to grow up and put an end of an unbearable humiliation, injustice and suffering!

I must admit, it is probably a very good thing to know how to look after oneself first. If you do not know how to take care of yourself; you would not be any good at all for anyone else either.

# Chapter Twelve

I sometimes sadly think of the stupidity of my Indian race. I know it is not much of any consequence now. But I just cannot help saying it though! Throughout British rule Indian troops acted more or less just like lap-dogs---loyal to the bone and blood of their British masters---gave their lives just to please the British rulers. They sacrificed their lives for the love of pleasing the British. That was their whole pleasure and satisfaction. I cannot imagine why they did it; but they did it all the same. It never came to their head that they were being used up for the worst possible selfish reason a human could think of! They were nothing more than stupid mercenaries fighting for the benefit of a country many thousand miles from their own; and they fought for a bare minimum of a bare bone. It is perhaps incredible, but it is absolutely true!

I really do not know what the British thought of them! Perhaps they came to believe that India was a wonderland where the people were all idiots without a faint trace of intellectual capacity, but were marvellous as perfect slaves---maybe even better than highly colourful spectacular toy-solders which were objects that could perform any performance which pleased them only. I doubt if the British ever thought that they were getting things for nothing, could they have honestly? I doubt very much if they ever really respected or, thanked the Indians for their services towards them. Amongst themselves they must have a big laugh about the silly Indians as a whole and come to regard them as a kind of sub-human low creature, which was very useful to use up.

Even now-a-days if one reads anything about India or Indians written by Europeans, this seems quite a bit apparent. They are accustomed to look down on Indians to some extent. One example: A book written on ancient Indian historical monuments. The photographs will invariably show up the spectacular remains of incredible skill and advanced sense of artistic and aesthetic balance of past India ---but the pictures will always have some starving poor Indians in such a way that will be definitely enough to throw an idea in the mind of the European readers that the monuments perhaps have nothing to do with the present inhabitants of India. If the present inhabitants look as wretched and helpless as they are seen in the picture---they could not possibly be the descendents of those people who constructed these monuments. Perhaps these spectacles were done by some disappeared branch of European origin or something like that to boost their own ego. Europeans never really feel much concern about other race anyway.

It never comes to their mind, of course, that deep down it must be something really terrible went on during their occupation of India which managed to drag India to the present stage! No never! Whatever, is discreditable, is India's own fault; whatever is nice, is the credit to themselves!

It is no good for the Indians to look anywhere really except to themselves. I wish no Indians read any book of India written by any biased European, and learn to develop an inferiority complex in its more serious form. One must learn how to respect oneself. Why should not one respect oneself? A human is a human---absolutely a human and nothing else! There is all the respects one needs to have are there! And nothing should undermine anybody's self respect. I wish I was an artist or I have an artist friend! I would have liked to make a book of India, in which all the pictures were the pictures of India presented with the Indians who would have suited the pictures most in the nicest possible way. Perhaps that might help us to build India so that the pictures would come true one day.

I believe in knowledge. Knowledge is far more powerful than action. Once you understand something, it is almost impossible to go back to the state of mind you left behind. And it is not so easy to make someone work against his or her belief.

That is why religion was once so potent to instigate action in the direction in which people were convinced. But knowledge will destroy that power and will make the world real. People will then have no excuse, they will have to take the responsibility of the consequence and its projection in their action. I personally prefer this than blind and fanatical burst of human energy and activities in any direction of human life.

It seems the most unbelievable mystery of life that people love so much of their own kind, things and pattern of life. Everybody is quite miserable, lonely and desperate in their own life without their own social environment. Some of the time they may be just a bit too loathing of their kind. Still they are very fond of themselves when it comes to choose between anything of theirs and someone else's things.

Their own belief, faith or, living style hardly made them that great or full of peace or, whatever. But they are too keen to destroy someone else's faith or belief. They do not hesitate slightest to look down on others' life and their understanding of life. They even proclaim that they are doing it to please God and also for the sake of their own faith.

They do not usually have any respect of the others, other peoples' understanding or ability to feel or seek knowledge. Maybe it is because they do not believe in them. Deep down in the subconscience maybe they do not have enough respect for their own mind; so they do not respect the others either. This deep need to destroy others' faith and understanding of life is very peculiar. Why don't they feel to give and take from each other, and improve things a little if possible! Maybe they would get happier and be able to make the others happier too in the process!

Europe is obsessed with their respective imperialism. It may be impossible for them to think without the thoughts of their kings and queens, their glorious past and power. Their subconscious is almost conditioned by it. They may never be out of it in their mind.

Similarly the Americans are somehow drowned in their superiority of military power, their strength in wealth; industrial and technological capacity overwhelmed their psyche. They may not be able to think beyond it.

The next struggle of the world may be between communal strength of China and the great appetite of the mystical aptitude of India. Both have enormous people power and variation of their cultural varieties. It would be interesting to see who comes up better off in the end. Any way it would definitely be a different picture from what went on before.

Life is so strange! We all walk through the time of our own space. It comes and then it ends. During this period we get so possessive, obsessive, energetic, aggressive, apathetic, and only you know what else and why! And maybe only you know whoever or whatever you really are! The fathomless mystery of life seems beyond anybody's grasp: what is life all about and why life exists and then it does not exist! It is absolutely pointless to seek for any answer. There isn't any; is there? But we human cannot help looking for it either! This maybe the absolute tragedy of us all!

The British media and public often seem too busy being flippant, witty and sexy. They seem to have not enough time to be anything else! Almost all of them are trying so hard to be clever in a strange way they appear too shallow and silly sometimes. I just can't make much sense out of what they are saying! It seems all too superficial, one-sided and hardly anything worthwhile or that deep!

They concentrate so much to be light-hearted, fashionable, well-dressed, interesting and looking-good; it all seems a farce and artificial, and a kind of making it all up without much effort, understanding or serious research. They all want to be great comedian first; everything else is second if not less! Anyway, emphasis appears to be on something not very clear and definitely not on the usual professional level or whatever!

Onetime the real power of England used to be in the hands of their Lords, Ladies and such people. They perhaps still do it to some extent; but quite a lot seems to be run by the people who are young; too much humorous and can talk a lot without much effort.

Out of all the jokes, comics, light-hearted humours, and whatever, there is hardly any programme in which I come across much about their real empirical past. They never seem to acknowledge the historical facts that the West became too strong and powerful because of the rest of the world was far too kind, generous and trusting to them. The West managed to bluff their ways. They managed to plunder and ruin those people, because these people were simple, nice and had great faith in humanity. They could not believe that any human could possibly be so false, harmful and bent on damaging them so harshly and ruthlessly too. It took them a very long time to get to know the true nature and intention of these shrewd, cunning and corrupt people of the Western society.

By the time they sensed the real truth of the nature of these people, it was too late to save them. The West had the upper hand and knew very well how to benefit them at the expense of these unprepared people of the poor nations. They did a very good job to make themselves very profitable, prosperous and powerful in deed. Sadly though they never ever acknowledged a slightest bit of gratitude to these unfortunate people! They just managed to make everybody believe that they got what they wanted and even more than what they expected, is only because they are superior people and God wanted them to have all these as they are His chosen people. And so it is their divine right to do and have whatever they want or wish!

Anyway, some people have bad luck. They have rather a lot of it. Some people on the other hand do not have so much of it. There might be some natural explanation in this naturally ill distribution of this phenomenon amongst humankind. I wish I knew it though! Because I am one of these unlucky ones and have, I think, too much of it too!

Maybe I bear the punishment of being too proud or just an awful idiot. This is the wrath of God or whatever! This is certain for anyone who is too proud or silly in life. It is the consequence of not knowing one's own place in this world.

Now I often feel everybody likes humiliating me. It seems that everyone enjoys trampling on me. It is painful to have to face it. However, it is much better to forget it. To remember the pain of humiliation does not do anybody any good at all. It must be realised that it is only human to trample on somebody who is down and appears to have no importance in people's eyes. It is only natural for everybody to hit the one who is in a position to be hurt! They probably feel it is their duty to kick me as I in their eyes have failed in procuring happiness for my own life! So they perhaps have the right to give me more unhappiness whenever it is possible for them to do so!

But I should not bear any grudge against them. It is only me who has really brought it on me. I no doubt deserve it. Whoever does not succeed in life, should end up in nothing except in a lot of pain and tear! Maybe one has to make use of others for one's own interest! I was not clever enough to understand it in time.

Loneliness is the greatest curse of all in life. I never thought it would catch up with me so badly. I never thought because I was slow and stupid no doubt. I should have known. I was heading this way for a long, long time. If I was clever enough I should have done something to stop it coming.

All the people, who end up unhappy and lonely as I am, must have only themselves to blame for it. The fault lies in themselves and no one else. There must be some kind of chemical imbalance in the physical chemistry of their mind. It is like a serious illness; you catch or produce it in your physical being. If you catch it mildly, understand the seriousness of it in time and take proper care to come out of it in really early stage, you may be lucky to be out of it sometimes.

But if you get it too badly and not realise it in the right time then, you just die of it. It must be the most painful waste of mind in life.

I wander what is this life! What is it really all about! I think now that it may be just a question of being able to make a choice. You just make a choice out of what is available to you. You choose but you choose in time. You spend your time in respecting and honouring your own choice. This is life. It is no joke! It is very hard to understand at first. It really needs a clear head to apprehend it! I did not understand well enough.

To wish and wait for something which is not available to you, is almost immoral. Nature punishes you for such perversion. Sooner or later you have to pay for such silly attitude of mind. It is after all quite a serious misgiving. It simply means rigidity of mind, unable to compromise, unable to adjust and hence unfit to survive. So you do not survive, at least not as a happy normal being. But before you really get totally extinct the whole process of dying goes on through a kind of existence, one describes it as unhappy lonely life. It is a period through the living shadow of death, or something similar.

All the people die like that must be faulty to start with. That is why they catch bad lucks in a basketful. Nothing ever goes right for them. As a matter of fact they breed bad lucks as they breathe!

Maybe discipline is vital in progressing successful life and living. The Western society is perhaps just about to degenerate to some extent. On one hand they are getting carried away with their high powered technology. They worship the mythology of computer system. Nothing intoxicates them more than the desire of running almost every sphere of everybody's life by the super sophisticated computer-power system. They seem to love and expect super human rigid discipline and accuracy of machine influencing their whole way of life.

On the other hand they do not appear to wish a lot to impose any discipline in their own individual life. They seem dislike practising discipline themselves. This dislike looks all the time on the increase. As they have views against discipline so it is quite fashionable and morally encouraging to justify their attitude and remain so. However, lack of discipline has lots of consequences. Society cannot have both ways. Lack of discipline can produce disorder. Lack of order and the absence of strictness in social life and living, bound to produce a number of delinquents and intellectual cabbages who are to some extent, protected and encouraged by the state to stay this way. This section of the society has no incentive to change their lazy-state of the growth of their mind. They will not have much grasp of the technology or of the mind to govern it. Hence the difference between the two groups of the society can only go on increasing until the two become completely incompatible.

I often think life is very strange indeed. Whatever it is, no one normally wishes to end it ever. For all its ups and downs life feels perhaps sweet enough somehow to everyone. Life knows only this world and people never wish to leave it from choice!

Long time ago I was thinking of Mathematics for some reason. I feel the whole structure of the study of Mathematics depends on the power of judgement and discrimination of some sort. This is in terms of Mathematical convention is what we mean by logical development or maybe attitude of mind. In the study of Mathematics one has to build up the learning set which will enable one to recognise the differences between patterns; one must observe distinctions, characteristics, similarities, differences and so on.

One has to see and appreciate the connections between all these patterns of symbolic ideas. A Mathematician is a person who is able to associate appropriate principles to appropriate symbolic or model situations. This requires judgement which depends on insight, experience, training and conditioning.

For the development of Mathematical intellect which is basically a matter of judgement and discrimination, it is absolutely necessary that the students should have confidence in their own ability. A teacher can improve a student's ability by giving encouragement and guidance with sufficient understanding.

More than anything else the students need motivation; an intellectual satisfaction by being naturally interested. The power or capacity to discriminate between patterns, objects, symbols, principles or rules, and to judge appropriately the necessary relationships, associations, characteristics and nature involved and implied in the exercise - these are developed in the students in the form of a kind of discovery, problem-solving games, and some discussion-type activities amongst the students. They must be encouraged to ask questions and explore as much as possible. The students must be made to feel secure, open and happy throughout these activities. Also they must enjoy and appreciate. The teacher should be always careful and aware that they are so. If not he or she should know why and find a remedy. A teacher must programme a learning situation in which the students respond actively, that is, they are brought into an atmosphere of self-involvement which they enjoy happily; and also they are trained to organise everything they have learned so that they are able to build up their knowledge structure appropriate for the level. This will equip them with the necessary standard of confidence and insight which in tern will help them to discriminate and judge successfully in the field of their study.

The teacher should see that the emotional stresses in the form of undue anxiety and frustration are kept to a minimum level.

It seems to me that knowledge has not got any end of it whatsoever. Man will never reach the ultimate truth; but his effort will never stop either. His sincere and honest thirst for knowledge will ever bring him more and more knowledge. The truth is not a fixed truth; it is an ever changing fact. Human conception or the power of analysis seems to be getting bigger and bigger. Hence, why should we assume that our knowledge about God has been reached the ultimate stage right about two thousand or so years ago in Jesus Christ and no more facts to be revealed about it any more, and just go on practising the same old faith for ever. Same thing applies to other faiths as well.

Anyway, how we can take it for granted logically that religion which concerns the most mysterious, delicate and totally unknown thing like God does not need any change in our understanding, while everything else is changing so much every day in our life. Life is a mystery no doubt!

When I was in the university, there was once a talk about something quite interesting. Afterwards I wrote about it:

Today there was a talk about equality in sexes amongst university students. It seems to me rather silly. Honestly I was a bit bored. I do not really know what they mean by equality and what do they mean by two sexes! I cannot understand what these people of the technically developed countries are talking about? Are they talking about some sort of machine or a particular class of animal or a certain type of forcing power? I am definite they are not certainly talking about human kind which consists of men and women, and each one of which whether it is he or she is distinctively unique in the world. One cannot compare individuality. It is simply individual in each case. Each is different from the rest in one way or other.

One can compare machine produced from the same factory. They are meant to be just the same; but human kind is not something produced by any mechanical factory. This is the speciality of it. One will never get a man or a woman who is exactly like one another. Comparing woman with man seems to me absolutely ridiculous, most silly thing to do in this world. How can one compare two entirely different things! I think the only thing to say about it maybe that, they are different; they are entirely different from each other. Men and women both build the human race; they have got different forms, different kind of functions, and different ways in life. But they have the same purpose to make life out of themselves, but the way they do it, is quite a bit different no doubt. A man can not normally be a woman; and a woman cannot naturally be a man. So what does it mean by equality between men and women! There should be a bit more specification; at least for some ignorant persons like me!

To my mind two different things are different and surely not equal. But if one talks about importance of men and women in human world, then according to my mathematical convention I must agree it should definitely be equal. Because, as the human world is made of men and women, each is as essential as the other; one cannot make it in the absence of one; so both are equally important whatever be their functions or forms. With one of them missing the human world is not half, it is zero. With both of them it is one; but we do not know actually whether they are half and half or zero and one or one and zero or anything else. But whatever it is they are equally essential to make a human life.

I wonder what sort of picture, does one have in their mind when they talk about two opposite sexes! Do they think of it as a certain kind of animal with two groups, male and female; and nobody has got anything except same instinct and so we are measuring the relative strength of instinct between the two groups! Human is little more than any animal in many respects. It has got a mind of its own and this mind varies person to person; and so what sort of work someone will be doing in one's life is just his or her own business of interest. The way of life or the field of interest has usually nothing to do with equality or inequality whatsoever. If a woman finds interest in the field where many men are interested, she will still be a woman; but whether those men will be pleased to have a woman there is a matter of these men's individual taste, background, social custom and more than anything else simply self interest. Men and women are not exactly a sort of forcing power meant to do exactly fixed kind of work. One just cannot generally fix it up. Different people will be doing different thing all the time. What sort of thing they would like to be doing, mostly depends on the form of the society they live in. It is again not a fixed one by any account. It varies time to time, and also place to place in the name of social interest or something like that.

When I came to England I was thinking about my situation. One day I was writing about it too. I cannot remember why exactly though! It was like this:

I am not too worried about my position in this foreign country. Whether I am accepted or not in a different society as one of them, is none of my concern. From logical point of view I cannot see why I should be. I am different in my culture and in my outlook. I have a very different background; with all these differences, I must be definitely different. Obviously I appear different too; and so I expect the people must accept me as different clearly. Maybe I can never be one of them for the simple reason that I am not one of them! And the desire to be treated like one of them would strike me as very immature, a symptom of lost personality or, something similar.

Whether I am appreciated or not does not bother me much at this moment. Maybe I have a very detached mind! I feel I myself cannot be anything more than an observer anywhere. However, I understand that from one's own personal point of view it would be preferable if one gets the opportunity to know the society, to know the way of living, to know the social pattern of a section of human race in certain environmental circumstances. It is not preferable because one is dying to fit oneself to that particular social pattern. Of course one always modifies oneself; but it should be preferable because it would help one to discover one's own true personality, and to achieve the stability of mind. The survival of a different but un-obsessed natural view in a different society is not only a very strong test for its genuine perception in the mind concerned. Also it is great by itself for the reason that it brings one to a wider view of life than that in a conventional living. It is always beneficial to be able to adjust one's mind with different approaches towards life that is to say it improves one because it improves one's knowledge.

The approaches towards life are all true in its own context. So the more truths one comes across, the better one makes oneself but in one's own way and not by copying blindly.

A man with reasonable respect for himself cannot copy life from anywhere, not even from God; it hurts his dignity; he must understand first and then follow his own judgement accordingly. It is nothing but cowardice, to follow things what one does not believe. Man must be honest to himself; he must follow his true sense that is all he can actually do if he wants to improve his life. He cannot do anything without his mind and his perception. If there is any truth, small or great, even God Himself; it cannot exist without a mind to perceive! I cannot see how a honest brave man can follow anything except what he realises sincerely or his knowledge allows him to believe it as right for him. Also one should always know that truth varies person to person, country to country and time to time as well.

It is only natural that man may be prejudiced or biased in certain respect; but so long he is not aware of the fact, nothing can be done about it. That is why it may be better for one to come away from conventional circumstances if possible. It might create some vacuum in the contentment or in the sentiment. Facing contrast or strange set up may therefore be able to create certain sharp enquiry in the consciousness of an able mind, which may need rethinking and readjustment; and that may in tern help him to realise and thereby overcome some of the unjustified prejudices. Otherwise prejudice just cannot be helped. One is a victim of one's own ignorance. We can only try to come out of it; and that is a gradual process of becoming a better being which perhaps is a continuous and constant process in the mind. The ultimate cannot be reached but can always be progressing nearer.

Prejudice is not really a disease; it is in fact an important factor of social health. Prejudice originates in the ignorance of mind; mind struggles to overcome it; and this constant process keeps the mind busy and perhaps provides the sense of living in the society in some ways.

I do not blame people being prejudiced against me; probably it cannot be helped. I do not mind at all if people do not like me. It is not very pleasant but I know it happens. Also I try to bear it if I am not appreciated. I am just as bad about some people too. Anyway, as long as one is honest about it, I can take it. I dislike it strongly and cannot tolerate it at all, if one just wants to play and try some tricks on me. It hurts me in my deeper being.

I do not understand or see sufficient reason why a normal human being would like to make me disturbed. Why people would like to destroy me or my stability! Are they jealous or are they annoyed? If so what is the real cause?

I cannot treat anybody with disrespect, because I respect myself. I am not a real coward! I will do anything what I consider best and what I sincerely like. But I respect discipline in life. I am a bit proud of being myself. I have built up my life as best as I could. I follow the dignity of my taste; I try to create harmony between my inner and outer beings. I am not a victim of my instincts; I posses self control to some extent. I do not think it is a kind of suppression; it may be just not too much self indulgence! Anyway, I do not see any reason why people must follow their instincts in the first place and not their reasons; after all human beings take pride in their power of reasoning. Also following the instincts blindly, one may lose the mind of reason first in some wards. One may loose completely all the things that make him different from an animal being. Otherwise, it is like being one and behaving like another; it is against nature which may not be of much value either.

I do not know a great deal about the East or the West. But I guess that there exist some differences between me and a young girl from England or, maybe from the Western world, at least to speak in general term. For instance, a smashing time for a Western girl is usually referred to the circumstances when she gets the opportunity to display some sort of association with men; it may well be physical, romantic and very sincere but it may be just physical and momentary. As long as she enjoys it, she thinks it is great to be close to a friendly man if she thinks he is nice. Usually she needs, of course, an artificial atmosphere, an excuse of a party or a dance. The main point is that she enjoys it and to her this is the best thing one can desire for an occasional enjoyment. She cannot see anything wrong in it at all.

I am not saying that it is wrong; I am not saying that it is right either. I cannot say anything really because I just do not know. All I can say is that it would not be the same for me. The main difference would be that I would not possibly be able to enjoy it. Circumstances like that usually would look very vulgar and distasteful to me; and naturally I would perhaps be withdrawn as a self defence and may refer to such a thing as the most disgraceful time of my life.

For God's sake, please do not misunderstand me for one thing. Do not get me wrong. I am not talking about the close atmosphere between two people who are really in love with each other. That is altogether a different matter in my eyes. When two people are in love; nothing to be said about them except that they love each other and perhaps everything between them! This is quite easy for me to understand because I guess that is the same in everywhere. But the smashing time for a Western girl is not necessarily the time with the man she loves. That is precisely the point puzzles me. She may be out to a party where, there may be several men all interested in her as a dance-partner for the time being and everything is forgotten after the party is over. But she says that she had a lovely time in the party.

I wonder what is this dance in the Western world; and why is it a part of their life! Is it an art! Is it the same thing what I would use the word 'dance' for? If not then how one tolerates it and why? For me this is the mystery of the Western world.

Please excuse me for my twisted enquiry. I am a bit ambitious; I want to discover the West, and I thought this is the starting point. I must confess that in my attempt to discover I came across to a disastrous suspicion. Is it possible that the Western society managed to create an excuse for the indulgence of their sexual impulses in disguise of dance; since dance as an art and as well as a social meeting is best suited for the purpose! But then what is hard to follow is that the West has not always been free like today; it had its puritanical past. How is it possible that no body ever been critical about this; or is it just that the Western social urges outweighed the barrier of sporadic sensitiveness by some mysterious Western way! Or is it just that the dance was not like this free before and the West today is making use of something for entirely different purpose. I wish I knew the answer. My motive, of course, is not to condemn but to know the very fact. In any case, I am old enough to realise that nothing depends on my opinion; on the other hand it is quite interesting to know, if possible, how things work in certain circumstances.

Long time ago I went to visit Manchester for some reason. I quite liked it. I know it is just a big crowded city in England; it hasn't got much to talk about. It was not even quite clean; but I liked its people. I did not care very much about how the city looks like. I did not mind if it is not very charming, clean and pleasant looking.

My home town Calcutta in India is big, horribly congested, terribly crowded and hopelessly dirty. It is still my home! I have a strong feeling for it! It is the place where people are rich, people are poor. Here I met clever people; here I met stupid people. I can see the whole of my India when I am in the most crowded part of Calcutta. I like to see different type of expression from people. I get bored very easily by the same sort of expression. People in Manchester and near about, are far more natural than the people in London. I know nothing is particularly wrong with London. It is a very big city with too many people in it; many of them are simply foreigners. It is actually quite nice and attractive too. I like to see more of it too. As a matter of fact every place is just the same. The only thing is, you must have to have the right type of eye to see it. And that comes from how you feel when you are there. That means how many friends and what sorts of people you are coming across there. So our eye to see a place is a delicate sense, developed from our state of mind relative to the people connected with the place in some ways.

# Chapter Thirteen

Maybe I talk the same thing over and over again; I just cannot help it. I am not happy about my life. My life is now almost completely wasted. I do not know why it has to end up like this. Perhaps it is my fault! Yes it must be my fault indeed. I do understand that it is up to oneself what one makes of one's own life.

Then again, I do not think I understood life at all! I think I used to feel that it is my life, I will make my life pure and beautiful; everybody is bound to be too keen to win me over and make me happy.

I did really make me high and mighty as best as I could. I concentrated on myself, did not take much notice of people, did not make any effort to make other people to love me.

The world now does not want to know me. No one really care for me anymore. Come to think of love, I do not now remember anybody ever loving me truly. Maybe I frightened them away! Strangely enough, I do not even remember now ever been hugged as a child, even by my mother or anybody else. Maybe it is all my imagination, and nothing else! I always had been a lonely child, always been a very lonely woman. Deep down in my heart I always desired to be loved deeply. The desire was too strong and passionate. It was so strong I had to hide it. I had to show that I am detached; to show the true feeling would hurt my pride; it would feel like I am begging for love from others and is not respectable enough for me.

The world must have misunderstood me from the start. No one ever knew me or, perhaps thought of any necessity to get to know my feeling. But I always expected them to be able to know what was going on in my mind.

The best time of my life is now gone.  I did not live a full-life; I did not achieve any fulfilment in my life.  At last I see myself as a woman with an empty life; a strange existence deprived of any normal environment and happy social atmosphere.  To other people now I am only a woman who lives in one's own world.

Is it not too pathetic!  Why should I become such as this!  Physiologically I was not inferior to any woman in general.  Intellectually I was probably capable of understanding all about this world and the people of this world quite a bit more than the most women.  Yet with all the power of my mind and body I am nothing more than a huge failure and a tragic waste in my life.  My life and my work all have gone sour.  I have no satisfaction, only bitterness and nothing else at all.

I joined the Bristol College of Technology as a Lecturer Grade 2 in Mathematics.  I joined in January 1967.  This is now many years ago.  I worked here.  I taught everything that was required of me.  In all these years I was given no responsibility which goes with power and prosperity of status.  I had to teach quite a lot of higher category of courses.  But I was ignored by my superiors.  My opinions were of no value to them.  I was absolutely without any power to bite at anything.  It was obvious that everyone knew it.  I was no body to any one there.

I did feel the humiliation in the bottom of my heart.  It just cut through my soul.  I did not know what I really could do.  All I did was just bear it and try to keep myself sane.  I never had the strength and way to challenge this attitude towards me.  Maybe this was an awful weakness and it was absolutely wrong.  People probably knew it and that was why they took the advantage of me in this way.

I saw it and I understood it.  But I could not protest it.  I simply thought I could not survive if I did protest.  I guess that it is not a simple matter; it must be very deep.  I felt that this was a deliberate policy to drive me mad so that I did leave the place.  It was a subtle and very serious hostile atmosphere around my prospect of working condition.  Nothing physical or too personal or it was not apparent to me anyway.  People were quite polite and helpful superficially.

But if you look beyond this nothing was right.  Everything was so painful; I was treated worse than a person just joined the profession in a far more junior position.

Perhaps they expect me to be grateful for providing me with a job which they would like to have back for one of their own people.  I do not really know.  I was glad to have the job.  I needed the job.  But I did the job with the pain of humiliation in my heart.  I felt I am living a worthless life for nothing of any proper consequence. I would have given anything to be able to change my position for something of reasonably respectable status.

Sometime I felt death might be much happier than my life like that. I felt I was suffering mainly because I am Indian and I identify with my Indian culture to some extent. So I do not fit. I am the odd one out. I have not been excepted as I am. I will not be accepted ever.

But where shall I go and what shall I do? This is the question I asked myself constantly. I have not found the answer yet.

I remember when I came for the job, all educated people in England, went to work for the industry. Hardly any qualified person came to work in Education. The pay was much better in the industry. So I had to do all the higher category of classes; there were many day-released pupils from industrial places for higher education. They were sincere, hard-working and matured people. They were delighted to be taught by me; the results were always excellent. I used to teach many of my colleagues, from my department and from quite a few others. I fitted in nicely. Everybody, colleagues, students and others, all were very happy with me. I thought I was doing a good job; and did not think I would ever need to change my job.

Things did change. British Industries collapsed. People started to come joining education; other jobs were gone. All my nice colleagues left. Top authority could not care less about me; they would rather have one of them in my place. Institutional racism must have been in the national blood. One of my students, not a very academic one either, was promoted as the Deputy Head of the Department, even though he was a Grade 1 Lecturer. My humiliation started. And there was no end of it either. Also time to change the job became almost impossible!

What a price I paid for earning a living in a foreign country! Not that I was lucky in my own country either! It was in the first place that I could not earn any living in my own country, is why I came to England.

I was young then. I was living at home. My parents provided for me. The boredom, the lack of opportunity was bad and boring; still I was able to tolerate it. I did not loose self-respect or nobody made me feel inferior.

So many years I am now living in England. I am earning but in exchange of my living I am always and everyday made to feel a fool, a peculiar inferior woman. The pain is intense, self-destroying, and simply unbearable! I do not know now what is worse than what; is it starvation or is it humiliation!

Food is essential for body. Lack of respect from fellow human and colleagues, is equally destructive for the human soul if not worse. What can money do? My life in England is so empty! It is simply an absolute waste. I have given the best years of my life away for nothing except a few worthless pounds. They do not want me; they want to get rid off me. Since quite sometime now they are probably carrying on a deliberate conspiracy against me only to drive me out of my job.

I feel that they show no respect of my opinion. They completely ignore my professional capacity and capability. I am being reduced to less and less everyday. I do the labour without any thank. I am selling my labour to the people who do not want it. I am not a privileged person. So I do not sell my labour at an advantageous price. I will have to accept the reality of being undervalued in this unfriendly market of labour. This is not the point though. In fact I am made to feel that I am imposing my worthless and useless labour on people who has no need for it. A feeling of inferiority and guilty consciences are being constantly poured on my ego. I am made to feel that I am tolerated here because they have to. Yet all my colleagues and the students value my work very much.

As a matter of fact, I know very well I would not have had the job if I came to try for it now. But when I applied for the job there were not many people wanted it. I did not compete with anyone. I was the only person who wanted the job.

I did the job without a hitch. I performed everything what was required of me with dignity and grace. Everybody was pleased with me. Students were very grateful. As I already mentioned I taught several of my colleagues. In fact, the Deputy Head I now work under was trained by me for two years. He passed the papers I taught in the first time; he took more than one chance to clear some other papers. I taught him in his Graduateship Institute of Mathematics Course.

Then, for some reason I suddenly lost all favour from the authority. They seemed to have changed their policy! There are of course quite a few qualified British people who are available for teaching post and would like to have the job I do. Maybe the departmental head now does not count me even as a penny. The power of the section is virtually vested on the person who was once my student. He does not miss a chance to order, discredit or, humiliate me on the slightest opportunity. Maybe somebody told him to do so.

This is now my life. This is what I do. And why do I do it! Could I not do without money? Money is killing me. I am living a slow and painful death. Should anybody blame me if I do not find any reason to be grateful for anything!

I was once not rich. But I am now a destitute! My joy of teaching is being taken off. I am being made to feel faulty, inadequate and consequently unsecured so badly that I feel I am not fit for anything. Yet the reason for all these is really so very trivial. Anybody could have these. And yet anybody would not feel the same or have the same consequence as me. I feel I am standing on a shaky ground, and any moment I will be broken down like a pile of roubles.

I wonder will I ever improve; will I ever feel happy again! I now do not really remember when I was actually happy last time. It must have been long, long time ago.

Still I was happy once, perhaps that is something I should remember! I have been so unlucky for so long, I cannot believe that it can ever be changed.

I cannot help wondering that the people of the society are in general, so very different from what they look to a pair of unaccustomed naïve eyes. The more successful the people are the bigger is the deception to the eyes.

It is fantastic; it is still incredible to me! No, I am far too inferior by their standard of this duality of nature; I could not possibly compete. It is no wander that I was doomed to failure. I am so straight, dull and stupid by their standard; I am not fit to live here really! Society could not be run by person like me; no one would really trust me, so what role can I play!

Maybe I do not know the rule of living. I never knew. I am no doubt a big failure. It is sad. It makes me cry. It must be too stupid that I do not know why I cry, for what or for whom. Still it probably makes me feel a bit relieved afterwards. Or at least I manage to go on living for a bit without crying. It is all too very peculiar.

If there were any God and if He was responsible for our happiness, I should have felt resentful no doubt for my luck. I guess I am the only one who is truly responsible for my own luck and action. So there is no blame and no body to help either. It is a very lonely old world in deed. Every time I tried to open my heart, I felt a sharp snap on my face. I do not know why this thing happens to me. Time and time again whenever I wanted to offer myself, no one wanted me. I seem to be some one everybody wants to stay clear off. Oh, people do not mind admiring me from a distance, but do not seem to want to have anything from me. Some like to take advantage of me; some like to play a little with me; and some may even pretend to like me too. That is how far it could go and not any further.

Is it not too strange! I always wander why! Everybody around me seems to have different experience. All the books, films and stories always are saying differently. Why can I not share other people's experience!

I do not seem to have any choice but to expect a very lonely life ahead of me. My heart gets full of sorrow and my eyes full of tear. I just cry and cry my heart out. Maybe it is my deep conviction that if I have a good cry, somehow all my sorrows will go away.

Anyway, mind is the source of multi-dimensional, versatile, incredibly resourceful and unimaginable imagination of human creativity and resourcefulness on this earth. Our mind is really the heaven, hell and anything else we can think of, of our world. The reality of all these and beyond, depends only on the mind and nothing else what-so-ever.

Our God lives in our mind, so do our Devil, the angels, the Fairies, all the Saints, and all whoever we care or do not care for. When our mind disappears, everything else also disappears too; where to or where not to we do not know. We do not exist beyond our mind. We do not know where it comes from or where it goes to! This is unfortunately the limitation of our life.

Another interesting truth in our world seems that the young always likes looking ahead; and the old likes looking back. That is life! It has to be like this always for the sake of nature itself!

As I am getting old, I do not work anymore. I am now retired. But I am getting more and more negative all the time. I just cannot help it. I understand life is a big struggle. It starts the day we are born. It goes on till the day we die. It simply goes on and on. However, one learns to live with it as you grow older. So somehow one gets a bit bold and takes a little cheer of some sort. This must be all our life about! Take it or leave it, there is no other choice!

I sometime think that the world we live in might not last too long. The whole human history seems based on so much crime, injustice, brutality, immoral activities, inhumanities, and who knows what else, it just should not last for ever. Or, maybe it does not deserve to last too long. There seems an inherent destructive yearn and desire in the human soul in general. I do not feel that the human race will stop until it kills itself and finishes with it all altogether. Maybe that is the fate befits the humanity best; and that is the fate it will follow up to the last breath of its life and living strength. It must be the justice of its eternal inherent core!

I took too long to grow up and then it was simply too late! I wish it was not so. It seems now that I have somehow managed to live rather a wasteful life. The futility of it all makes me very sad but there is nothing I can do about it now.

Maybe in this world none of us can achieve anything without the help and blessings of our God or, fate or, whatever one would like to call it!

As I already mentioned it before, nothing ever works in my life; and nothing is easy for me either. I only get some glimpse of hope sometimes, only a kind of distant hope. It does not usually become a reality for me though. It fades away, and I stay exactly the same as before.

I do not know why it should be so or, if it is the same with other people too! If it is the same with everybody, I do like to know how they cope with it in their life.  I find it so hard, it is almost unbearable.

I did manage to bear my hard life before but it is getting very difficult indeed.  I cannot cope with such anxiety any more, I just cannot, I must be too old!  People find faults in me, I am getting faultier everyday!  It is very easy for anybody to find fault in me now-a-days.  And it is very hard for me to see them finding fault in me.  It makes me feel small, inadequate, useless and unworthy.  It drains out the joy of living from me completely.

I think it is because I am becoming hypersensitive.  The lack of love, hope and security in my life is probably the cause of it all.  But what can I do about it now.  Is it not far too late?  I wander what happens to people like me in the end!  Do they all commit suicide or, do they all have to be destined to go insane in the end?  Or, is it possible for anybody to live through this deadly dull, unloved and unnecessary hopeless life?  What is at the end of it all this painful useless living?  No one cares, no one wants; still it has to go on; but for what?  I wish I knew the answer; it might make it just a little interesting to bear this most uninteresting life of mine.  If I write about my miserable feeling, I feel little better with the thought that my experience might help another person to avoid his or her misery in time.  After all it is all a matter of right calculation at the right time!  One's experience should at least teach another a lesson.  Hope some one else will benefit by my failure in my life.  So all is not wasted, there may be some value even in a great failure; maybe my failure will make other lives look a bit shiny and successful.  Maybe darkness is necessary for the existence and meaning of some bright light.

Oh!  Well!  Maybe or maybe not; what has it to do with me!  I have to live my own life; no one can live it for me!  And how am I to make my suffering any lighter?  If I cannot do it then, it is going to break my heart and that is in fact the end of me; is it not?  So does that mean, some lives are meant to be destroyed before time?  Perhaps it is so!  That is why some lives end abruptly.  Life does stop suddenly and slowly in time and before time.  It does stop by disease of the mind and of the body.  It then simply means that some people are lucky to have the joy of living and some are unlucky to miss the joy of life and living.  We surely owe respect for the living; and also we definitely owe truth only for the dead!

The state of my nerves are so bad, they are simply getting worse.  I do not know if I am about to break down or not.  I heard people do break down.  But I do not know what it is supposed to be and if I am really heading that way.  All I can guess is that I am feeling very strange.

I cannot concentrate.  I cannot pull through myself and get on with what I am supposed to be doing.  I have no will power, no hope, no energy and no determination to get on.  My mind is in a perpetual state of misery and helplessness. I cannot help crying bitterly and a strong feeling of loneliness is over me; I am being over powered by a sad sensation as being forsaken by everybody including God, if there is any such meaning in our life.

I am so low, I feel so badly abandoned by the world. I have no consolation. I feel I myself have brought this state upon myself. I am responsible for my misfortune. I am incapable of living successfully. There is and there was always something built-in in my make-up which must be the root of it all.

I wish I could quieten or pacify my emotion a little bit and go on living as a mechanical robot. For no apparent reason I am finding it so difficult recently; I wish I knew why and what I should do about it. The only remedy I found so far is that if I start writing, I somehow do calm down.

All my life I have been drifting away. No body, no place, no personal security, no taste of personal happiness or any joy; only emptiness and real loneliness made me loose all my pride. I wish now I had a child who would waste all my money for the love of mankind, which I failed to do in my life. That is all I would like now. All my ambitions are now finished.

I spent my life thinking of my next step. It sounds sad now. It is sad. But this is what I made of the life I got. We all like to think we are quite clever. But it does not seem so when things turn up differently. Everybody likes a winner. No body thinks much of a looser. The looser are the stupid of the world. Nothing works for them. Life is for the living those are clever enough to make things work. Death is all the looser can win for them. This must be the law of nature. No good denying the fact. There is no place for the looser in life.

I made myself a stupid and useless life. It has no purpose to serve, only to bear more and more humiliation and pain of a fruitless life.

I did aspire to be intellectual. I thought I could improve my mind with education and aspiration. But I was a fool. I did not realise that basically I am nothing but a naïve and gullible. I am too easily impressed. I am just a coward who gets easily carried away by words and have no strength of mind to pursue action which bears fruits and real sense. Also the saddest thing of it all in this world is the lack of love in one's life.

My mind often cries in deep sorrow for the fate I have brought upon me. I remember I used to be so proud, high-minded, self-satisfied, bold, and never ever had a shed of doubt that I can one day be unhappy. Over the years, however, I have gradually lost all that. Now, I am full of self- pity. Never can I think for a moment that I can still be happy after all. It seems so nice to be ordinary. Ordinary things in ordinary life appear, to be so precious and beyond my reach. By comparison I do not have anything which other people do. It is so extraordinary, and so wretched! Almost inhuman! I have no hope, no confidence, no courage, and nothing any more! Is it not sad that even I could have been quite natural and ordinary if I acted differently in time with right people!

It is bad to have to go without; but it is much worse to be mocked as well. I do not know the reason but it seems to me that God of my life is a cold and cruel God! Maybe I should be punished for something I did or, maybe for being very stupid. I have to bear the punishment of my fate. The price to pay for the loneliness must be the worst punishment in life! Still, it will all end one day. We all have to go! Happiness and unhappiness, all have to stop! And thank God for that!

When I came to England I was young, not very smart but quite bright. I was so full of hopes. I wanted to see the world and grow up big, rational and noble. I wanted to prepare myself, and I wanted the future to be proud of me.

I did not come to England as an immigrant. I came as a visitor only to open up my mind and expand my intellectual capability. I had no intention to integrate into the foreign society. I came simply to modify myself. I never had any true desire to loose my identity. I could not possibly identify with England. I always thought that would be sheer madness and definitely a physical non-reality no doubt. As a matter of fact the thought never entered in my mind! Wrong people wanted to attract me at the wrong time. True that I earned my living in England, but I have often made to bleed for it quite badly too. And I could never forget that what a miserable rotten old, dull and fruitless life I have chosen!

The talk about values of human dignity is just the luxury of the privileged ones, who do not know the pain of not having the basic need of life!

Indians in the West always drag India into almost every conversation. I do not always feel happy about it. I feel we aught to let India breathe a little bit of fresh air while we talk about something else! There are people who like to parallel India with everything they come across or, imagine to come across. This must be a sign of sickness what I feel may be an inferiority complex. Almost every Indian man and woman in the West suffers to some extent from this complex which is really a pity.

Inferiority complex makes a man so stupid and hopelessly inactive! He only suffers from the humiliation of his own soul in his own mind. He destroys himself, and he destroys the world around him. He is acidic, twisted; and he is greatly unhappy. What a shame! But he does not know that he is sick. He does not know the remedy either. He is imprisoned to his own prison, victim of the venom of his own mind. This complex destroys the soul; and the destroyed soul cannot create.

Happiness is a positive creation. So he cannot make anybody really happy. He is bitter. He likes to expose only the black side of everything.

Man identifies everything with himself; if he is negative then everything is negative too. What a waste! What a poor country India is! Most of her children who are lucky enough to be in a wider open world, with greater variety of lives, become only resentful and shut themselves into a very narrow and false cell built up as a refuge for themselves for purely selfish reason of their coward mind. They do not contribute to the dignity of mankind. They do not at all enrich their life in wider context either. They only hide themselves to a dark corner just like an awl afraid of being lost in the light. That is why they try to show off their concern about India only to justify their self defence. This is nothing but a fashion in real sense; just a false weapon which provides some impact in their intoxicated mind. It is not love for their country; it may be the perverted hate, an unconscious disrespect for their country of origin.

This is a sad human story! Why man does not respect himself! He is surely a man; he is capable of creation, he can elevate himself as high as he wants irrespective of his nationality or the land of origin. Nationality does not make a man anything but a man! Man must respect himself. He has nothing to be ashamed off! He can choose the path he thinks best for him. He is free, he has his reason; he is not a child; why he has to be protected by an artificial means? Being a man, he must be brave enough to face the reality; he must be able to modify himself according to his knowledge. The knowledge is nothing to protect in the closed iron chaste, it is to be identified in the open world with open sincere mind.

Poor old India! What an irony! From time immemorial India cried to her children, saying: Man! Your identity is God, you are God; raise yourself to the full consciousness of your greatness. Yet India suffers from the indignation of self pity! Perhaps Indians became deaf by too much cry for too long. In fact the old India does not exist in the positive sense anymore, for most of the Indians of the present time. Probably they have not managed to grow up for some unfortunate reason; and that is why they loose their identity too easily, and use the name of India and her past heritage just to cover up their own impotence. They do behave like children; nice and gentle superficially, but underneath very unrealistic, unchallenged, septic and also a bit immoral.

I am ever so doubtful! I feel there must be something wrong somewhere. Now and then, I cannot help wandering about if all Indians are somewhat either stupid or they possess dead brains and dead hearts. Or, is it me who is dead and therefore see the reflection of me everywhere? I really do not know the answer.

But I am sure if the Indians were alive then, Indian economist could not possibly make fun out of "economics of India". I could not help finding Indian economists are the most happily concentrated, cheerful and laughing people in India. They seem to be terribly fond of making funny comments on Indian economic affairs, and just too satisfied with whatever is going on in India.

I just feel that they are too fond of playing with too much of the ordinary theories in their theoretical world which seemed too remote from the practical life and action there. It may not mean anything to them personally. India is a poor country; Indian population is such a big figure which makes them proud when they handle it in their study or in the course of some conversation; it is supposed to be a topic for big talk by big people.

They like to play with India's problem; they just talk, but they may not know what exactly they are talking about. Some maybe just like a parrot, just saying what had already been told many times by many people in many places; a kind of true slave characteristic either in the core of the national brain or in the heart.

I am positive that life thinks, life understands and above all life feels. So if the Indians are alive, they must have at least a faint sign showing that they can build up an original idea and cannot just be proud enough with the imitation one or, at least be terribly sorry for not being able to have one.

It is so painful for one who has a country full of insincere people who could not care much for the vast number of poverty stricken population there. The rich India does not seem to care much about the poor India. And too much corruption looks to be appearing everywhere in India.

Some people in the West may like to believe that poverty is a peculiar characteristic of the East; something like a bad habit of the Eastern people which is because these people are primitive. It may not touch their heart too much. Maybe it does not bring much compassion in their conscience either. It only helps them to despise and contempt the Eastern people who to them is nothing but a somewhat inferior species. All the talk and concern are really nothing more than a kind of pretence, which somehow make them feel good, complacent, self-righteous and on the whole a very superior species indeed. Perhaps they want to point out that they themselves are really the topmost species who came out of the entire natural evolution of life on earth; and only they deserve the blessings, protections and resourcefulness of their Creator!

The Western Power perhaps laughs at us the poor nations to some extent. They call us the third world, maybe they mean to say the third rate nations of the world. In some way they maybe right. We do not have unity among us; of course, it is impossible to have unity amongst us. We do not yet have the opportunity or maturity to grasp the complexity of the world politics. We are yet to grow up. We are still to develop enough to stand up to our adversity.

The West may not see it like that. They may think we are not clever enough to unite against them, because we are quite stupid; and it will remain so because they think we are genetically stupid!

In their pride of superiority they confidently and consistently cheated every nation. All these nations obviously do understand that they have been cheated, patronised or badly treated one way or other. When they will have the chance they will naturally have no love for the West.

One day the West may not have many friends in the third world. The West may have to compete too hard amongst them. They might discover then that they do not have much unity amongst them either!

Maybe confidence is the magic and the miracle of a nation. Western people are so confident, they always appear too clever, able and intellectually superior amongst mankind. However, the West has been interfering in the world affairs so much for so long, in anything and everything possible in this world! People got used to it; it seems right and reasonable. But is it so?

They are so afraid of immigration to their own country. But for a long period of time Western population from different countries and different period of times had been migrated to anywhere they wished or wanted to in order to improve themselves and help themselves materially. It helped their population to benefit and prosper; but now they are too sharp to stop the people from poorer nations to move in to better countries.

Superiority is a big factor in human mind, full of too many conceits. Anyway, everybody is inferior unless or until they help to profit and make your world a better place for yourself. Then, of course, it is ever so wonderful; and we all become tolerant, brotherly and very close indeed in every possible way; culturally, economically and in any other way one can possibly think off.

It is much more self satisfying to think that anybody from different culture to be less than you yourself. It is simply human instinct and helpful for one's own self preservation, if not anything else! Money is the source and centre of too many possibility, glamour and cover up of all evils!

People talk of purer breed! What exactly is the purer breed? The European people are proud of their purer breed. But do they not know that there is no such thing as purer breed. All the human races all over the world are the production of mix up of different people from different parts of the world over many, many centuries of time.

The only purer breed, at least purer than human are the monkeys, chimpanzees, gorillas, orang-utans and so on. They are the breeds before human evolved into what they are today. Maybe the theory of evolution is nothing to be proud off, but just a matter of natural facts and nothing else. We cannot ignore it though.

Good and bad are really the two sides of the same thing, the life; like life and death is exactly the same thing of this world; just two expression of our natural existence in this world.

There is no such thing as Devil and Angel; they are only the imaginary expression of our mind and nothing else! I wish I knew the magic to put all nasty things in the ditch, and hopefully make everybody remember only to watch the lovely world going round, and feel full of joy. No one should live in a lonely dark wardrobe, no matter how many good things in it.

We offer our appreciation by offering our best creative artistic creativity only to show our admiration of our Omni power God's vast creative activities all around us. Difference between Science Camps and philosophers in truly ancient time, is in their time and environment. As far as they were concerned, they were truly seekers of whatever they wanted to know.

There were no difference between their quest for spiritual goal and their knowledge of the truth of life. They were just like the scientist. There was nothing or nobody to colour their curiosity about truth. They did not work between two or more groups. Nothing to dominate their views, except whatever they were able to reveal for themselves, and not for profiteering!

They probably were not very experienced in serious politics. They were only up to their own goal. The deep insight in the mature future enlightenment needs foresight, liberalism and understanding of the world in real sense, not just one's own short term, isolated benefit.

To know the truth is not an easy job for any one. Newton exclaimed it in a beautiful way: "If I have seen further than the others, it's only because I am looking standing on the shoulder of the giant".

In medieval time the amount of selfishness, brutality, savage and extreme cruelty performed in this world must be far away exceeded the little bit of nicety happened in this world. Yet everybody is so fond of their life and cannot imagine leaving it ever. I wonder if anybody keeps a record of all this.

Maybe one of the purposes of organised religion in the olden days, was to keep the ordinary people busy worshiping and following through all the set rules and rituals of the religion, while the upper ruling class being busy helping and enjoying themselves all the things they could get hold of for their own enjoyment and comfort. They had life of glorious luxury, setting up a sort of example for the common and religious people, what they could expect in heaven in their next life.

Germany was a bit too late; conquering Europe was not that easy. English, France, and a few others had much easier time in Asia, Africa, America; the people there were not trained in their powerful ways.

Some people are lucky; things go right for them. Some people are unlucky; things do not go right for them. It may be a matter of miscalculation, a miss judgement! Or, it may be something else! It is very difficult to say. Obviously no one would like to choose bad luck for oneself if one has a choice. When one has an unlucky life, one cannot do anything about it except perhaps blaming God! Perhaps it helps to invent something or someone to blame for one's own misery. Everybody, however, blames the miserable person himself. People believe there is something wrong with the unlucky person, may be there is!

I do not know if there is any such thing as God! Oh God, please give me the strength to bear the boredom of this miserable life! I know, I am the source and cause of the misery of my own miserable life. I did not play the game of my life with success. I am simply a failure. I must have chosen to fail, but I was unable to choose otherwise; it is a fate, I could not escape. I led myself blindly right into it! No matter whom I blame for it, God or, myself; it does not really help me now. Miserable life is painful, it hurts badly.

Analysis of failure does not soften the pain. Still, may be it helps a little to bear it. Life never suited me. I have never been happy even when there was no reason to be unhappy. I never understood life or, what it is all about! I have always been stupid and naïve. I always took everything at its face value; I more or less, believed in all the values society preaches superficially. I trusted all the beauties and the romances people want you to see. I understand now that this can never do; I did not see the true nature and the meaning of my sight! I was blind with open eye! I understand now that it was a big failure of most serious nature. No one could have helped me.

I guess that those people who go through life successfully they do so instinctively. Most people follow their instinct; that is why most people are on the whole reasonably successful. There was something wrong with my instinct, and so I did not succeed in life. I must be quite a bit unbalanced then, I do not know how to compromise, and everything makes me shocked to some extent.

I believed in the purity, virtues, kindness and grace; but they do not really exist at all! They are all only pretence, they have no function in a real society. Their invention and use as pretence is useful but they are nevertheless false in true sense!

The more sophisticated the society is the more obsolete the spiritual values and the values of morality there. I am so surprised that I can see so clearly nowadays the true nature of the whole society. I wish I could do it earlier!

Indians were just a pawn for the foreign power. They just wanted to use this pawn to the best of their own selfish interest; and they did it very well indeed. Indians were at that stage not politically matured enough to understand or, counter act sufficiently to prevent the power struggle against their own destruction. They were not able to preserve their unity, peace and sanity in their national life.

Vietnam fought tooth and nail with the capitalist imperial power. They suffered hideously and lost the lives of many of their people. Yet they managed to win and were able to keep their country united.

Many countries did not succeed doing it. India failed miserably. Her land had been dissected ruthlessly by foreign interest and very clever tactics. India was not clever enough to resist and stop this division. So she had to face the tragedy and the pain of all these cuts of her own body. It would take India a long, long time to overcome all these loss of limbs and who knows what. India is still going through a lot of muddle like delusions, illusions, Myth-factories, soda aristocrats, and God knows what else!

Even Gandhi could not save India from the pain of division. I am not sure if people generally understand the historic significance of Gandhi in India. So far in our modern world everybody is excited about blood for blood. Forgiveness is just a paper talk and spoken in diplomatic term and used as a tactics only.

Gandhi was the only one who said I do not want blood for blood; if you want my blood you have it. But I do not want your blood. It is below the dignity of my humanity. I will follow non-violence to the last of my existence on earth.

He came from India. India was deprived, oppressed and not considered as human enough for the power of the world at the time. She was regarded as backward, uncivilised and abominable in many respects by many of the respectable people of the world, who thought they were the lords of this world and should rule this earth as a divine right.

It simply amazed me how India produced anybody like Gandhi. But it seems now quite natural as if he came out of ancient India bearing all the ancient heritage and values of India.

For many centuries India suffered from foreign uncaring overlords. The Rajas, Maharajas, Nowabs and most of the upper crusts were mainly the collaborators. They were too busy to look after their own places and interests. Majority of the rest of the population were nobody and no one to look after them. They were almost invisible to almost all practical sense or, purposes.

Life still goes on. It is not really possible to stop life and living, no matter where you are or what period of human existence one can think of. Capitalist countries still wish to ride on the broken back of their former colonies.

Anything is possible if times were infinite. Anybody would be able to do anything if there was no shortage of time; if time was limitless and time was truly infinite. But it is not true for any individual; not for any life form on earth. Time is too short for all lives. Life starts and goes on only for a limited time; that is for everybody and everything we know of in our universe. This is nature; and nothing can change it or, maybe nothing should change it. Nothing lasts for ever. Life does go on but it is not the same life though.

Interestingly, can one think of anything elevating human spirit more than mountain, as the manifestation of divine attributes? Intensity of life and its evolution are so strange and incredibly peculiar indeed! Each human individual comes to this world so happy, excited and full of life! None, however, wants to leave this life whenever the time comes, willingly or, happily. Yet no one feels glad, fulfilled or proudly satisfied about the things they have gone through; all too miserable and cantankerous about everything all around them. They never leave this world happily. They blame everything except themselves.

I sometimes felt that Pure Mathematics may come from a kind of concept of abstract impression of the entire physical universal impression of human mind! And art is perhaps some sort of subconscious attempt of the expression of the same thing in a kind of symbolic gesture! I feel that unique creativity comes from the depth of one's own personality. Nothing could be more important for one in one's own life.

Life is quite strange! Most of us people are usually too selfish without a doubt. However, people love pretending otherwise most of the time. I remember once I was watching television. It was quite sometime ago. It must have been in 1975.

Everybody was talking about foreign doctors. I was wondering why suddenly so much talk against overseas doctors! There must be a hidden reason behind it all! To me it was obvious that they, that is, the British doctors at least wanted to get rid off them. But why was it? I was guessing that somehow the overseas doctors must have been in the way of the British doctors.

Perhaps the British doctors were fighting hard to improve the status of the doctors in England very much better. They probably have had nearly succeeded in doing so. The doctors in England included overseas doctors as well. So it means that from then on the doctors from the poor countries there would have the benefit, same as the doctors in the rich countries. Theoretically it sounded alright! But in practice, in the mind of the real British people it perhaps had stricken as disastrously all wrong!

For centuries British were used to exploit people of the other nations. They exploited people in a very interesting manner; the exploited people remained unaware of the true nature of the British interest and were obliged to feel most grateful for having the chance of being exploited by the clever and gracious British. The British played the role of a nation of great and gracious benefactors of the poor wretched world!

The British-role pattern remained undisturbed so long. Britain was filled with low-paid unskilled labourers who came from poor countries and who did all the dirty jobs which no British wished to do anymore. It was quite welcomed for the doctors to come over to England from any corner of the poor world as long as they did remain as the lowest category doctors and earned a meagre salary for the professional jobs which British doctors did not wish to do for that sum of money.

However, things were then changed a little, for the British and for the others as well!

British charity sprang from the bottom of their heart for the unprivileged; but they do not know how to share with people who claim to have the same status as them. Their diplomatic sense of craftiness would immediately compel them to invent means under the disguise of a suitable excuse which will help them to strike a hard blow to change the situation for their interest.

However, coming back to my own job experience in England, I was never happy here. People were nice to me; my students were very appreciative of me and my help. But the authority could never seem to care for me at all, and I never received any thanks for all my hard and sincere work.

At the beginning the situation was different, they were happy to have me. It was not easy to get one as qualified as me. I helped them with almost all of their courses for higher qualification. I produced nearly 100% success rate. Everybody was happy; and I was happy. So I did not look for moving out for a better place.

I stayed here too long. Things have changed for the worse. I gradually realised that I was in the wrong place. I seemed to be in such a vulnerable position. Only one wrong kind of student had to pick up a bit of courage and pronounced that he or she does not understand me or my teaching, everybody would immediately fall backward to jump to the conclusion that he or she must definitely be right. All my records would seem to be overlooked for some reason. It would appear just too convincing for them, because they want to believe it. They could easily then say that my accent was not right, my expression was really very foreign to the students; maybe I did not teach in the way other teachers did there. They could justify their belief in many ways than one.

Probably they were right; I might not know. My question was why I was there! How did I produce so much success rate for so many years! Why suddenly I am a complete waste! I understood I was not wanted. My appearance obviously always gives way to the fact that I am an odd person there.

It was so hard. And it was getting harder and harder. Everything seemed to be closing in on me. I could not find a way to escape from all these miseries of my life. Why did I have to have such suffering!

No one would be going to believe me. No one has any idea of the true situation. Only I know but I cannot prove anything. My mind was almost loosing ground. I was getting very tired of the whole thing. One thing I really never understood though that how did I manage to teach so many years in the same place! I might have one or two problems now and then, but who would not! On the whole it was not at all too unsatisfactory. Most of my students always got through their examination. Many of them did very well indeed. Sometimes they even did show their appreciation and praised my teaching.

I was often able to help a number of weak students and produce remarkable improvement. But none of these seemed ever have drawn any proper attention to the authority. No one seemed to notice any of these. All my achievements and successes were always appeared unknown to everybody.

However, it needed only one rough and bold student to say that he did not understand me, and everything blew up like explosion. It did not matter if this particular student did much worse with other teachers. His complain would always hit me, and hit me badly. It seemed just want to destroy me. It nearly had, a few times!

No one ever appeared to question into the motive of the student. No one seemed to want to see the background of the student's complaint; the whole thing always looked like getting out of perspective and completely out of proportion. The fact that the rest of the class was doing well and happy with my teaching seemed to have no bearing on the matter! I was always almost accused of not doing my job properly. I was made to feel helpless and cornered. I am no diplomat; I know no tactics to overcome the humiliation. It is simply too easy to humiliate me. All these humiliations were getting too much for me. It was really eating up my soul! I was fed up of pleading not guilty of this or that. All these guilt I was not at all sure if they were true or imaginary. Maybe higher authority invented them as a weapon to help them to get rid off me! They did not succeed though. I was there until I retired. I did not enjoy but I had no choice.

Life is a life; no matter where ever it may be, and whose life it exactly is! Life may be good or bad, glorious or not so glorious; it maybe mystical, saintly or nothing of the sort, just very simple indeed. It is still some one's life in our world all the same. It is important, significant and valuable beyond our mind and meaning.

We should therefore exclaim philosophers' exclamation:
Life is a gift, take it
Life is a chance, make the most of it
Life is an opportunity, use it, and
Life is an experience, enjoy it.

Life or living is all too short! Nothing last forever for anybody or for anything whatsoever!

www.ingramcontent.com/pod-product-compliance
Lightning Source LLC
Chambersburg PA
CBHW030310290526
45785CB00001B/297